THE SOCIOLOGY STUDENT
WRITER'S MANUAL

THE SOCIOLOGY STUDENT WRITER'S MANUAL

William A. Johnson, Jr.

University of Central Oklahoma

Richard P. Rettig

University of Central Oklahoma

Gregory M. Scott

University of Central Oklahoma

Stephen M. Garrison

University of Central Oklahoma

PRENTICE HALL, UPPER SADDLE RIVER, NEW JERSEY 07458

Library of Congress Cataloging-in-Publication Data

The sociology student writer's manual/William A. Johnson, Jr....
  [et al.].
       p.   cm.
     Includes bibliographical references and index.
     ISBN 0-13-462961-2
       1. Sociology—Authorship—Handbooks, manuals, etc.   2. Sociology—
Research—Handbooks, manuals, etc.   3. Report writing—Handbooks,
manuals, etc.   I. Johnson, William Archer.
HM73.S637   1998
301—dc21   97-30514
                                                              CIP

Editorial director: Charlyce Jones Owen
Acquisitions editor: Nancy Roberts
Editorial assistant: Pat Naturale
Marketing manager: Christopher DeJohn
Editorial/production supervision
    and electronic page makeup: Kari Callaghan Mazzola
Interior design: John P. Mazzola
Cover design: Wendy M. E. Alling
Buyer: Mary Ann Gloriande

This book was set in 10/12 Cheltenham Book by Big Sky Composition
and was printed and bound by Hamilton Printing Company.
The cover was printed by Phoenix Color Corp.

 © 1998 by Prentice-Hall, Inc.
Simon & Schuster/A Viacom Company
Upper Saddle River, New Jersey 07458

Printed in the United States of America
10   9   8   7   6   5   4   3

ISBN 0-13-462961-2

PRENTICE-HALL INTERNATIONAL (UK) LIMITED, *London*
PRENTICE-HALL OF AUSTRALIA PTY. LIMITED, *Sydney*
PRENTICE-HALL CANADA INC., *Toronto*
PRENTICE-HALL HISPANOAMERICANA, S.A., *Mexico*
PRENTICE-HALL OF INDIA PRIVATE LIMITED, *New Delhi*
PRENTICE-HALL OF JAPAN, INC., *Tokyo*
SIMON & SCHUSTER ASIA PTE. LTD., *Singapore*
EDITORA PRENTICE-HALL DO BRASIL, LTDA., *Rio de Janeiro*

To
Janice
Margaret
Chris
Melissa

CONTENTS

TO THE STUDENT

Successful students, like successful social scientists, are competent writers. As sociology students, we observe social institutions and behavior. We write to record what we observe, to explain what we record, and to defend what we explain. As citizens, we write to take part in making decisions that direct our nation, our community, and our private lives. From the Declaration of Independence to the Emancipation Proclamation, from the United Nations Charter to President Kennedy's Inaugural Address, writing has brought us the freedom we enjoy today.

The Sociology Student Writer's Manual is designed to help you do two things: (1) learn how to research and write in sociology, and (2) improve your writing ability. These objectives are addressed in the four major sections of this book. The "Introduction" tells you what sociology is all about. Intended for both first-time and experienced sociology students, it offers a basic historical orientation and a challenging account of current theoretical perspectives in the field.

"Part I: A Handbook of Style for Sociology" addresses fundamental concerns of all writers, exploring the reasons we write, describing the writing process itself, and examining those elements of grammar, style, and punctuation that most often cause confusion among writers in general. It also explains the importance of formatting the research paper properly—the title page, table of contents, and so on—along with citing and referencing sources using the American Sociological Association's *Style Guide* or the new Student Citation System. A vital concern throughout this part, and the rest of the book as well, is the three-way interrelationship among writer, topic, and audience. Our discussion of this relationship aims at building your self-confidence as you clarify your goals. Writing is not a magical process beyond the control of most people. It is instead a series of interconnected skills that any writer can improve with practice, and the end result of this practice is power. Part I of this manual treats the act of writing not as an empty exercise undertaken only to produce a grade, but as a powerful learning tool, as well as the primary medium by which sociologists accomplish their goals.

"Part II: How to Conduct Research in Sociology" focuses on the research process. The first chapter in this part, Chapter 5, describes the research process in detail, explaining how you can maintain self-confidence by establishing control over your project and assume the crucial responsibility of every writer to use source material ethically. Chapter 6 lists and describes traditional sources of information for sociology researchers, including libraries, government agencies, and private research organizations that may provide you with information not available in your library. Chapter 7 is an introduction to a major new source of information: the Internet and World Wide Web. It demonstrates how to find and obtain resources in this burgeoning new territory that are important to your topic. And finally, Chapter 8 deals with conducting quantitative research in sociology. It examines several common research designs utilized to conduct quantitative research in sociology, while focusing on the scientific method and critical thinking.

The four chapters in "Part III: How to Write Different Types of Sociology Papers" explain different types of papers that are commonly assigned in sociology classes. Each chapter begins by exploring the purposes and characteristics of the paper covered. Next, the steps for writing a successful paper are spelled out and typical formats provided. Each chapter encourages you to use your imagination and resourcefulness in confronting the paper's requirements.

Your professor may give you a specific writing assignment from one of these chapters. If your assignment is not specific, you may want to select an assignment and discuss your selection with your instructor before proceeding.

This manual is a reference book. It was written to help you become a better writer. We wish you all success as you accept a primary challenge of academic and professional life: to write and write well.

*William A. Johnson, Jr., Richard P. Rettig,
Gregory M. Scott, and Stephen M. Garrison*

TO THE INSTRUCTOR

How many times have you assigned papers in your sociology classes and found yourself teaching the class how to write the paper—not only content, but form and grammar as well? This text—which may accompany the primary text you assign in any sociology class or may stand on its own—allows you to assign one of the papers explained in Part III with the understanding that virtually everything the student needs to know—from grammar to sources of information to citing sources—is here within one book.

We have outlined four projects commonly assigned by sociology instructors: (1) book reviews (can also be used as guidelines for reviewing articles), (2) social issue analysis papers (with guidelines for both introductory and advanced papers), (3) case studies (including different types of sociology case studies), and (4) surveys (with statistical analysis for the more advanced students). For example, you might direct your students in Introductory Sociology to write a social issue analysis paper according to the directions in Chapter 10, following the instructions in Part I for formatting, grammar, and source citations, and those in Part II for organizing the research process and utilizing available resources. Most questions a student could ask about the paper are answered in this book, but it also allows you to supplement your assignment with special instructions. Examples are included.

Writing an analysis paper following the directions in Chapter 10 is an excellent exercise for beginning students, as social issue analysis papers are exercises in logic and problem solving. Our directions help students do the following:

1. define an actual existing social issue or problem
2. identify and evaluate possible theoretical contributions to understanding that issue or problem
3. formulate a recommendation for solving the problem

By using the guidelines in this manual to complete a social issue analysis paper—or any of the other assignments that are included—your students will learn to define and focus clearly on issues or problems that are germane to their world. They will become more competent problem solvers and develop skills that are important in every profession.

As you know, writing skills are essential to professional success in sociology, as in other professions. By combining the latest sociology research and writing techniques with a broad spectrum of writing activities—based on a total of over seventy-five years of experience teaching courses in sociology, criminal justice, political science, and English—we have written this book to assist you in leading students toward success.

We would like to thank the following reviewers for their helpful comments: William M. Cross, *Illinois College*; Larry D. Crawford, *Morehouse College*; Valerie Brown, *Cuyahoga Community College*; Harriett Romo, *Southwest Texas State University*; Steven L. Vassar, *Mankato State University*; and Carol Stix, *Pace University*. A special thanks goes to Shelby Johnson, a film and dance major at Middlebury College in Vermont, for carefully reading and editing the manuscript. Her many excellent suggestions improved this manual significantly.

William A. Johnson, Jr., Richard P. Rettig,
Gregory M. Scott, and Stephen M. Garrison

INTRODUCTION

Of making many books there is no end; and much study is a weariness of the flesh.

—Isaiah 12:12

WELCOME TO THE STUDY OF SOCIOLOGY

If you are about to write your first paper in sociology, this introduction is for you. It will enhance your confidence and ability to present ideas and issues at every level of the discipline, from Introductory Sociology to Sociological Theory and Advanced Sociological Research. Reading this section will help you understand what sociology is all about and what sociologists are trying to achieve when they write. It provides a brief overview of the discipline, which will help you understand basic sociological concepts, methods, and theories and apply them in your writing. The knowledge it offers can save you time, energy, and confusion.

Sociology is taught under different conditions at different colleges and universities by instructors who have varying amounts and types of resources at their disposal. If you have already studied sociology in some detail, you may choose to skip this introduction and read Chapters 1 through 8 before selecting the chapters in Part 3 that provide directions for the specific type of paper you have been assigned. However, you may find that reading this introduction will help to refresh your memory and establish your writing efforts more firmly within the broader framework of the discipline. Wherever you are in your progress toward mastering the methods and contributing to the rich tradition of sociology, we encourage you to read this section.

WHAT IS SOCIOLOGY?

Sociology, the study of human interaction, attempts to remove the "mystery" from human behavior. Although we, like the Hebrew prophet Isaiah, often become weary of finding the answers we seek, we continue nonetheless, for the price of ignorance has far too often proven—not only for the Jews—too costly. Because it deals with the effects of social systems on people's behavior, there is virtually no topic that sociology does not touch. Therefore, it is sometimes difficult to see where sociology is distinct from other disciplines. Perhaps the best way to begin is with an example from everyday life taken from Hess, Markson, and Stein (1988):

> Sometime this week you will probably eat at a luncheonette or restaurant. As you pay your bill, you will probably leave a tip. Why do that? Do you have a deep psychological urge to give money to people who provide a service? Is it biological? Do you have a "tipping gene" that programs your actions? Or has some divine power commanded you to do so? The answer to all three questions is, of course, "no." Then why, in our society, is this behavior almost automatic? Students pondering this question typically give such responses as, "It's expected," "I was taught to," "If you don't, they'll spill soup on you the next time you eat there," or "It's the way they make a living because their wages are so low." Regarding the amount of the tip, some students will point to group pressure and to "wanting to be taken as a big shot" by restaurant personnel, other customers, or their dates. And some will point out that if the size of the tip is directly related to the quality of service, it serves to motivate high levels of performance.
>
> Notice that all of these answers involve some form of interaction; they assume that your behavior is linked to that of other people, and that you are acting within expectations and mutual influence. Under some circumstances—when trying to impress someone, or eating in a crowd—we will probably leave larger tips than when dining alone. Tipping also varies according to the eating place—the more expensive the meal, the proportionately higher the tip. In general also, men tend to tip more generously than do women. And if you have traveled across this country or abroad, you will probably have noticed regional and national variations in tipping expectations.
>
> Once you realize that these differences have little to do with how hungry you are or how you were toilet trained, you can begin to grasp the essence of the sociological perspective: Human beings live in groups; these groups are characterized by rules that govern behavior; the rules are learned; and we take other people into account when we choose how to behave. In other words, our thoughts and actions are largely shaped by forces outside ourselves—by the social context and how we interpret it.

But notice also that we can choose not to tip, and that the amount we leave depends on a number of considerations—what we think is customary, a fear of retaliation or of looking like a cheapskate, what we consider a fair reward for service, or a means of adding to the income of low-paid workers. Thus, although there is an outside patterning or structure to which we are reacting, human beings are not robots or puppets; we can choose not to react or we can give varying meanings to our actions. Nevertheless, the raw material on which our choices are based also comes from what we have learned as members of the society. (Pp. 2–3)

From this example, we can see that sociology is the systematic study of the social behavior of individuals. It is the examination of the workings of social groups, organizations, cultures, and societies.

DIFFERENT KINDS OF SOCIOLOGY

There is no one sociology. Instead, there are several different sociological approaches to the study of human behavior in society. Unlike disciplines more limited in scope, such as economics or political science, sociology can deal with all aspects of society and human behavior, a fact that adds to the excitement of the field. The discipline's diversity virtually ensures that every student will find something of particular interest to study—from urban sociology to the sociology of art.

A sociologist who is asked, "What kind of sociologist are you?" will likely respond by listing his or her specialties; for example, some aspect of human behavior such as deviance, or some characteristic of social life such as politics. Although most sociologists have a theoretical preference, many utilize several approaches, depending on what's being studied.

SOME FUNDAMENTAL IDEAS OF SOCIOLOGY

SOCIAL CHANGE

Most sociologists agree that it is the actions and behaviors of humans that create social settings and social laws, and that these settings also influence the way people act. For example, consider the widespread use of slavery in developing countries and the widespread abolition of slavery in developed countries. Changes in women's right to vote, in the legal and illegal use of drugs, in the legal custody of minor children, and in the family system itself are just a few of the myriad examples of social change.

Every day people affirm or modify their social settings and thus maintain or change them. Each time a major change occurs, some people resist. Sociology is concerned with the way individuals and groups support or change their social surroundings.

THE SOCIOLOGICAL IMAGINATION

Some sociologists believe that society can be understood only by looking at both the subjective/personal and the objective/historical side of any given period. The sociological imagination demands that thinking people (1) view their world by locating themselves in their time period, and (2) become conscious of how the broader social structure directly affects their lives (Mills 1959).

People often view their personal lives in narrow frames that tend to exclude the effects of structural transformations like population migration to the sunbelt or evolution of local industries from textile manufacturing to high technology products. They may feel stifled by an inability to handle society's rapid pace of change. The sociological imagination allows people to envision what happens among them in society. It helps them to distinguish their personal problems from broader social issues and to thereby understand the effect of cultural values and norms on their own lives. In other words, personal problems can be better understood by "seeing" them within the social structure in which they occur.

Three basic questions frame the classic study of people in particular societies:

> What is the structure of the society in general?
> Where does the society stand in human history?
> What types of men and women prevail in this society and period of time?

Social issues—such as unemployment, divorce, and terrorism—are directly related to personal problems. Linking people to their social surroundings and the historical period in which they live tells us about their individual and social potentials. This linking activity requires sociological imagination, and this book will help you identify and sharpen your own social imagination.

CREATING THE PERSON

Socialization refers to the process in which people learn to conform to their society's norms, values, and roles. All social settings influence or constrain our behavior. Primary socialization refers to the process by which the newborn baby is molded into a social being. Secondary socialization occurs later in childhood and adolescence, as the young person is influenced by adults and peers outside the family. Our personal attitudes, beliefs, and behaviors about everything—morality, politics, religion, work, entertainment, and so on—are formed and changed by social settings.

Different stages of our lives instigate the change process, as do educational opportunities, a new job, new surroundings, and new historical times. Moving from one stage to another is often accompanied by a *rite of passage*, especially if the change is considered very important in that society. Graduation from high school marks a significant shift for some individuals in

American society: The graduation ceremony, or ritual, is the traditional rite of passage that illuminates the transition from adolescence to adulthood.

In advanced technological societies like the United States, the movement from one stage of cultural evolution to another is often more subtle than in societies where the current stage is relatively primitive, such as the Aborigines of the Australian outback. Their "walkabout" rite of passage requires that each postpubescent male adolescent be left alone in an unfamiliar place far from the village with only a spear. If he is able to make his way back to the village—a trip, often filled with life-threatening events, that sometimes takes up to two weeks—he is welcomed home with a ceremony that christens his arrival to adult status within the Aborigine society.

Looking further into understanding the socialization process, we find many unsolved issues that may be of interest to you as a student. One example centers around the relative strength of biological and/or social influences on human development—a critical issue in many areas of sociology, including criminology and social psychology. This discussion is known as the nature versus nurture debate. It questions the impact of heredity on the sense of self, versus how social environments affect socialization over time and within social circumstances. As sociologists study human behavior, they often discover that facts run contrary to popular beliefs. For example, within the context of the nature versus nurture debate, popular belief often holds that criminals are "born" with a predisposition to break laws. However, most social scientists agree that criminals are "socially constructed," or affected by numerous external influences, not "born that way."

CULTURAL RELATIVISM

The concept that cultures are "blueprints for living," drawn from particular environmental and situational conditions, is called *cultural relativism*. In a now classic study demonstrating cultural eccentricities and underscoring the idea of cultural relativism, Horace Miner (1956) describes the way of life of the Nacirema, a North American group whose chief lives on the banks of the Camotop River. The tribe is obsessed with rituals centered on deforming the human body: changing its color, its smell, and its shape. Under the guidance of "holy mouth men," whom they seek out once or twice a year, the Nacirema engage in a daily ritual of inserting bundles of hogs' hair and magical powders into the mouth and "then moving the bundle in a highly formalized series of gestures." Nacirema ceremonies can be quite painful, as when the men scrape their faces with sharp instruments and the women bake their heads in small ovens.

Described in this way, such customs appear very strange. Perhaps you'd be tempted to call them "primitive." Surely a person from the modern industrial world would not behave in this fashion. Yet Miner was simply looking at American (Nacirema backwards) society from a different perspective. Can you see it?

Look at some of our other behaviors. Consider tattooing, a process that is far from painless and is supposed to make the bearer's body both more attractive and somehow more powerful for having endured the pain. Another painful process, hair transplanting, is a fairly involved procedure designed to counter baldness.

No behavior should be considered out of the context of the culture in which it originates because what is natural to us will not necessarily be so to members of other societies (Hess et al. 1988).

Awareness and understanding of other cultures is important today because we all live in an international and global community. Cross-cultural studies involving reports and descriptions of societies other than our own allow students to become aware of and knowledgeable about how other societies function, which in turn diminishes ethnocentrism—the idea that one's own culture or group is best.

A BRIEF HISTORY OF SOCIOLOGY

EMERGENCE OF THE DISCIPLINE

As a discipline, sociology emerged in Europe as a direct result of the political, economic, demographic, social, and scientific changes precipitated by the Industrial Revolution in the late eighteenth and early nineteenth centuries. The Industrial Revolution, along with the French and other political revolutions, and a desire to apply the scientific method to the study of society, provided the vision to view society as a whole and the resources to accomplish that task. According to Charon (1996):

> Not only was sociology born in a time of science, but also in a time when industrialization and urbanization were transforming the very basis of society. [This led some sociologists to view] industrialization as they saw science: a means by which the problems that plagued humanity would be banished.... Other sociologists, such as Karl Marx, reacted to the extremes of inequality and poverty that the Industrial Revolution telescoped, while still others, such as Durkheim and Weber, saw basic changes in the old ways of society occurring—changes such as the declining importance of traditional religion and the growing bureaucratic organization of society. (P. 12)

STANDING ON THE SHOULDERS OF GIANTS

Many modern sociologists believe the aforementioned French and German scholars, with a few exceptions, laid the foundation for the basic issues and concepts that define sociology today. They spoke directly to the effects of social change and stability that were inherent in the revolutions on both continents. Robert K. Merton (1910–) notes that sociology has progressed to its current position as a scientific discipline by (borrowing Sir Isaac Newton's phrase) "standing on the shoulders of giants." The following is a brief summary of the contributions of several of these "giants."

Frenchman Auguste Comte (1798–1857) is often called the founder of sociology because he gave the emergent discipline its name—from the Latin *socius*, meaning companion with others, and the Greek *logos*, meaning the study of reason. A child of the Age of Enlightenment, Comte subscribed to its ideals of progress, political and economic freedom, individualism, the scientific method, and a profound belief in the ability of human beings to solve social problems. Highly influenced by the French Revolution and the tremendous changes it brought to European societies, Comte sought to help restore order and tranquillity to French society. Comte believed that sociology should be recognized as the science of society, beneath which all other sciences should be placed. He had tremendous faith in science as a means to solve such social problems as war, revolution, crime, and poverty, and rejected theological and philosophical approaches (although traces of them remained in his work).

Many of the ideas and concepts that are still germane to sociology sprang from scholars' attempts to explain the social milieu of their time. They defined economic aspects of social life, such as class, status, and power, and described the growing gap between urban and rural life, and rational and traditional thinking.

German philosopher Karl Marx (1818–1883) drew attention to the class conflict that arises between those who own the means of production and those who do not—the "haves" versus the "have-nots." He focused on the conflict that generated the change process. For Marx the superstructure of society—a cultural foundation composed of politics, religion, law, education, government, and family—constitutes a level of social life that is shaped primarily by economics.

Although it would not be entirely appropriate to label Marx a sociologist, his social analysis and political philosophy laid the foundation for *conflict theory*, which along with *functionalism* and *symbolic interactionism* (which we will discuss later) are the three major models or perspectives of sociological explanation today. Marx̓s analysis of social change proved to be a watershed of ideas for thinkers like Weber and Durkheim.

Max Weber (1864–1920) disagreed with Marx that the superstructure was always a product of economic institutions, and that economic conflict was always the precursor of social change. His classic work *The Protestant Ethic and the Spirit of Capitalism* (1930) supports the hypothesis that capitalism as an economic system was dependent on and flourished within the normative structure of Protestant religion, and that the Protestant ethic became the precursor of capitalism because it supported the belief that God approves of working hard, enjoying the material benefits of labor, and subsequently being generous to others.

Weber also believed that the emerging rationality of the modern age would ultimately transform social institutions into bureaucracies, wherein occupational specialization and the rational ordering of people would become a way of life. From a technical point of view, the bureaucratic type of administrative organization is the most rational, efficient, precise, and disciplined means of exerting control over human beings. No one recognized and feared the possible consequences of this trend more than Weber (1969):

> [I]t is still more horrible to think that the world could one day be filled with nothing but those little cogs, little men clinging to little jobs and striving towards bigger ones—a state of affairs which is to be seen once more, as in the Egyptian records, playing an ever-increasing part in the spirit of our present administrative system, and specially of its offspring, the students. This passion for bureaucracy ... is enough to drive one to despair. It is as if ... we were deliberately to become men who need "order" and nothing but order, who become nervous and cowardly if for one moment this order wavers, and helpless if they are torn away from their total incorporation in it. That the world should know no men but these: it is in such an evolution that we are already caught up, and the great question is therefore, not how we can promote and hasten it, but what can we oppose to this machinery in order to keep a portion of mankind free from this parceling-out of the soul, from this supreme mastery of the bureaucratic way of life. (P. 455)

Much of what Weber predicted has come to pass. Bureaucratic organizations have become dominant in most institutions of the modern world, including the military, religions, universities, government, and the economy.

French sociologist Emile Durkheim (1858–1917) examined the economic changes of the nineteenth century in a somewhat different light. His classic work *La Suicide* (1897) linked personal actions to much larger social forces—mainly the degree of social integration experienced by the individual. His work demonstrated for the first time that a personal act such as suicide could be properly understood only in terms of social facts such as religious beliefs and marital status.

Durkheim generated many insights related to social order and social relations. He believed that social solidarity is maintained by similar ideals internalized by people's personalities, and that complex social relations are governed by negotiations between individuals.

Ferdinand Toennies (1855–1936) emphasized the widening gap between the *Gemeinschaft* (traditional, communal relationships that exist in small, rural societies and are based on personal emotions and long-standing customs) and *Gesellschaft* (large, urban societies characterized by a modern type of associational relationship that is based on impersonal, rational, secondary group relations). He believed that as science uncovers the laws of nature, some of the wonder and mystery of existence is destroyed, and social organization moves from the *Gemeinschaft* to the *Gesellschaft*. He called this process the "disenchantment of the world."

Herbert Spencer (1820–1903), an English social historian, was one of the first to suggest that social scientists should suspend their own opinions and wishes when studying the facts of society. Spencer applied the predominant economic and biological models already available to the emergent discipline of sociology. Using the theory of evolution originated by English naturalist Charles Darwin (1809–1882) to help explain social change, Spencer's social evolution model provided critical justification for the growth of capitalism. He was influential for decades because his explanations supported rather than challenged the economy and social structure in which they were based.

Sigmund Freud (1854–1939), the founder of psychoanalysis, is considered the creator of the medical model of mental illness. His works *Totem and Taboo* (1913) and *Civilization and Its Discontents* (1930), among others, significantly influenced the creators of modern sociological theory. He stressed the interplay between internal (conscious and unconscious) personality forces and external social factors. Freud's contribution to sociology is important particularly because he stressed the ongoing conflict between the individual and society. For Freud, the socialization process consists of the progressive development of a social conscience (superego) through the increasing submission of individual impulses (sublimation) to societal wishes and requirements.

THE RISE OF AMERICAN SOCIOLOGY

By the turn of the nineteenth century, the Industrial Revolution had begun in the United States. Industrial expansion brought waves of immigrants from Europe, and America experienced a tremendous population increase. The period from 1880 to 1920 produced not only a rapid increase in population but also a dramatic change in the composition of the population. As droughts and crop failures plagued the nation's heartland, the United States became primarily urban for the first time, and urban life assumed new dimensions of social and technological challenge.

Responding to these developments, American sociologists first examined social changes, urbanization, racism, and crime. They also explored the gap between personal action and social structure, borrowed liberally from European influences, and generated new ideas of their own.

Charles Horton Cooley (1864–1929) and George Herbert Mead (1863–1931) were two major influences in the development of this new social psychology from a sociological perspective. In his classic work *Human Nature and the Social Order* (1902), Cooley rejected the belief that human nature is determined predominantly by genetic heritage and biological maturation. He argued that human development is a product of interaction with other humans in social group situations.

George Herbert Mead, in his book *Mind, Self and Society* (1934), published posthumously by his students, argued that both mind and self are social products that represent the outcomes of interactions with others in social situations rather than biological inheritance. He emphasized that the use of significant symbols—namely, language—is fundamental to human development. For Mead, socialization is never a finished product. His three-stage process—play, game, and identification with the generalized other (rules of society)—ultimately provides the frame of reference from which the child views him or herself. Mead argued that the self is never a finished product but rather is subject to significant modification throughout one's lifetime.

From the 1920s through the early 1970s, sociology enjoyed considerable growth as an academic discipline at major universities and colleges in the United States. Many sociology departments were formed, faculties hired and theory and research programs developed. While the field remains a highly abstract intellectual enterprise, it has also supplied the theoretical and methodological structure for more applied disciplines such as social work and criminal justice. This alignment with these more applied disciplines has great potential in both the discipline of sociology and in the amelioration of significant problems in the world.

MAJOR SOCIOLOGICAL PERSPECTIVES

According to Farley (1995:59), a perspective is usually composed of three elements (1) an approach to a topic that helps to determine the kinds of questions that are asked about the topic; (2) a theory or set of theories describing what are believed to be the realities of the topic; and (3) stated or unstated values concerning potentially controversial issues related to the topic.

We shall close this section by reexamining and expounding on the three major sociological perspectives introduced earlier: functionalism, conflict theory, and symbolic interactionism. Each perspective has unique assumptions and consequently different explanations or theories about social structure and human behavior. The first two perspectives, functionalism and conflict theory, compete with one another within what is known as the order versus conflict debate—a disagreement concerning whether society's institutions are the outgrowth of natural human impulses to order or conflict.

FUNCTIONALISM

Functionalism—often labeled structural-functionalism, equilibrium theory, consensus theory, or systems theory—is a product of Durkheim's attempt to show that Marx was mistaken in many of the assumptions and explanations that he associated with class conflict. Functionalism has been further developed, refined and elaborated by such modern American theorists as Talcott Parsons (1902–1975) and Robert K. Merton (1910–   ).

Functionalism emphasizes the order perspective, which assumes that every pattern of activity or structure in a given society makes some contribution—positive (functional) or negative (dysfunctional)—to the overall maintenance of that society. Functionalists view social structure as a regular pattern of social interaction and persistent social relationships, such as the patterned social relationship between races and ethnic groups, or the patterns of family organization. Functions represent a positive purpose or consequence, one necessary for the continued existence of the society. Manifest functions are intended and well-recognized, while latent functions are less obvious and often unintended. Major criticisms of this perspective center around its difficulty in explaining social change, and its tendency to affirm established power and the status quo.

CONFLICT THEORY

The Marxist model of power and class struggle is the bastion for the conflict perspective in the order versus conflict debate. A central assumption of Marxist theory is that "the distribution of wealth ... determines other aspects of society, such as the political system and the culture, including social norms, values and beliefs" (Farley 1995:61). These norms, values, and beliefs were labeled ideology by Marx, who believed that conflict is inevitable because of the scarcity of economic resources in society. Differences in access to these scarce economic resources allow one group or class (the haves) to dominate the other (the have-nots). The dominant social class is always the one that controls the means of economic production. Divergent values and interests create struggle that ensures the disenfranchisement and impoverishment of the weak. Since the ideological superstructure supports the dominant class (the middle class in a capitalistic system), the subordinate laboring class eventually experiences alienation—especially from work—and the potential for revolution increases. Conflict theory has been refined and elaborated on by such modern American theorists as C. Wright Mills and Ralf Dahrendorf.

SOCIAL PSYCHOLOGY

Symbolic interactionism is mainly a product of American sociology, and stems mostly from the ideas of Cooley, Mead, W. I. Thomas (1863–1947), and Florian Znaniecki (1882–1957). It focuses on the role of symbols—especially those embodied in language—that communicate meanings among people, and on a common "definition of the situation." According to this social-psychological perspective, people in a given society share an understanding of most commonly used symbols. Humans have a unique ability to use words. As they grow, word learning moves from the concrete to the abstract. We are influenced initially by the significant others in our lives, such as relatives and friends, who help us develop a sense of self. As we grow and mature, we adopt a perspective within the generalized other—society's values and normative structure. By understanding the meanings people attach to things through the use of words and other symbols, it is possible to understand much of human behavior.

A FINAL NOTE

The key proposition of all sociological thought is that human behavior—wherever you find it—is mediated, shaped, channeled, and influenced by social relationships and social systems. According to all sociological perspectives, answers to the human condition are not found in the genes or the phases of the moon but in the structure of social life, among the variations of social institutions and organizations such as the family, education, religion, ethnicity, social status, and nationality.

Sociology develops its understanding of all propositions through writing. Ideas do not crystallize until they are set forth on paper or in electronic form. This manual was written to help and encourage you to make your own unique contribution to society's understanding of how we live together, to join the marvelous pursuit of the branch of knowledge known as sociology.

CHAPTER 1

WRITING AS COMMUNICATION

Pilate had a notice prepared and fastened to the cross. It read:

JESUS OF NAZARETH, THE KING OF THE JEWS

Many of the Jews read this sign…. The chief priests of the Jews protested to Pilate, "Do not write 'The King of the Jews,' but that this man claimed to be king of the Jews."
     Pilate answered, "What I have written, I have written."
                              —*The Gospel According to John (19:19–22)*

Writing increaseth rage….

                              —*Fulke Greville, Lord Brooke, 1554–1628*

1.1   WRITING TO LEARN

Writing is a way of ordering your experience. Think about it: No matter what you are writing—a paper for your Introductory Sociology class, a short story, a limerick, or a grocery list—you are putting pieces of your world together in new ways and making yourself freshly conscious of these pieces. This is one of the reasons writing is so hard. From the infinite welter of data that your mind continually processes and locks in your memory, you are selecting only certain items significant to the task at hand, relating them to other items, and phrasing them in a new coherence. You are mapping a part of your universe that has hitherto been unknown territory. You are gaining a little more control over the processes by which you interact with the world around you.

This is why the act of writing, no matter where it leads, is never insignificant. It is always communication, a way of making a fresh connection with your world. Writing, therefore, is also one of the best ways to learn. This statement, at first, may sound odd. If you are an unpracticed writer, you may share a common notion that the only purpose writing can have is to express what you already know or think. Any learning that you as a writer might do has already been accomplished by the time your pen meets the paper. In this view, your task is to inform or even surprise the reader. But if you are a practiced writer, you know that at any moment as you write, you are capable of surprising yourself. And it is surprise that you look for: the shock of seeing what happens in your own mind when you drop an old, established opinion into a batch of new facts or bump into a cherished belief from a different angle. Writing synthesizes new understanding for the writer. E. M. Forster's famous question "How do I know what I think until I see what I say?" is one that all of us could ask. We make meaning as we write, jolting ourselves by little, surprising discoveries into a larger and more interesting universe.

1.1.1   THE IRONY OF WRITING

Good writing often helps the reader become aware of the ironies and paradoxes of human existence. One such paradox is that good writing expresses that which is unique about the writer and, at the same time, that which is common, not to the writer alone, but to every human being. Many of our most famous political statements share this double attribute of mirroring the singular and the ordinary. For example, read the following excerpts from President Franklin Roosevelt's first inaugural address, spoken on March 4, 1933, in the middle of the Great Depression. Then answer this question: Is what Roosevelt said famous because its expression is extraordinary, or because it appeals to something that is basic to every human being?

> This is pre-eminently the time to speak the truth, the whole truth, frankly and boldly. Nor need we shrink from honestly facing conditions in our country today. This great nation will endure as it has endured, will revive and will prosper.
>
> So first of all let me assert my firm belief that the only thing we have to fear is fear itself—nameless, unreasoning, unjustified terror which paralyzes needed efforts to convert retreat into advance.
>
> In every dark hour of our national life a leadership of frankness and vigor has met with that understanding and support of the people themselves which is essential to victory. I am convinced that you will again give that support to leadership in these critical days.
>
> In such a spirit on my part and on yours we face our common difficulties. They concern, thank God, only material things. Values have shrunken to fantastic levels; taxes have risen; our ability to pay has fallen; government of all kinds is faced by serious curtailment of income; the means of exchange are frozen in the currents of trade; the withered leaves of industrial enterprise lie on every side; farmers find no markets for their produce; the savings of many years in thousands of families are gone.

More important, a host of unemployed citizens face the grim problem of existence, and an equally great number toil with little return. Only a foolish optimist can deny the dark realities of the moment.

Yet our distress comes from no failure of substance. We are stricken by no plague of locusts. Compared with the perils which our forefathers conquered because they believed and were not afraid, we have still much to be thankful for. Nature still offers her bounty and human efforts have multiplied it. Plenty is at our doorstep, but a generous use of it languishes in the very sight of the supply....

The measure of the restoration lies in the extent to which we apply social values more noble than mere monetary profit.

Happiness lies not in the mere possession of money; it lies in the joy of achievement, in the thrill of creative effort.

The joy and moral stimulation of work no longer must be forgotten in the mad chase of evanescent profits. These dark days will be worth all they cost us if they teach us that our true destiny is not to be ministered unto but to minister to ourselves and to our fellow-men. (Commager 1963:240)

The benefits of writing in learning and in controlling what we learn are why sociology instructors will require a great deal of writing in their classes. Learning the complex and diverse world of sociology takes more than a passive ingestion of facts. You have to understand and come to grips with social issues and with your own attitudes toward them. When you write in an Introductory Sociology or Minorities in American Society class, you are entering into the world of the sociologist in the same way he or she does—testing theory against fact, fact against belief, belief against reality.

Writing is the entryway into social and political life. Virtually everything that happens in education, politics, and so on, happens on paper first. Documents are wrestled into shape before their contents can affect institutions and/or the public. Great speeches are written before they are spoken. Meaningful social programs must be spelled out before they are implemented. The written word has helped free slaves, end wars, create new opportunities in the workplace, and shape the values of nations. Often, gaining recognition for our ourselves and our ideas depends less on what we say than on how we say it. Accurate and persuasive writing is absolutely vital to the sociologist.

1.1.2 LEARNING BY WRITING

Here is a way to test the notion that writing is a powerful learning tool: Rewrite the notes you have taken from a recent class lecture. It does not matter which class—it can be history, chemistry, or advertising. Choose a difficult class, if possible, one in which you are feeling somewhat unsure of the material, and one in which you have taken copious notes. As you rewrite, provide the transitional elements (connecting phrases, such as *in order to, because of, and, but, however*) that you were unable to supply in class because of time constraints. Furnish your own examples or illustrations of the ideas expressed in the lecture.

This experiment forces you to make your own thought processes coherent. See if the time it takes you to rewrite the notes is not more than compensated for by a gain in your understanding of the lecture material.

1.1.3   CHALLENGING YOURSELF

There is no way around it—writing is a struggle. Do you think you are the only one to feel this way? Take heart! Writing is hard for everyone, great writers included. Bringing order into the world is never easy. Isaac Bashevis Singer, winner of the 1978 Nobel Prize in literature, once wrote, "I believe in miracles in every area of life except writing. Experience has shown me that there are no miracles in writing. The only thing that produces good writing is hard work" (Lunsford and Connors 1992:2). Hard work was evident in the words of John F. Kennedy's inaugural address. Each word is crafted to embed an image in the reader's mind. As you read the following excerpts from Kennedy's speech, what images come to mind? Historians tend to consider a president "great" when his words live longer than his deeds in the minds of the people. Do you think this will be true of Kennedy?

> We observe today not a victory of party but a celebration of freedom—symbolizing an end as well as a beginning—signifying renewal as well as change. For I have sworn before you and Almighty God the same solemn oath our forebears prescribed nearly a century and three-quarters ago.
>
> The world is very different now. For man holds in his mortal hands the power to abolish all forms of human poverty and all forms of human life. And yet the same revolutionary beliefs for which our forebears fought are still at issue around the globe—the belief that the rights of man come not from the generosity of the state but from the hand of God.
>
> We dare not forget today that we are the heirs of that first revolution. Let the word go forth from this time and place, to friend and foe alike, that the torch has been passed to a new generation of Americans—born in this century, tempered by war, disciplined by a hard and bitter peace, proud of our ancient heritage—and unwilling to witness or permit the slow undoing of those human rights to which this nation has always been committed, and to which we are committed today at home and around the world....
>
> In the long history of the world, only a few generations have been granted the role of defending freedom in its hours of maximum danger. I do not shrink from this responsibility—I welcome it. I do not believe that any of us would exchange places with any other people or any other generation. The energy, the faith, the devotion which we bring to this endeavor will light our country and all who serve it—and the glow from that fire can truly light the world.
>
> And so, my fellow Americans: ask not what your country can do for you—ask what you can do for your country.
>
> My fellow citizens of the world: ask not what American will do for you, but what together we can do for the freedom of man. (Commager 1963:688–689)

One reason for the difficulty of writing is that it is not actually a single activity, but a process consisting of several activities that can overlap each other, with two or more sometimes operating simultaneously as you labor to organize and phrase your thoughts (this will be discussed in greater detail later in this chapter). The writing process tends to be sloppy for everyone—an often frustrating search for the best way to articulate meaning.

Frustrating though that search may sometimes be, however, it need not be futile. Remember that the writing process makes use of skills that we all have. In other words, the ability to write is not some magical competence bestowed on the rare, fortunate individual. While few of us may achieve the proficiency of Isaac Singer, we are all capable of phrasing thoughts clearly and in a well-organized fashion. But learning how to do so takes practice: The one sure way to improve your writing is to write.

Remember also that one of the toughest but most important jobs in writing is to maintain enthusiasm for your writing project. Commitment may sometimes be hard to come by given the difficulties inherent in the writing process—difficulties that can be made worse when the project assigned is unappealing at first glance. For example, how can you be enthusiastic about having to write a paper analyzing welfare reform, when you know little about the American welfare system and see no real use in doing the project?

One of the worst mistakes that unpracticed writers sometimes make is failing to assume responsibility for keeping themselves interested in their writing. No matter how hard it may seem at first to drum up interest in your topic, you have to do it—that is, if you want to write a paper you can be proud of, one that contributes useful material and a fresh point of view to the topic. One thing is guaranteed: If you are bored with your writing, your reader will be, too.

So what can you do to keep your interest and energy level high? Challenge yourself. Think of the paper not as an assignment for a grade, but as a piece of writing that has a point to make. Getting this point across persuasively is the real reason that you are writing, not the simple fact that a teacher has assigned a project.

If someone were to ask you why you are writing your paper, what would you answer? If your immediate, unthinking response is, "Because I've been given a writing assignment," or "Because I want a good grade," your paper may be in trouble. If, on the other hand, your first impulse is to explain the challenge of your main point—"I'm writing to show how welfare reform will benefit both welfare recipients and the American taxpayer"—then you are thinking usefully about your topic.

1.1.4 MAINTAINING SELF-CONFIDENCE

Having a sense of confidence in your ability to write well about your topic is essential for good writing. This does not mean that you will always know what the end result of a particular writing activity will be. In fact, you have to cultivate your ability to tolerate a high degree of uncertainty while weighing evidence, testing hypotheses, and experimenting with organizational strategies and wording. Be ready for temporary confusion, for seeming dead ends, and remember that every writer faces them. It is from your struggle to combine fact with fact, to buttress conjecture with evidence, that order arises.

Do not be intimidated by the amount and quality of work already done in your field of inquiry. The array of opinion and evidence that confronts you in the published literature can be confusing. But remember that no important topic is ever exhausted. There are always gaps—questions that have not yet been satisfactorily explored either in the published research on a subject or in the prevailing popular opinion. It is in these gaps that you establish your own authority, your own sense of control.

Remember that the various stages of the writing process reinforce one another. Establishing a solid motivation strengthens your sense of confidence about the project, which in turn influences how successfully you organize and write. If you start out well, using good work habits, and give yourself ample time for the various activities to gel, you should produce a paper that will reflect your best work, one that your audience will find both readable and useful.

1.2   THE WRITING PROCESS

As you engage in the writing process, you are doing many different things at once. While planning, you are no doubt defining the audience for your paper at the same time that you are thinking about the paper's purpose. As you draft the paper, you may organize your next sentence while revising the one you have just written. Different parts of the writing process overlap, and much of the difficulty of writing is that so many things happen at once. Through practice—in other words, through writing—it is possible to learn how to control those parts of the process that can be controlled and to encourage those mysterious, less controllable activities.

No two people go about writing in exactly the same way. It is important for you to recognize routines—modes of thought as well as individual exercises—that help you negotiate the process successfully. And it is also important to give yourself as much time as possible to complete the process. Procrastination is one of the writer's greatest enemies. It saps confidence, undermines energy, and destroys concentration. Working regularly and keeping as close as possible to a well-thought-out schedule often make the difference between a successful paper and an embarrassment.

Although the various parts of the writing process are interwoven, there is, naturally, a general order to the work you have to do. You have to start somewhere! What follows is a description of the various stages of the writing process—planning, drafting, revising, editing, and proofreading—along with suggestions as to how to get the most out of each.

1.2.1   PLANNING

Planning includes all activities that lead up to the writing of the first draft. These activities differ from person to person. For instance, some writers prefer to compile a formal outline before writing that draft. Others perform brief writing exercises to jump-start their imaginations. Some draw diagrams; others doodle. Later on we'll look at a few starting strategies and you can determine which may be of help to you.

Right now, however, let us discuss some early choices that all writers must make during the planning stage. These choices concern topic, thesis, purpose, and audience—four elements that help make up the writing context, the terms under which we all write. Every time you write—even if you are writing a diary entry or a note to the delivery person—these four elements are present. You may not give conscious consideration to all of them in each piece of writing that you do, but it is extremely important to think carefully about them when writing a sociology paper. Some or all of these defining elements may be dictated by your assignment, yet you will always have a degree of control over them.

Selecting a Topic   No matter how restrictive an assignment may seem to be, there is no reason to feel trapped by it. Within any assigned subject you can find a range of topics to explore. What you are looking for is a topic that engages your own interest. Let your curiosity be your guide. For example, if you have been assigned the subject of welfare reform, then try to find some issue(s) concerning welfare reform that interests you. (How does receiving something for nothing affect an individual's self-esteem? What would be the repercussions of limiting the amount of time anyone could receive welfare benefits?) Any good topic comes with a set of questions; you may well find that your interest picks up if you simply begin asking questions.

One strong recommendation: Ask your questions on paper. Like most other mental activities, the process of exploring your way through a topic is transformed when you write down your thoughts as they come instead of letting them fly through your mind unrecorded. Remember the old adage from Louis Agassiz: "A pen is often the best of eyes" (Pearce 1958:106).

While it is vital to be interested in your topic, you do not have to know much about it at the outset of your investigation. In fact, having too heartfelt a commitment to a topic can be an impediment to writing about it; emotions can get in the way of objectivity. Often it is better to choose a topic that has piqued your interest yet remained something of a mystery to you—a topic discussed in one of your classes, perhaps, or mentioned on television or in a conversation with friends.

Narrowing Your Topic   The task of narrowing your topic offers you a tremendous opportunity to establish a measure of control over the writing project. It is up to you to hone your topic to just the right shape and size to suit both your own interests and the requirements of the assignment. Do a good job of it, and you will go a long way toward guaranteeing yourself sufficient motivation and confidence for the tasks ahead of you. Do it wrong, and somewhere along the way you may find yourself directionless and out of energy.

Generally, the first topics that come to your mind will be too large to handle in your research paper. For example, the topic of a national health policy has generated a tremendous number of news articles and reports recently published by experts in the field. Despite all the attention turned toward this topic, however, there is still plenty of room for you to investigate it on a level that has real meaning to you and that does not merely recapitulate the published research. What about an analysis of how one of the proposed U.S. health policies might affect insurance costs in a locally owned company?

The problem with most topics is not that they are too narrow or too completely explored; it is that they are too rich. There are so many useful ways to address a topic that choosing the best focus is often difficult. Take your time narrowing the topic. Think through the possibilities that occur to you, and—as always—jot down your thoughts.

The following is a list of topics assigned to undergraduate students in a course on social theory. Their task was to choose a topic and write an essay of 2,500 words. Next to each topic is an example of how a student narrowed it to make it a manageable paper topic.

General Topic	Paper Topic
Plato	Plato's philosophy of the role of women in politics
Freedom	A comparison of Rousseau's concept of freedom with John Locke's
Community	Arguments for the necessity of community used by Amitai Etzioni
Max Weber	Weber's definition of bureaucracy

Finding a Thesis   As you plan, be on the lookout for an idea that would serve as your thesis. A thesis is not a fact that can be immediately proven by recourse to recorded information, but a hypothesis worth discussing, an argument with more than one possible conclusion. Your thesis sentence will reveal to your reader not only the argument you have chosen, but also your orientation toward it—the conclusion that your paper will attempt to prove.

In looking for a thesis, you do many jobs at once:

1. You limit the amount and kind of material that you must cover, making it manageable.
2. You increase your own interest in the narrowing field of study.
3. You work to establish your paper's purpose—the reason that you are

EXERCISE

Without taking time to research them, see what kinds of viable narrowed topics you can make from the following general topics:

crime in America	political corruption
international terrorism	military spending
education	affirmative action hiring policies
freedom of speech	freedom of religion
gun control	abortion rights

Example

general topic   the family

narrowed topics   cultural demands that keep family members isolated

substance abuse and the family

the Waltons and *Mommie Dearest*: elements of the American family

writing about your topic. (If the only reason you can see for writing is to earn a good grade, then you probably won't!)

4. You establish your notion of who your audience is and what sort of approach might best catch their interest.

In short, you gain control over your writing context. For this reason, it is a good idea to establish a thesis early on—a working thesis—that will very probably change as your thinking deepens but that will allow you to establish a measure of order in the planning stage.

The Thesis Sentence   The introduction of your paper will contain a sentence that expresses in a nutshell the task that you intend to accomplish. This thesis sentence communicates your main idea—the one you are going to support or defend or illustrate. The thesis sets up an expectation in the reader's mind that you must satisfy. But it is more than just the statement that informs your reader of your goal; in the planning stage, the thesis is a valuable tool to help you narrow your focus and confirm in your own mind your paper's purpose.

Developing a Thesis   A class on Crime and Society was assigned a twenty-page paper studying a problem currently being faced by the municipal authorities in their own city. The choice of the problem was left up to the students. One student, Richard Gonzales, decided to investigate the problem posed by the city of the large number of abandoned buildings in a downtown neighborhood that he drove through on his way to the university.

Richard's first working thesis was: "Abandoned houses result in negative social effects to the city."

The problem with this thesis, as Richard found out, was that it was not an idea that could be argued, but a fact corroborated easily by the sources Richard began to consult. As he read reports from various sources, such as the Urban Land Institute and the City Planning Commission, and talked with representatives from the Community Planning Department, Richard began to get interested in the dilemma faced by his city in responding to the problem of abandoned buildings.

Richard's second working thesis was: "Removal of abandoned buildings is a major problem facing the city."

This thesis narrowed the topic somewhat and gave Richard an opportunity to use material gleaned from his research, but there was still no real comment attached to it. It still states a bare fact, easily proved. At this point, Richard became interested in the still narrower topic of how building removal should best be handled. He found that the major issue was funding and that different civic groups favored different methods of funding the demolition. As Richard explored the arguments for and against funding plans, he began to feel that one of them might be best for the city.

Richard's third working thesis was: "Assessing a 'demolition fee' to each sale of a property offers a viable solution to the city's building removal problem."

Note how this thesis narrowed the focus of Richard's paper still further than the other two yet presents an arguable hypothesis. This thesis told Richard what he had to do in his paper, just as it tells his reader what to expect.

At some time during your preliminary thinking on a topic, you should consult the library to see how much published work has already been done. This search is beneficial in at least two ways:

1. It acquaints you with a body of writing that will become very important in the research phase.
2. It gives you a sense of how your topic is generally addressed by the community of scholars you are joining. Is the topic as important as you think it is? Has there already been so much research on the topic as to make your inquiry, in its present formulation, irrelevant? These questions can be answered by reviewing the literature.

As you go about determining your topic, remember that one goal of sociology writing in college is to enhance your own understanding of the social and/or social-psychological process, to build an accurate model of the way societies work. Let this goal help you: Aim your research into those subject areas that you know are important to your understanding of the discipline.

Defining a Purpose   There are many ways to classify the purposes of writing, but in general most writing is undertaken either to inform or to persuade an audience. The goal of informative or expository writing is, simply, to impart information about a particular subject, whereas the aim of persuasive writing is to convince your reader of your point of view on an issue. The distinction between expository and persuasive writing is not hard and fast. Most sociology writing has elements of both exposition and persuasion. However, most effective writing has a clearly chosen focus of either exposition or persuasion. When you begin writing, consciously select a primary aim of exposition or persuasion, and then set out to achieve that goal.

Suppose you have been required to write a paper explaining how parents' attitudes affect their children's choice of college. If you are writing an expository paper, your task could be to describe in a coherent and impartial way the attitudes of the parents and the choices of their children.

If, however, your paper attempts to convince your reader that parental attitudes often result in children making poor choices, you are now writing to persuade, and your strategy is radically different. You will now need to explain the negative effects of parental attitudes. Persuasive writing seeks to influence the opinions of its audience toward its subject.

Writing assignments in sociology may break down the distinction between expository and persuasive writing in a number of ways. You may be called on to analyze sociopolitical situations, evaluate government programs, speculate on directions in social policy, identify or define problems within a range of fields, or suggest solutions and predict results. It is very important to spend planning time sharpening your sense of purpose.

Know what you want to say. By the time you begin working on your final draft, you must have a very sound notion of the point you wish to argue or the position you wish to support. If, during the writing of the final draft, someone were to ask you to state your thesis, you should be able to give a satisfactory answer with a minimum of delay and no prompting. On the other hand, if you have to hedge your answer because you cannot easily form a notion of your thesis in your own mind, you may not yet have arrived at a final draft.

For example, two writers have been asked what point they wish to make in their papers. One of these writers has a better grip on her writing task.

Writer 1: "My paper is about tax reform for the middle class."

Writer 2: "My paper argues that tax reform for the middle class would be unfair to the upper and lower classes, who would then have to share more responsibility for the cost of government."

The second writer has a clear view of her task; the first knows what her topic is—tax reform for the middle class—but may not yet know what it is about tax reform that she wishes to support. It may be that you will have to write a draft or two or engage in various prewriting activities to arrive at a secure understanding of your task.

Watch out for bias! There is no such thing as pure objectivity. You are not a machine. No matter how hard you may try to produce an objective paper, every choice you make as you write is influenced to some extent by your personal beliefs and opinions. What you tell your readers is influenced—sometimes without your knowing—by a multitude of factors: your environment, upbringing, and education; your attitude toward your audience; your political affiliation; your race and gender; your career goals; and your ambitions for the paper you are writing. The influence of these factors can be very subtle, and it is something you must work to identify in your own writing as well as in the writing of others in order not to mislead or be misled. Remember that one of the reasons you write is for self-discovery. The writing you will do in sociology classes—as well as the writing you will do for the rest of your life—will give you a chance to discover and confront honestly your own views on your subjects. Responsible writers keep an eye on their own biases and are honest with their readers about them.

Defining Your Audience   It may sometimes be difficult to remember that the point of your writing is not simply to jump through the technical hoops imposed by the assignment. The point is communication—the transmission of your knowledge and your conclusions—to the reader in a way that suits you. Your task is to pass to your reader the spark of your own enthusiasm for the topic. Readers who were indifferent to your topic should look at it in a new way after reading your paper. This is the great challenge of writing: to enter into your reader's mind and leave behind new knowledge and new questions.

It is tempting to think that most writing problems would be solved if the writer could view her writing as if it had been produced by another person. The ego barrier between writer and audience is the single greatest impediment to accurate communication. To reduce the discrepancy between your understanding and that of your audience, it is necessary to consider the audience's needs. By the time you begin drafting, most—if not all—of your ideas have begun to attain coherent shape in your mind, so that virtually any words in which you try to phrase those ideas will reflect your thought accurately—to you. Your reader, however, does not already have in mind the conclusions that you have so painstakingly achieved. If you leave out of your writing the material that is necessary to complete your reader's understanding of your argument, he may not be able to supply that information himself.

The potential for misunderstanding is a given for any audience—whether it is made up of general readers, experts in the field, or your professor, who is reading, in part, to see how well you have mastered the constraints that govern the relationship between writer and reader. Make your presentation as complete as possible, writing always as if to an audience whose previous knowledge of your topic is limited to information easily available to the general public.

John F. Kennedy's Pastry Mistake

President Kennedy was one of America's greatest speechmakers. He had a gift for understanding and speaking directly to the audience he was to address. At one point during the Cold War, the Soviet Union banned shipments of supplies across East Germany to West Berlin, the part of the city governed by the Western, noncommunist countries. It was a tense moment in East-West relations.

Going to Berlin, on June 26, 1963, Kennedy spoke to the besieged people as if he were one of them. The people responded warmly, cheering his speech continuously. At the climactic moment, Kennedy boldly proclaimed, in words that became famous, "Ich bein ein Berliner." He was attempting to say, in German, "I am a citizen of Berlin," meaning, "I am one of you; I share your concerns in this moment of crisis."

What he said instead was German for, "I am a pastry." His mistake was in inserting the article ein—ein Berliner is a kind of pastry in Germany.

Knowing your audience can sometimes be more difficult than it first appears.

1.2.2   USING INVENTION STRATEGIES

In this chapter, we have discussed methods of selecting and narrowing the topic of a paper. As your focus on a specific topic sharpens, you naturally begin to think about the kinds of information that will go into the paper. In the case of papers not requiring formal research, that material comes largely from your own recollections. Indeed, one of the reasons why instructors assign unresearched papers is to convince you of the incredible richness of your memory, the vastness and variety of the "database" you have accumulated and which, moment by moment, you continue to build.

So vast is your horde of information that it is sometimes difficult to find within it the material that would best suit your paper. In other words, finding out what you already know about a topic is not always easy. Invention—a term borrowed from classical rhetoric—refers to the task of discovering, or recovering from memory, information about your topic. As we write, all of us go through some sort of invention procedure that helps us explore our topic. Some writers seem to have little problem coming up with material; others need more help. Over the centuries writers have devised different exercises that can help locate useful material housed in memory. We shall look at a few of these briefly.

Freewriting   Freewriting is an activity that forces you to get something down on paper. There is no waiting around for inspiration. Instead, you set yourself a time limit—three minutes or five minutes—and write for that length of time without stopping, not even to lift the pen from the paper or your hands from the typewriter or computer keyboard. Focus on the topic, and don't let the difficulty of finding relevant material stop you from writing. If necessary, you may begin by writing, over and over, some seemingly useless phrase, like, "I cannot think of anything to write about," or perhaps the name of your topic. Eventually, something else will occur to you. (It is surprising how long a three-minute freewriting

can seem to take!) At the end of the freewriting, look over what you have produced for anything of use. Granted, much of the writing will be unusable, but
there may be an insight or two that you did not know you possessed.

In addition to its ability to recover usable material for your paper,
freewriting yields a few other benefits. First, it takes little time to do, which
means you may repeat the exercise as often as you like within a relatively
short span of time. Second, it breaks down some of the resistance that stands
between you and the act of writing. There is no initial struggle to find something to say; you just write.

An Example of Freewriting

The professor in Shelby Johnson's second-year Family as a Social
Institution class assigned a paper focusing on some aspect of American
family life. Shelby, who felt her understanding of the family as an institution
was modest, tried to get her mind started on the job of finding a topic that
interested her with a two-minute freewriting. Thinking about the family and
child development, Shelby wrote steadily for three minutes without lifting
her pen from the paper. Here is the result of her freewriting:

> Okay, now, what do I know about the family? I was raised in
> one. I have a father, mother and sister. Both parents were pre-
> sent all my life. Both worked. Professionals. Sometimes I wished
> Mom was at home. That might be interesting: working parents,
> the effects on kids. Two-paycheck families. I like it. Where to
> start. I could interview my parents. I need to find some recent
> statistics on two-paycheck families.

Brainstorming   Brainstorming is simply making a list of ideas about a
topic. It can be done quickly and, initially, without any need to order items
into a coherent pattern. The point is to write down everything that occurs to
you quickly and as briefly as possible, as individual words or short phrases.
Once you have a good-sized list of items, you can then group the items
according to relationships that you see among them. Brainstorming allows
you to both uncover ideas stored in your memory and make useful associations among those ideas.

A professor in a political sociology class asked her students to write a 700-
word paper, in the form of a letter to be translated and published in a Warsaw
newspaper, giving the Polish readers useful advice about living in a democracy.
Carrie Nation, a student in the class, started thinking about the assignment by
brainstorming. First, she simply wrote down anything that occurred to her:

Life in a Democracy

voting rights	welfare	freedom of press
protest movements	everybody equal	minorities
racial prejudice	American Dream	injustice
the individual	no job security	lobbyists and PACs
justice takes time	psychological factors	aristocracy of wealth
size of bureaucracy	market economy	

Thinking through her list, Carrie decided to rearrange her list into two, one devoted to positive aspects of life in a democracy, the other to negative aspects. At this point she decided to discard some items that were redundant or did not seem to have much potential. As you can see, Carrie had some questions about where some of her items would fit.

Positive	Negative
voting rights	aristocracy of wealth
freedom of the press	justice takes time
everybody equal	racial prejudice
the American Dream	welfare
psychological factors	lobbyists and PACs
protest movements (positive?)	size of bureaucracy

At this point, Carrie decided that her strongest inclination was to explore the ways in which money and special interests affect a democratically elected government. Which of the remaining items in her two lists would be of help to Carrie?

Asking Questions   It is always possible to ask most or all of the following questions about any topic: Who? What? When? Where? Why? How? These questions force you to approach the topic the way a journalist does, setting the topic within different perspectives that can then be compared to discover insights within the material.

For a class in the sociology of law, a professor asked her class to write a paper describing the impact of Supreme Court clerks on the decision-making process. Here are some questions that a student in the class might logically ask to begin thinking about a thesis.

- Who are the Supreme Court's clerks? (How old? What racial and sexual mix are they? What are their politics?)
- What are their qualifications for the job?
- What exactly is their job?
- When during the court term are they most influential?
- Where do they come from? (Is there any geographical pattern discernible in the way they are chosen? Any pattern regarding religion? Do certain law schools contribute a significantly greater number of clerks than any others?)
- How are they chosen? (Are they appointed? elected?)
- When in their careers do they serve?
- Why are they chosen as they are?
- Who have been some influential court clerks? (Have any gone on to sit on the bench themselves?)

Can you think of other questions that would make for useful inquiry?

Being Flexible   As you engage in invention strategies, you are also doing other work. You are still narrowing your topic, for example, as well as making decisions that will affect your choice of tone or audience. You move forward on all fronts, with each decision you make affecting the others. This means you must be flexible enough in your understanding of the paper's development to allow for adjustments or alterations in your understanding of your goal. Never be so determined to prove a particular theory that you fail to notice when your own understanding of it changes. Stay objective.

1.2.3   ORGANIZING YOUR WRITING BY OUTLINING

A paper that contains all the facts but provides them in an ineffective order will confuse rather than inform or persuade. While there are various methods of grouping ideas, none is potentially more effective than outlining. Unfortunately, no organizing process is more often misunderstood.

Outlining for Yourself   There are really two jobs that outlining can do. First, it can serve as a means of forcing you, the writer, to gain a better understanding of your ideas by arranging them according to their interrelationships. As the following model indicates, there is one primary rule of outlining: Ideas of equal weight are placed on the same level within the outline. This rule requires you to determine the relative importance of your ideas. You must decide whether one idea is of the same type or order as another and which subtopic each idea best fits into.

In the planning stage, if you arrange your ideas with care in a coherent outline, your own grasp of your topic will be greatly enhanced. You will have linked your ideas together logically and given a skeleton to the body of the paper. This sort of subordinating and coordinating activity is difficult, however, and as a result, inexperienced writers sometimes fail to pay the necessary attention to the outline. They begin writing their first draft without an effective outline, hoping for the best. That hope usually disappears, especially in complex papers involving research.

Garcia, a student in a second-year class in government management, researched the impact of a worker-retraining program in his state and came up with the following facts and theories. Number them in logical order.

1. A growing number of workers in the state do not possess the basic skills and education demanded by employers.
2. The number of dislocated workers in the state increased from 21,000 in 1982 to 32,000 in 1992.
3. A public policy to retrain uneducated workers would allow them to move into new and expanding sectors of the Oklahoma economy.
4. Investment in high technology would allow the state's employers to remain competitive in the production of goods and services in both domestic and foreign markets.
5. The economy is becoming more global and more competitive.

Outlining for Your Reader   The second job of an outline is aimed not at the writer's understanding, but at the reader's. An outline accompanying your paper can serve the reader as a blueprint of the paper—a summary of the paper's points and their interrelationships. A busy person can consult your outline to quickly get a sense of your paper's goal and the argument you have used to promote it. This accompanying outline, then, is very important, since its clarity and coherence helps to determine how much attention your audience will give to your ideas.

As sociology students, you will be given a great deal of help with the arrangement of your material into an outline to accompany your paper. A look at the model presented in other chapters of this manual will show you how strictly these formal outlines are structured. But while you must pay close attention to the requirements of the accompanying outline, do not forget that an outline is a powerful tool in the early planning stages of your paper.

Formal Outline Pattern   Following this pattern accurately during the planning stage of your paper helps to guarantee that your ideas are placed logically:

Thesis sentence (prefaces the organized outline).

I.   First main idea
　　A. First subordinate idea
　　　　1. Reason, example, or illustration
　　　　2. Reason, example, or illustration
　　　　　　a. Detail supporting reason #2
　　　　　　b. Detail supporting reason #2
　　　　　　c. Detail supporting reason #2
　　B. Second subordinate idea
II. Second main idea

Notice that each level of the paper must have more than one entry: For every A there must be at least a B (and, if required, a C, D, etc.); for every 1 there must be a 2. This arrangement forces you to compare ideas, looking carefully at each one to determine its place among the others. The insistence on assigning relative values to your ideas is what makes your outline an effective organizing tool.

The structure of any particular type of sociology paper is governed by a formal pattern. When rigid external controls are placed on their writing, some writers tend to feel stifled; their creativity impeded by this kind of paint-by-numbers approach to structure. It is vital to the success of your paper that you never allow yourself to be overwhelmed by the pattern rules of a particular type of paper. Remember that such controls are placed on papers not to limit your creativity but to make the paper immediately and easily useful to its intended audience. It is as necessary to write clearly and confidently in a social issue paper or a case study as it is in a term paper for English literature, a résumé, a short story, or a job application letter.

1.2.4   WRITING DRAFTS

The Rough Draft   After the planning comes the writing of the first draft. Using your thesis and outline as direction markers, you must now weave your amalgam of ideas, researched data, and persuasion strategies into logically ordered sentences and paragraphs. Though adequate prewriting may make the drafting easier than it might have been, it will still not be easy. Writers establish their own methods of encouraging themselves to forge ahead with the draft, but here are some tips to bear in mind:

1. Remember that this is a rough draft, not the final draft. At this stage, it is not necessary that every word you write be the best possible word. Do not put that sort of pressure on yourself; you must not allow anything to slow you down now. Writing is not like sculpting, in which every chip is permanent—you can always go back to your draft later and add, delete, reword, or rearrange. No matter how much effort you have put into planning, you cannot be sure how much of this first draft you will eventually keep. It may take several drafts to get one that you find satisfactory.

2. Give yourself sufficient time to write. Don't delay the first draft by telling yourself there is still more research to do. You cannot uncover all the material there is to know on a particular subject, so don't fool yourself into trying. Remember that writing is a process of discovery. You may have to begin writing before you can see exactly what sort of final research you need to do. Keep in mind that there are other tasks waiting for you after the first draft is finished, so allow for them as you determine your writing schedule. Giving yourself time is very important for another reason: The more time that passes after you write a draft, the better your ability to view it with greater objectivity. It is very difficult to evaluate your writing accurately soon after you complete it. You need to cool down, to recover from the effort of putting all those words together. The "colder" you get on your writing, the better able you are to read it as if it were written by someone else, which helps you acknowledge the changes needed to strengthen the paper.

3. Stay sharp. It is important to keep in mind the plan you created for yourself as you narrowed your topic, composed a thesis sentence, and outlined the material. But if as you write you feel a strong need to change the plan a bit, do not be afraid to do so. Be ready for surprises dealt you by your own growing understanding of your topic. Your goal is to render your best thinking on the subject as accurately as possible.

Authority   To be convincing, your writing needs to be authoritative; that is, you have to sound as if you have confidence in your ability to convey your ideas in words. Sentences that sound stilted or that suffer from weak phrasing or the use of clichés are not going to win supporters for the aims that you express in your paper. So sounding confident becomes a major concern. Consider the following points as you work to convey to your reader that necessary sense of authority.

LEVEL OF FORMALITY. Tone is one of the primary methods by which you signal to the reader who you are and what your attitude is toward him and toward your topic. The major choice you make has to do with the level of language formality that you feel is most appropriate for your audience. The informal tone you would use in a letter to a friend might well be out of place in a paper called "Waste in Military Spending" written for your sociology professor. Remember that tone is only part of the overall decision that you make about how to present your information. To some extent, formality is a function of individual word choices and phrasing. Is it appropriate to use contractions like "isn't" or "they'll"? Would the strategic use of a sentence fragment for effect be out of place? The use of informal language, the personal "I," and the second person "you" is traditionally forbidden—for better or worse—in certain kinds of writing. Often, part of the challenge of writing a formal paper is, simply, how to give your prose bite while staying within the conventions.

JARGON. One way to lose readers quickly is to overwhelm them with jargon—phrases that have a special, usually technical meaning within your discipline, but that are unfamiliar to the average reader. The occasional use of jargon may add an effective touch of atmosphere, but anything more than that will severely dampen a reader's enthusiasm for the paper. Often a reason for jargon is the writer's desire to impress the reader by sounding lofty or knowledgeable. Unfortunately, all jargon usually does is make for confusion. In fact, jargon is often an index of the writer's lack of connection to his audience.

Sociology writing is a haven for jargon. Perhaps writers of professional journals and certain issue papers believe their readers are all completely attuned to their terminology. It may be that these writers occasionally hope to obscure faulty information or potentially unpopular ideas in confusing language. Or the problem could simply be fuzzy thinking on the writer's part. Whatever the reason, sociology papers too often sound like prose made by machines to be read by machines.

Some students may feel that, in order to be accepted as sociologists, their papers should conform to the practices of their published peers. This is a mistake. Remember that it is always better to write a clear sentence than a cluttered or confusing one, and that burying your ideas in jargon defeats the effort that you went through to form them.

CLICHÉS. In the heat of composition, as you are looking for words to help you form your ideas, it is sometimes easy to plug in a cliché—a phrase that has attained universal recognition by overuse. (Note that clichés differ from jargon in that clichés are part of the general public's everyday language, while

jargon is specific to the language of experts in a particular field.) Our vocabu-
laries are brimming with clichés:

> It's raining cats and dogs.
> That issue is dead as a doornail.
> It's time for the governor to face the music.
> Angry voters made a beeline for the ballot box.

The problem with clichés is that they are virtually meaningless. Once
colorful means of expression, they have lost their color through overuse, and
they tend to bleed energy and color from the surrounding words. When revising, replace clichés with words that more accurately convey the specific
impression that you wish to create.

Descriptive Language   Language that appeals to the reader's senses
will always engage his or her interest more fully than language that is abstract.
This is especially important for writing in disciplines that tend to deal in
abstracts—such as sociology. The typical sociology paper—with its discussions of abstract principles, demographics, or deterministic outcomes—is
often in danger of floating off on a cloud of abstractions, drifting farther away
in each paragraph from the tangible life of the reader. Whenever appropriate,
appeal to your reader's sense of sight, hearing, taste, touch, or smell. Consider
the effectiveness of the second sentence below, as opposed to that of the first.

1. The housing project had deteriorated since the last inspection.
2. Since the last inspection, deterioration of the housing project had
   become evident in stench rising from the plumbing, grime on the walls
   and floors, and the sound of rats scurrying in the hallways.

Bias-Free and Gender-Neutral Writing   Language can be a very powerful method of either reinforcing or destroying cultural stereotypes. You
should try to avoid gender bias and ethnic stereotyping in your writing. By
treating the sexes in subtly different ways in your writing, you may unknow-
ingly be committing an act of discrimination. A common example is the use of
the pronoun *he* to refer to a person whose gender has not been identified. But
there are many other writing situations in which sexist and/or ethnic bias may
appear. To avoid gender bias, the American Sociological Association (1996)
recommends replacing words like *man, men,* or *mankind* with *person, people,*
or *humankind.* When both sexes must be referred to in a sentence, use *he or
she, her or him,* and *his or hers* instead of *he/she, him/her,* and *his/hers.*
Consider the following examples of sexist and nonsexist language:

> *Sexist:* A lawyer should always treat his client with respect.
> *Corrected:* A lawyer should always treat his or her client with respect.
> *or:* Lawyers should always treat their clients with respect.

Sexist: Man is a political animal.

Corrected: People are political animals.

There are other methods of avoiding gender bias in your writing. Some writers, faced with the aforementioned pronoun dilemma, alternate the use of male and female personal pronouns, identifying to the unknown referent as he in one section of their text, then as she in the next (a strategy used in this manual). You can also change the subject to plural—there is no gender bias in *they.*

Sexist language denies to a large number of your readers the basic right to fair and equal treatment. Be aware of this subtle form of discrimination. Remember that language is more than the mere vehicle of your thoughts; your words shape perceptions for your reader. How well you say something will profoundly affect your reader's response to it.

1.2.5 REVISING

After all the work you have gone through writing it, you may feel "married" to the first draft of your paper. However, revising is one of the most important steps in assuring your paper's success. While unpracticed writers often think of revision as little more than making sure all the *i*'s are dotted and *t*'s are crossed, it is much more than that. Revising is reseeing the paper, looking at it from other perspectives, trying always to align your view with the view that will be held by your audience. Research in the process of composition indicates that we are actually revising all the time, in every phase of the writing process as we reread phrases, rethink the placement of a item in an outline, or test a new topic sentence for a paragraph. Subjecting your entire hard-fought draft to cold, objective scrutiny is one of the most difficult activities to master in the writing process, but it is absolutely necessary. You must make sure that you have said everything that needs to be said clearly and in logical order. One confusing passage, and the reader's attention is deflected from where you want it to be. Suddenly she has to become a detective, trying to figure out why you wrote what you did and what you meant by it. You don't want to throw such obstacles in the path of meaning.

Here are some tips to help you with revision:

1. Give yourself adequate time to revise. As mentioned previously, you need time to become "cold" on your paper in order to analyze it objectively. After you have written your draft, spend some time away from it. Try to come back to it as if it had been written by someone other than yourself.

2. Read the paper carefully. This is tougher than it sounds. One good strategy is to read it aloud or to have a friend read it aloud while you listen. (Note: Having friends critique your writing may be helpful, but friends do not usually make the best critics. They are rarely trained in revision techniques and are usually so close to you that they are unwilling—often unconsciously so—to risk disappointing you by giving your paper a really thorough examination.)

3. Prepare a list of specific items to check. It is important to revise in an orderly fashion—in stages—looking first at large concerns, such as the overall structure, then rereading for problems with smaller elements, such as paragraph organization or sentence structure.

4. Check for unity—the clear and logical relation of all parts of the essay to its thesis. Make sure that every paragraph relates well to the whole paper and that it is in the right place.

5. Check for coherence. Make sure there are no gaps among the different parts of the argument and that you have adequate transition everywhere it is needed. Transitional elements are markers indicating places where the paper's focus or attitude changes. Transitional elements can be one word long—*however, although, unfortunately, luckily*—or as long as a sentence or a paragraph: *In order to fully appreciate the importance of democracy as a shaping presence in post-cold-war Polish politics, it is necessary to examine briefly the Poles' last historical attempt to implement democratic government.* Transitional elements rarely introduce new material. Instead, they are direction pointers, either indicating a shift to new subject matter or signaling how the writer wishes certain material to be interpreted by the reader. Because you—the writer—already know where and why your paper changes direction and how you want particular passages to be received, it can be very difficult for you to determine where transition is needed.

6. Avoid unnecessary repetition.

Avoiding Repetition   There are two types of repetition that can annoy a reader: repetition of content and repetition of wording. Repetition of content leads to redundancy. Ideally, you want to cover a topic once, memorably, and then move on to your next topic. Organizing a paper is a difficult task, however, one that usually occurs through a process of enlightenment as to purposes and strategies. It is possible for an early draft to circle back to a subject you have already covered, and to begin to treat the same material over again. This sort of repetition can happen even if you have made use of prewriting strategies. What is worse, it can be difficult for you as a writer to acknowledge the repetition—to admit to yourself that the material you have worked so hard to shape on page 2 returns on page 5 in much the same shape. As you write and revise, bear this in mind: Any unnecessary repetition of content that you allow into your final draft is a potential annoyance to your reader, who is working to make sense of the argument she or he is reading and does not want to be distracted by a passage that repeats material already encountered. Train yourself, through practice, to read through your draft, looking for material that you have repeated unnecessarily.

Repetition of wording results in boring material. Make sure that you do not overuse any phrases or individual words. This sort of repetition can make your prose sound choppy and uninspired. It is important that your language sound fresh and energetic. Before you turn in your final draft, make sure to read through your paper carefully, looking for such repetition. Here are some examples of repetition of wording:

The subcommittee's report on education reform will surprise a number of people. A number of people will want copies of the report.

The chairman said at a press conference that he is happy with the report. He will circulate it to the local news agencies in the morning. He will also make sure that the city council has copies.

I became upset when I heard how the committee had voted. I called the chairman and expressed my reservations about the committee's decision. I told him I felt that he had let the teachers and students of the state down. I also issued a press statement.

The last passage illustrates a condition known by composition teachers as the *I*-syndrome. Can you hear how such duplicated phrasing can make a paper sound disconnected and unimaginative?

Note that not all repetition is bad. You may wish to repeat a phrase for rhetorical effect or special emphasis: *I came. I saw. I conquered.* Just make sure that any repetition in your paper is intentional—placed there to produce a specific effect.

1.2.6   EDITING

Editing is sometimes confused with the more involved process of revising. But editing happens later, after you have wrestled through your first draft—and maybe your second and third—and arrived at the final draft. Even though your draft now contains all the information you want to impart and the information is arranged to your satisfaction, there are still many factors to check, such as sentence structure, spelling, and punctuation.

It is at this point that an unpracticed writer might let down his guard. After all, most of the work on the paper is finished; the big jobs of discovering material and organizing and drafting it have been completed. But watch out! Editing is as important as any other step in the writing process. Any error that you allow in the final draft will count against you in the reader's mind. It may not seem fair, but a minor error—a misspelling or the confusing placement of a comma—will make a much greater impression on your reader than perhaps it should. Remember that everything about your paper is your responsibility, including getting even the supposedly little jobs right. Careless editing undermines the effectiveness of your paper. It would be a shame if all the hard work you put into prewriting, drafting, and revising were to be damaged because you carelessly allowed a comma splice!

Most of the preceding tips for revising hold for editing as well. It is best to edit in stages, looking for only one or two kinds of errors each time you reread the paper. Focus especially on errors that you remember committing in the past. For instance, if you know you have a tendency to misplace commas, go through your paper looking at each comma carefully. If you have a weakness for writing unintentional sentence fragments, read each sentence aloud to make sure that it is, indeed, a complete sentence. Have you accidentally shifted verb tenses anywhere, moving from past to present tense for no reason? Do all the subjects in your sentences agree in number with their verbs? Now is the time to find out.

Watch out for miscues—problems with a sentence that the writer can easily overlook. Remember that your search for errors is hampered in two ways:

1. As the writer, you hope not to find any errors with your writing. This desire can lead you to miss sighting them when they occur.
2. Because you know your material so well, it is easy, as you read, to unconsciously supply missing material—a word, correct punctuation—as if it were present.

How difficult is it to see that something is missing in the following sentence?

Unfortunately, legislators often have too little regard their constituents.

We can even guess that the missing word is probably *for*, which should be inserted after *regard*. However, it is quite possible that the writer of the sentence will supply the missing *for* automatically as he reads it, as if he has seen it on the page. This is a miscue, and miscues can be hard for the writer to spot because he is so close to his own material.

Editing is the stage in which you finally answer those minor questions that you put off earlier when you were wrestling with wording and organization. Any ambiguities regarding the use of abbreviations, italics, numerals, capital letters, titles (for example, when do you capitalize the title *president*?), hyphens, dashes (usually created on a typewriter or computer by striking the hyphen key twice), apostrophes, and quotation marks have to be cleared up. You must check to see that you have used the required formats for footnotes, endnotes, margins, and page numbers.

Guessing is not allowed. Sometimes unpracticed writers who realize that they don't quite understand a particular rule of grammar, punctuation, or format often do nothing to fill that knowledge gap. Instead they rely on guesswork and their own logic—which is not always up to the task of dealing with so contrary a language as English—to get them through problems that they could solve if only they referred to a writing manual. Remember that it does not matter to the reader why or how an error shows up in your writing; it only matters that you as the writer have dropped your guard. You must not allow a careless error to diminish your hard work.

One tactic for catching mistakes in sentence structure is to read the sentences aloud, starting with the last one in the paper, moving to the next to last, then the previous sentence, thus going backward through the paper (reading each sentence in the normal, left-to-right manner, of course) until you reach the first sentence of the introduction. This backward progression strips each sentence of its rhetorical context and helps you to focus on its internal structure.

1.2.7   PROOFREADING

Before you hand in your final version of the paper, it is vital that you check it over one more time to make sure there are no errors of any sort. This job is called proofreading or proofing. In essence, you are looking for many of the same things you checked for during editing, but now you are doing it on the last draft, which has been typed and is about to be submitted to your audience. Proofreading is as important as editing; you may have missed an error in the previous stages, or an error may have been introduced when the draft was recopied or typed for the last time. Like every other stage of the writing process, proofreading is your responsibility.

At this stage, it is essential that you check for typing mistakes—letters transposed or left out of words, or missing words, phrases, or punctuation. If you have had the paper professionally typed, you still must check it carefully. Do not rely solely on the typist's proofreading abilities. If you typed your paper on a computer or a word processor, it is possible that you unintentionally inserted a command that alters your document drastically—slicing out a word or a line or a sentence at the touch of a key. Make sure such accidental deletions have not occurred.

Above all else, remember that your paper represents you. It is a product of your best thoughts, your most energetic and imaginative response to a writing challenge. If you have maintained your enthusiasm for the project and worked through the different stages of the writing process honestly and carefully, you should produce a paper you can be proud of and one that will serve its readers well.

CHAPTER 2

WRITING COMPETENTLY

Read over your compositions, and where ever you meet with a passage which you think is particularly fine, strike it out.

—*Dr. Samuel Johnson, 1709–1784*

2.1 GUIDELINES FOR THE COMPETENT WRITER

Good writing places your thoughts in your reader's mind in exactly the way you want them to be there. It tells your reader just what you want her or him to know without revealing anything you do not wish to say. That may sound odd, but the fact is that writers have to be careful not to let unwanted messages slip into their writing. For example, look at the following passage, taken from a paper analyzing the impact of a worker-retraining program. Hidden within the prose is a message that jeopardizes the paper's success. Can you detect the message?

> Recent articles written on the subject of dislocated workers have had little to say about the particular problems dealt with in this paper. Since few of these articles focus on the problem at the local level.

Chances are, when you reached the end of the second "sentence," you sensed something missing, a gap in logic or coherence, and your eye ran back through both sentences to find the place where things went wrong. The second sentence is actually not a sentence at all. It does have certain features of a sentence—a subject, for example (few), and a verb (focus), but its first word (Since) subordinates the entire clause that follows, taking away its ability to stand on its own as a complete idea. The second "sentence," which is properly called a subordinate clause, merely fills in some information about the first sentence, explaining why recent articles about dislocated workers fail to deal with problems discussed in the present paper.

This sort of error is commonly called a sentence fragment, and it conveys to the reader a message that no writer wants to send: that the writer either is careless or—worse—has not mastered the language she is using. Language errors, such as fragments, misplaced commas, or shifts in verb tense send up little red flags in the reader's mind. The result is that the reader loses a little of his concentration on the issue being discussed. He becomes distracted and begins to wonder about the language competency of the writer. The writing loses effectiveness.

Remember that whatever goal you set for your paper—whether you want it to persuade, describe, analyze, or speculate—you must also set another goal: to display language competence. Without it, your paper will not completely achieve its other aims. Language errors spread doubt like a virus; they jeopardize all the hard work you have done on your paper.

Credibility in the job market depends on language competence. Anyone who doubts this should remember the beating that Dan Quayle took in the press when he was vice president of the United States for misspelling the word *potato* at a Trenton, New Jersey, spelling bee. His error caused a storm of humiliating publicity for the hapless Quayle, and contributed to an impression of his general incompetence.

Although they may seem minor, these sorts of language errors—which are often called surface errors—can be extremely damaging in certain kinds of writing. Surface errors come in a variety of types, including misspellings, punctuation problems, grammar errors, and the inconsistent use of abbreviations, capitalization, or numerals. They are an affront to your reader's notion of correctness—and therein lies one of the biggest problems with surface errors. Different audiences tolerate different levels of correctness. You already know that you can get away with surface errors in, say, a letter to a friend, who will not judge you harshly for them, while those same errors in a job application letter might eliminate you from consideration for the job. Correctness depends to an extent on context.

Another problem is that the rules governing correctness shift over time. What would have been an error to your grandmother's generation—the splitting of an infinitive, for example, or the ending of a sentence with a preposition—is taken in stride today by most readers. So how do you write correctly when the rules shift from person to person and over time? Following are some tips.

2.1.1   CONSIDER YOUR AUDIENCE

One of the great risks of writing is that even the simplest of choices you make regarding wording or punctuation can sometimes prejudice your audience against you in ways that may seem unfair. For example, look again at the old grammar "rule" forbidding the splitting of infinitives. After decades of counseling students to *never* split an infinitive (something this sentence has just done), composition experts now concede that a split infinitive is not a grammar crime. But suppose you have written a position paper trying to convince your city council of the need to hire security personnel for the library, and half of the council members—the people you wish to convince—remember their eighth-grade grammar teacher's outdated warning about splitting infinitives. How will they respond when you tell them, in your introduction, that librarians are ordered to always accompany visitors to the rare book room because of the threat of vandalism? How much of their attention have you suddenly lost because of their automatic recollection of a non-rule? It is possible, in other words, to write correctly and still offend your readers' notions of language competence.

Make sure that you tailor the surface features of your writing to the level of competency that your readers require. When in doubt, take a conservative approach. The same goes for the level of formality you should assume. Your audience might be just as distracted by contractions as by a split infinitive.

2.1.2   AIM FOR CONSISTENCY

When dealing with a language question for which there are different answers—such as whether to place a comma after the second item in a series of three (*The mayor's speech addressed taxes, housing for the poor, and the job situation.*)—always use the same strategy. If, for example, you avoid splitting one infinitive, avoid splitting all infinitives in your paper.

2.1.3   HAVE CONFIDENCE IN WHAT YOU ALREADY KNOW ABOUT WRITING

It is easy for unpracticed writers to allow their occasional mistakes to discourage them about their writing ability. But, most of what we know about writing is right. For example, we are all capable of writing sentences that are grammatically sound—even if we cannot identify the grammar rules by which we achieve coherence. Most writers who worry about their chronic errors have fewer than they think. Becoming distressed about errors makes writing more difficult. In fact, you already know more about grammar than you think you do. As various composition theorists have pointed out, the word *grammar* has several definitions. One meaning is "the formal patterns in which words must be arranged in order to convey meaning." We learn these patterns very early in life and use them spontaneously without thinking about them. Our understanding of grammatical patterns is extremely sophisticated, despite the fact that few of us can actually cite the rules that the patterns follow.

Patrick Hartwell (1985:111) tested grammar learning by asking native English speakers of different ages and levels of education, including high school teachers, to arrange these words in natural order:

French   the   young   girls   four

Everyone he asked could produce the natural order for this phrase: *the four young French girls.* Yet none of Hartwell's respondents said they knew the rule that governs the order of the words.

2.1.4   ELIMINATE CHRONIC ERRORS

The question then arises: If just thinking about our errors has a negative effect on our writing, how do we learn to write with greater accuracy? One important way is simply to write as often as possible. Give yourself practice in putting your thoughts into written shape, and get lots of practice in revising and proofing your work. And as you write and revise, be honest—and patient—with yourself. Chronic errors are like bad habits; getting rid of them takes time. You probably know of one or two problem areas in your writing that you could have eliminated but have not done so. Instead, you have "fudged" your writing at the critical points, relying on half-remembered formulas from past English classes or trying to come up with logical solutions to your writing problems. (Warning: Rules governing the English language are not always logical.) You may have simply decided that comma rules are unlearnable or that you will never understand the difference between the verbs *lay* and *lie.* And so you guess—and get the rule wrong a good part of the time. What a shame, when just a little extra work would give you mastery over those few gaps in your understanding and boost your confidence as well.

Instead of continuing with this sort of guesswork, instead of living with the gaps, why not face the problem areas now and learn the rules that have heretofore escaped you? What follows is a discussion of those surface features of a paper in which errors most commonly occur. You will probably be familiar with most—if not all—of the rules discussed, but there may be a few you have not yet mastered. Now is the time to do so.

2.2   RULES OF PUNCTUATION

2.2.1   APOSTROPHES

An apostrophe is used to show possession; when you wish to say that something belongs to someone or to another thing, you add either an apostrophe and an *s* or an apostrophe alone to the word that represents the owner.

When the owner is singular (a single person or thing), the apostrophe precedes an added *s*:

> According to Mr. Pederson's secretary, the board meeting has been canceled.
>
> The school's management team reduced crime problems last year.
>
> Somebody's briefcase was left in the classroom.

The same rule applies if the word showing possession is a plural that does not end in *s*:

The women's club provided screening services for at-risk youth and their families.

Professor Logan has proven himself a tireless worker for children's rights.

When the word expressing ownership is a plural ending in *s*, the apostrophe follows the *s*:

The new procedure was discussed at the youth workers' conference.

There are two ways to form the possessive for two or more nouns:

1. To show joint possession (both nouns owning the same thing or things), the last noun in the series is possessive:
   Billy and Richard's first draft was completed yesterday.

2. To indicate that each noun owns an item or items individually, each noun must show possession:
   Professor Wynn's and Professor Camacho's speeches took different approaches to the same problem.

The apostrophe is important, an obvious statement when you consider the difference in meaning between the following two sentences:

Be sure to pick up the psychiatrist's things on your way to the airport.

Be sure to pick up the psychiatrists' things on your way to the airport.

In the first of these sentences, you have only one psychiatrist to worry about, while in the second, you have at least two!

2.2.2   CAPITALIZATION

When to Capitalize   Following is a brief summary of some hard-to-remember capitalization rules.

Rule 1: You may, if you choose, capitalize the first letter of the first word in a sentence that follows a colon (but remember to be consistent throughout your paper).

Correct: Our instructions are explicit: Do not allow anyone into the conference without an identification badge.

Also correct: Our instructions are explicit: do not allow anyone into the conference without an identification badge.

Rule 2: Capitalize proper nouns (nouns naming specific people, places, or things) and proper adjectives (adjectives made from proper nouns). A common noun following the proper adjective is usually not capitalized, nor is a common adjective preceding the proper adjective (such as *a*, *an*, or *the*):

Proper Nouns	**Proper Adjectives**
England	English sociologists
Iraq	the Iraqi educator
Shakespeare	a Shakespearean tragedy

Proper nouns include:

- names of famous monuments and buildings: the Washington Monument, the Empire State Building, the Library of Congress

- historical events, eras, and certain terms concerning calendar dates: the Civil War, the Dark Ages, Monday, December, Columbus Day

- parts of the country: North, Southwest, Eastern Seaboard, the West Coast, New England (Note that when words like north, south, east, west, northwest are used to designate direction rather than geographical region, they are not capitalized: "We drove east to Boston and then made a tour of the East Coast.")

- words referring to race, religion, and nationality: Islam, Muslim, Caucasian, White (or white), Asian, African American, Black (or black), Slavic, Arab, Jewish, Hebrew, Buddhism, Buddhists, Southern Baptists, the Bible, the Koran, American

- names of languages: English, Chinese, Latin, Sanskrit

- titles of corporations, institutions, businesses, universities, and organizations: Dow Chemical, General Motors, the National Endowment for the Humanities, University of Tennessee, Colby College, Kiwanis Club, American Association of Retired Persons, the Oklahoma State Senate (Note: Some words once considered proper nouns or adjectives have, over time, become common: french fries, pasteurized milk, arabic numerals, italics, panama hat.)

Rule 3: Titles of individuals should be capitalized when they precede a proper name; otherwise, titles are usually not capitalized.

The committee honored Chairperson Furmanski.

The committee honored the chairperson from the sociology department.

We phoned Doctor MacKay, who arrived shortly afterward.

We phoned the doctor, who arrived shortly afterward.

A story on Queen Elizabeth's health appeared in yesterday's paper.

A story on the queen's health appeared in yesterday's paper.

Pope John Paul's visit to Colorado was a public relations success.

The pope's visit to Colorado was a public relations success.

When Not to Capitalize   In general, do not capitalize nouns when your reference is nonspecific. For example, you would not capitalize the phrase *the senator*, but you would capitalize *Senator Smith*. The second reference is as much a title as it is a term of identification, while the first reference is a mere identifier. Likewise, there is a difference in degree of specificity between the phrase the state treasury and the Texas State Treasury.

Note that the meaning of a term may change somewhat depending on capitalization. What, for example, might be the difference between a Democrat and a democrat? (When capitalized, the word refers to a member of a specific political party; when not capitalized, the word refers to someone who believes in a democratic form of government.)

Capitalization depends to some extent on the context of your writing. For example, if you are writing a policy analysis for a specific corporation, you may capitalize words and phrases—Board of Directors, Chairperson of the Board, the Institute—that would not be capitalized in a paper written referring to boards of directors, chairpersons, and institutes in general. Likewise, in some contexts it is not unusual to see titles of certain powerful officials capitalized even when not accompanying a proper noun: The President's visit to the Oklahoma City bombing site was considered timely. In this case the reference is to a specific president, President Clinton.

2.2.3   COLONS

There are uses for the colon that we all know. For example, a colon can separate the parts of a statement of time (4:25 A.M.), separate chapter and verse in a biblical quotation (John 3:16), and close the salutation of a business letter (Dear Senator Keaton:). But there are other uses for the colon that writers sometimes don't quite learn that can add an extra degree of flexibility to sentence structure.

The colon can introduce into a sentence certain kinds of material, such as a list, a quotation, or a restatement or description of material mentioned earlier in the paper.

- List: The committee's research proposal promised to do three things: (1) establish the extent of the problem, (2) examine several possible solutions, and (3) estimate the cost of each solution.
- Quotation: In his speech, the mayor challenged us with these words: "How will your council's work make a difference in the life of our city?"
- Restatement or description: Ahead of us, according to the senator's chief of staff, lay the biggest job of all: convincing our constituents of the plan's benefits.

2.2.4   COMMAS

The comma is perhaps the most troublesome of all punctuation marks, no doubt because so many variables govern its use, such as sentence length, rhetorical emphasis, or changing notions of style. Following are the most common problems.

Comma Splices   Joining two complete sentences by only a comma makes a comma splice. Examine the following examples of comma splices:

An impeachment is merely an indictment of a government official, actual removal usually requires a vote by a legislative body.

An unemployed worker who has been effectively retrained is no longer an economic problem for the community, he has become an asset.

It might be possible for the city to assess fees on the sale of real estate, however, such a move would be criticized by the community of real estate developers.

In each of these passages, two complete sentences (also called independent clauses) have been "spliced" together by a comma. When a comma splice is taken out of context, it becomes easy to see what is wrong: The break between the two sentences is inadequate. Simply reading the draft through to try to "hear" the comma splices may not work, however, since the rhetorical features of your prose—its "movement"—may make it hard to detect this kind of sentence error.

There is one foolproof way to check your paper for comma splices. Locate the commas in your draft and then read carefully the structures on both sides of each comma to determine whether you have spliced together two complete sentences. If you find a complete sentence on both sides of a comma, and if the sentence following the comma does not begin with a coordinating connective (*and, but, for, nor, or, so,* or *yet*), then you have found a comma splice.

There are five commonly used ways to correct comma splices.

1. Place a period between the two independent clauses:

   Splice: A physician receives many benefits from his or her affiliation with clients, there are liabilities as well.

   Correction: A physician receives many benefits from his or her affiliation with clients. There are liabilities as well.

2. Place a comma and a coordinating connective (*and, but, for, or, nor, so,* or *yet*) between the sentences:

   Splice: The chairperson's speech described the major differences of opinion over the department situation, it also suggested a possible course of action.

   Correction: The chairperson's speech described the major differences of opinion over the departmental situation, and it also suggested a possible course of action.

3. Place a semicolon between the independent clauses:

   Splice: Some people believe that the federal government should play a large role in establishing a housing policy for the homeless, many others disagree.

   Correction: Some people believe that the federal government should play a large role in establishing a housing policy for the homeless; many others disagree.

4. Rewrite the two clauses of the comma splice as one independent clause:

Splice: Television programs play some part in the development of delinquent attitudes, however they were not found to be the deciding factor in determining the behavior of juvenile delinquents.

Correction: Television programs were found to play a minor but not a decisive role in determining the delinquent behavior of juveniles.

5. Change one of the two independent clauses into a dependent clause by beginning it with a subordinating word. A subordinating word introducing a clause prevents the clause from being able to stand on its own as a complete sentence. Words that can be used as subordinators include *although, after, as, because, before, if, though, unless, when, which*, and *where*.

   Splice: The student meeting was held last Tuesday, there was a poor turn out.

   Correction: When the student meeting was held last Tuesday, there was a poor turnout.

Comma Missing in a Compound Sentence   A compound sentence is comprised of two or more independent clauses—two complete sentences. When these two clauses are joined by a coordinating conjunction, the conjunction should be preceded by a comma. (In the previous section, the second solution for fixing a comma splice calls for the writer to transform the splice into this sort of compound sentence.) The error is that writers sometimes fail to place the comma before the conjunction. Remember, the comma is there to signal the reader that another independent clause follows the coordinating conjunction. In other words, the comma is like a road sign, telling a driver what sort of road she is about to encounter. If the comma is missing, the reader does not expect to find the second half of a compound sentence and may be distracted from the text. As the following examples indicate, the missing comma is especially a problem in longer sentences or in sentences in which other coordinating conjunctions appear.

Missing comma: The senator promised to visit the hospital and investigate the problem and then he called the press conference to a close.

With the comma added: The senator promised to visit the hospital and investigate the problem, and then he called the press conference to a close.

Missing comma: The water board can neither make policy nor enforce it nor can its members serve on auxiliary water committees.

With the comma added: The water board can neither make policy nor enforce it, nor can its members serve on auxiliary water committees.

Notice how the comma sorts out the two main parts of the compound sentence, eliminating confusion. However, an exception to the rule must be noted. In shorter sentences, the comma may not be necessary to make the meaning clear:

The mayor phoned and we thanked him for his support.

Placing a comma between the independent clauses after the conjunction is never wrong, however. If you are the least bit unsure of your audience's notions about what makes for "proper" grammar, it is a good idea to take the conservative approach and use the comma:

The mayor phoned, and we thanked him for his support.

Missing Comma or Commas with a Nonrestrictive Element   A nonrestrictive element is part of a sentence—a word, phrase, or clause—that adds information about another element in the sentence without restricting or limiting the meaning of that element. In other words, a nonrestrictive element simply says something about some other part of the sentence without changing radically our understanding of it. While the information it carries may be useful, we do not have to have the nonrestrictive element for the sentence to make sense. To signal the nonessential nature of the element, we set it off from the rest of the sentence with commas.

Failure to indicate the nonrestrictive nature of an element by using commas can cause confusion. For example, see how the presence or absence of commas affects our understanding of the following sentence:

The judge was talking with the police officer, who won the outstanding service award last year.

The judge was talking with the police officer who won the outstanding service award last year.

Can you see that the comma changes the meaning of the sentence? In the first version of the sentence, the comma makes the information that follows it incidental: The judge was talking with the police officer, who happens to have won the service award last year. In the second version of the sentence, the information following the term police officer is important to the sense of the sentence; it tells us, specifically, which police officer—presumably there are more than one—the judge was addressing. The lack of a comma has transformed the material following the term police officer into a restrictive element—meaning one necessary to our understanding of the sentence. Be sure that in your paper you make a clear distinction between nonrestrictive and restrictive elements by setting off the nonrestrictive elements with commas.

Missing Comma in a Series   A series is any two or more items of a similar nature that appear consecutively in a sentence. The items may be individual words, phrases, or clauses. One of the rules that we all learned a long time ago is that the items in a series of three or more items are separated by commas. The series items are in italics:

The senator, *the mayor*, and *the police chief* all attended the ceremony.

Because of the new zoning regulations, *all trailer parks must be moved out of the neighborhood*, *all small businesses must apply for recertification and tax status*, and *the two local churches must repave their parking lots*.

The final comma, the one before the *and*, is sometimes left out, especially in newspaper writing. This practice, however, can make for confusion, especially in longer, complicated sentences like the second example. Here is the way the sentence would read without the final comma:

> Because of the new zoning regulations, all trailer parks must be moved out of the neighborhood, all small businesses must apply for recertification and tax status and the two local churches must repave their parking lots.

Notice how the second *and*, which is not set off from the sequence in front of it, seems at first to be an extension of the second clause in the series instead of the beginning of the third. This is the sort of ambiguous structure that can cause a reader to backtrack and lose concentration.

To avoid the possibility of causing this sort of confusion, it is a good idea always to include that final comma. And remember that if you do decide to include it, be consistent; make sure it appears in every series in your paper.

2.2.5   DANGLING MODIFIERS

A modifier is a word or group of words used to describe—to "modify" our understanding of—another word in the sentence. A dangling modifier is one that appears either at the beginning or ending of a sentence and seems to describe some word other than the one the writer obviously intended. The modifier "dangles," disconnected from its intended meaning. Because the writer knows what she wishes to say, it is often hard for her to spot a dangling modifier. But other readers find them, and the result can be disastrous for the sentence.

> *Incorrect:* Flying low over Washington, the White House was seen.
> *Corrected:* Flying low over Washington, we saw the White House.
> *Incorrect:* Worried about the cost of the program, sections of the bill were trimmed in committee.
> *Corrected:* Worried about the cost of the program, the committee trimmed sections of the bill.
> *Corrected:* The committee trimmed sections of the bill because they were worried about the cost of the program.
> *Incorrect:* To lobby for prison reform, a lot of effort went into the TV ads.
> *Corrected:* The lobby group put a lot of effort into the TV ads advocating prison reform.
> *Incorrect:* Stunned, the television network broadcast the defeated senator's concession speech.
> *Corrected:* The television network broadcast the stunned senator's concession speech.

You will note that in the first two incorrect sentences, the confusion is largely due to the use of passive voice verbs: *the White House was seen, sec-*

tions of the bill were trimmed. Often, though not always, the cause of a dangling modifier is the fact that the actor in the sentence—*we* in the first example, *the committee* in the second—is either distanced from the modifier or obliterated by the passive voice verb. It is a good idea to avoid passive voice unless you have a specific reason for using it.

One way to check for dangling modifiers is to examine all modifiers at the beginnings or endings of your sentences. Look especially for *to be* phrases ("to lobby") or for words ending in *-ing* or *-ed* at the start of the modifier. Then check to see whether the word being modified is in plain sight and close enough to the phrase to be properly connected.

2.2.6   PARALLELISM

Series of two or more words, phrases, or clauses within a sentence should be structured in the same grammatical way. Parallel structures can add power and balance to your writing by creating a strong rhetorical rhythm. Here is a famous example of parallelism from the U.S. Constitution. (The capitalization, preserved from the original document, follows eighteenth-century custom. Parallel structures have been italicized.)

Preamble to the Constitution

We the People of the United States, in Order to *form a more perfect Union, Establish Justice, insure Domestic Tranquillity, provide for the common defense, promote the general Welfare,* and *secure the Blessings of Liberty to ourselves and our Posterity,* do ordain and establish this Constitution for the United States of America.

Note that there are actually two series in this sentence, the first composed of several phrases that each complete the infinitive phrase beginning with the word *to* ("to form," "[to] Establish," "[to] insure"), the second consisting of two verbs ("do ordain and establish"). These parallel series appeal to our love of balance and pattern, and give an authoritative tone to the sentence. We feel the writer has thought long and carefully about the subject, and has taken firm control of it.

We find a special satisfaction in balanced structures and so are more likely to remember ideas phrased in parallelisms than in less highly ordered language. For this reason—as well as for the sense of authority and control that they suggest—parallel structures are common in well-written speeches. Consider the following examples:

We hold these truths to be self-evident, that all men are created equal, that they are endowed by their Creator with certain unalienable Rights, that among these are Life, Liberty, and the pursuit of Happiness.

—Declaration of Independence

But, in a larger sense, we can not dedicate—we can not consecrate—we can not hallow—this ground. The brave men, living and dead, who struggled here, have consecrated it, far above our poor power to add or detract.

> The world will little note, nor long remember what we say here, but it can never forget what they did here.
>
> —Abraham Lincoln, Gettysburg Address

> Let us never negotiate out of fear. But never let us fear to negotiate.... Ask not what your country can do for you; ask what you can do for your country.
>
> —John F. Kennedy, Inaugural Address

If the parallelism of a passage is not carefully maintained, the writing can seem sloppy and out of balance. To check for parallelism, scan your writing for any series of two or more items in a sentence. These items should be parallel in structure. In other words, if one item depends on an *-ing* construction, as in the second example following, so should its partners. Any lists in your paper should consist of items that are parallel in structure. Note the following examples of incorrect and correct constructions:

> *Incorrect:* The mayor promises not only to reform the police department, but also the giving of raises to all city employees.
>
> *Corrected:* The mayor promises not only to reform the police department, but also to give raises to all city employees. [Connective structures such as *not only ... but also* introduce elements that should be parallel.]
>
> *Incorrect:* The cost of doing nothing is greater than the cost to renovate the apartment block.
>
> *Corrected:* The cost of doing nothing is greater than the cost of renovating the apartment block.
>
> *Incorrect:* Here are the items on the committee's agenda: (1) to discuss the new property tax, (2) to revise the wording of the city charter, and (3) a vote on the city manager's request for an assistant.
>
> *Corrected:* Here are the items on the committee's agenda: (1) to discuss the new property tax, (2) to revise the wording of the city charter, and (3) to vote on the city manager's request for an assistant.

2.2.7   FUSED (RUN-ON) SENTENCES

A fused sentence is one in which two or more independent clauses (passages that can stand as complete sentences) have been joined together without the aid of any suitable connecting word, phrase, or punctuation; the sentences run together. As you can see, there are several ways to correct a fused sentence:

> *Incorrect:* The council members were exhausted they had debated for two hours.
>
> *Corrected:* The council members were exhausted. They had debated for two hours. [The linked independent clauses have been separated into two sentences.]
>
> *Corrected:* The council members were exhausted; they had debated for two hours. [A semicolon marks the break between the two clauses.]

Corrected: The council members were exhausted, having debated for two hours. [The second independent clause has been rephrased as a dependent clause.]

Incorrect: Our policy analysis impressed the committee it also convinced them to reconsider their action.

Corrected: Our policy analysis impressed the committee by convincing them to reconsider their action. [The second clause has been rephrased as part of the first clause.]

Corrected: Our policy analysis impressed the committee, and it also convinced them to reconsider their action. [The two clauses have been separated by a comma and a coordinating word.]

While a fused sentence is easily noticeable to the reader, it can be maddeningly difficult for the writer to catch in proofreading. Unpracticed writers tend to read through the fused spots, sometimes supplying the break that is usually heard when sentences are spoken. To check for fused sentences, read the independent clauses in your paper carefully, making sure that there are adequate breaks among all of them.

2.2.8 PRONOUN ERRORS

The Difference between Its and It's   Do not make the mistake of trying to form the possessive of *it* in the same way that you form the possessive of most nouns. The pronoun *it* shows possession by simply adding an *s*:

The prosecuting attorney argued the case on its merits.

The word *it's* is a contraction, meaning *it is*:

It's the most expensive program ever launched by the prison.

What makes the *its/it's* rule so confusing is that most nouns form the singular possessive by adding an apostrophe and an *s*: *The jury's verdict startled the crowd.* When proofreading, any time you come to the word *it's*, substitute the phrase *it is* while you read. If the phrase makes sense, you have used the correct form. Consider the following examples:

If you have used the word *it's*:

The newspaper article was misleading in it's analysis of the election.

Then read it as *it is*:

The newspaper article was misleading in it is analysis of the election.

If the phrase makes no sense, substitute *its* for *it's*:

The newspaper article was misleading in its analysis of the election.

Vague Pronoun Reference   Pronouns are words that stand in place of nouns or other pronouns that have already been mentioned in your writing. The most common pronouns include *he, she, it, they, them, those, which,* and *who.* You must make sure that each pronoun reference is clear; in other words, that there is no confusion about the reference. Examine the following clear pronoun references:

> The mayor said that he would support our bill if the city council would also back it.
>
> The piece of legislation that drew the most criticism was the bill concerning housing for the poor.

The word that is replaced by the pronoun is called its antecedent. To check the accuracy of your pronoun references, ask yourself this question: To what does the pronoun refer? Then answer the question carefully, making sure that there is not more than one possible antecedent. Consider the following sentence:

> Several special interest groups decided to defeat the new health care bill. This became the turning point of the government's reform campaign.

To what does the word *This* refer? The immediate answer seems to be the word *bill* at the end of the previous sentence. It is more likely the writer was referring to the attempt of the special interest groups to defeat the bill, but there is no word in the first sentence that refers specifically to this action. The reference is unclear. One way to clarify the reference is to change the beginning of the second sentence:

> Several special interest groups decided to defeat the new health care bill. Their attack on the bill became the turning point of the government's reform campaign.

Here is another example:

> When John F. Kennedy appointed his brother Robert to the position of U.S. Attorney General, he had little idea how widespread the corruption in the Teamsters Union was.

To whom does the word *he* refer? It is unclear whether the writer is referring to John or to Robert Kennedy. One way to clarify the reference is simply to repeat the antecedent instead of using a pronoun:

> When President John F. Kennedy appointed his brother Robert to the position of U.S. Attorney General, Robert had little idea how widespread the corruption in the Teamsters Union was.

Pronoun Agreement   Remember that a pronoun must agree in gender and in number with its antecedent. This rule is generally easy for us to remember. Study the following examples of pronoun agreement:

> Mayor Smith said that he appreciated our club's support in the election.
>
> One reporter asked the senator what she would do if the President offered her a cabinet post.

Having listened to our case, the judge decided to rule on it within the week.

Engineers working on the housing project said they were pleased with the renovation so far.

The following words, however, can become troublesome antecedents. They may look like plural pronouns but are actually singular:

everybody	nobody	everyone
no one	somebody	each
someone	either	anyone

A pronoun referring to one of these words in a sentence must be singular, too. Pronoun agreement errors appear in the following examples:

Incorrect: Each of the women in the support group brought their children.

Correct: Each of the women in the support group brought her children.

Incorrect: Has everybody received their ballot?

Correct: Has everybody received his or her ballot? [The two gender-specific pronouns are used to avoid sexist language.]

Correct: Have all the delegates received their ballots? [The singular antecedent has been changed to a plural one.]

Shift in Person   It is important to avoid shifting among first person (*I, we*), second person (*you*), and third person (*she, he, it, one, they*) unnecessarily. Such shifts can cause confusion:

Incorrect: Most people [third person] who seek a job find that if you [second person] tell the truth during your interviews, you will gain the voters' respect.

Correct: Most people who seek a job find that if they tell the truth during their interviews, they will win the voters' respect.

2.2.9   QUOTATION MARKS

It can be difficult to remember when to use quotation marks and where they go in relation to other marks of punctuation. When faced with a gap in their knowledge of the rules, unpracticed writers often try to rely on logic rather than referring to a rule book. But the rules governing quotation marks do not always seem to us to rely on logic. The only way to make sure of your use of quotation marks is to memorize the rules. There are not many.

When to Use Quotation Marks   Use quotation marks to enclose direct quotations, if they are four typed lines or less:

In his farewell address to the American people, George Washington warned, "The great rule of conduct for us, in regard to foreign nations, is, in extending our commercial relations, to have with them as little political connection as possible." (U.S. Senate 1991)

Longer quotes are indented left and right and single-spaced—without quotation marks:

> Lincoln explained his motive for continuing the Civil War clearly in his response to Horace Greeley's open letter:
>
>> I would save the Union. I would save it the shortest way under the Constitution. The sooner the National authority can be restored, the nearer the Union will be "the Union as it was. If there be those who would not save the Union unless they could at the same time save Slavery, I do not agree with them. If there be those who would not save the Union unless they could at the same time destroy Slavery, I do not agree with them." (Lincoln 1862)

Use single quotation marks to set off quotations within quotations: "I intend," said the professor, "to use in my lecture a line from Frost's poem, 'The Road Not Taken.'" Note that when the interior quote occurs at the end of the sentence, both single and double quotation marks are placed outside the period. Use quotation marks to set off the following kinds of titles:

- the title of a short poem: "The Second Coming," by William Butler Yeats [But note that the title of a long poem published as a book does not appear in quotation marks: The Dark Sister, by Winfield Townley Scott]
- the title of a short story
- the title of an article or essay
- the title of a song
- an episode of a television or radio show

Use quotation marks to set off words or phrases used in special ways:

- to convey irony: The so-called "liberal" administration has done nothing but cater to big business.
- to set off a technical term: To have "charisma," Weber would argue, is to possess special powers. Many believe that John F. Kennedy had great charisma. [Note that once the term is defined, it is not placed in quotation marks again.]

Placement of Quotation Marks in Relation to Other Punctuation   Always place commas and periods inside closing quotation marks:

> "My fellow Americans," said the President, "there are tough times ahead of us."

Place colons and semicolons outside closing quotation marks:

> In his speech on voting, the sociologist warned against "an encroaching indolence"; he was referring to the middle class.

There are several victims of the government's campaign to "Turn Back the Clock": the homeless, the elderly, and the mentally impaired.

Place question marks, exclamation points, and dashes inside or outside closing quotation marks, depending on context. If the punctuation is part of the quotation, it goes inside the quotation mark:

"When will the tenure committee make up its mind?" asked the dean.
The demonstrators shouted, "Free the hostages!" and "No more slavery!"

If the punctuation is not part of the quotation, it goes outside the quotation mark:

Which president said, "We have nothing to fear but fear itself"?

Note that although the quote was a complete sentence, you do not place a period after it. There can only be one mark of "terminal" punctuation (punctuation that ends a sentence).

2.2.10   SEMICOLONS

The semicolon is another little used punctuation mark that is worth incorporating into your writing strategy because of its many potential applications. A semicolon can be used to correct a comma splice:

Incorrect: The union representatives left the meeting in good spirits, their demands were met.
Corrected: The union representatives left the meeting in good spirits; their demands were met.
Incorrect: Several guests at the fund-raiser had lost their invitations, however, we were able to seat them, anyway.
Corrected: Several guests at the fund-raiser had lost their invitations; however, we were able to seat them, anyway.

It is important to remember that conjunctive adverbs like *however, therefore*, and *thus* are not coordinating words (such as *and, but, or, for, so,* and *yet*) and cannot be used with a comma to link independent clauses. If the second independent clause begins with *however*, it must be preceded by either a period or a semicolon. As you can see from the second example, connecting the two independent clauses with a semicolon instead of a period preserves the suggestion that there is a strong relationship between the clauses.

Semicolons can separate items in a series. Usually commas separate items in a series; for example: We ate breakfast, lunch, and dinner in the hotel. But when the series items themselves contain commas, the items may be separated from one another with semicolons. For example: The newspaper account of the rally stressed the march, which drew the biggest crowd; the mayor's speech, which drew tremendous applause; and the party afterwards in the park.

Avoid misusing semicolons. Do not use a semicolon to separate an independent clause from a dependent clause:

> *Incorrect:* Students from the college volunteered to answer phones during the pledge drive; which was set up to generate money for the new arts center.
>
> *Corrected:* Students from the college volunteered to answer phones during the pledge drive, which was set up to generate money for the new arts center.

While you can use a semicolon to separate two independent clauses, you should use a comma to separate an independent clause from a dependent clause. Do not overuse semicolons. Useful though semicolons are, if too many of them appear in your writing they can distract your reader's attention. Avoid monotony by using semicolons sparingly.

2.2.11   SENTENCE FRAGMENTS

A fragment is a part of a sentence that is punctuated and capitalized as if it were an entire sentence. It is an especially disruptive kind of error, because it obscures the kinds of connections that the words of a sentence must make in order to complete the reader's understanding.

Students sometimes write fragments because they are concerned that a particular sentence is growing too long and needs to be shortened. Remember that cutting the length of a sentence merely by adding a period somewhere along the way often creates a fragment. When checking your writing for fragments, it is essential that you read each sentence carefully to determine (1) whether there is a complete subject and a verb, and (2) whether there is a subordinating word preceding the subject and verb, making the construction a subordinate clause rather than a complete sentence.

Some fragments lack a verb:

> *Fragment:* The chairperson of our committee, having received a letter from the mayor. [It may look as if there is a verb in this passage, but the word *having*, which can be used as a verb, is used here as a gerund introducing a participial phrase. Watch out for words that look like verbs but are used in another way.]
>
> *Corrected:* The chairperson of our committee received a letter from the mayor.

Some fragments lack a subject:

> *Fragment:* Our study shows that there is broad support for improvement in the health care system. And in the unemployment system.
>
> *Corrected:* Our study shows that there is broad support for improvement in the health care system and in the unemployment system.

Some fragments are subordinate clauses:

> *Fragment:* After the latest edition of the newspaper came out. [This clause
> has the two major components of a complete sentence: a subject (edition)
> and a verb (came). Indeed, if the first word (After) were deleted, the clause
> would be a complete sentence. But that first word is a subordinating word,
> which acts to prevent the following clause from standing on its own as a
> complete sentence. Watch out for this kind of construction. It is called a
> subordinate clause, and it is not a sentence.]

> *Corrected:* After the latest edition of the newspaper came out, the mayor's
> press secretary was overwhelmed with phone calls. [A subordinate clause
> is connected in meaning to the independent clause either before or after it.
> A common method of revising a subordinate clause that has been punctu-
> ated as a complete sentence is to connect it to the complete sentence to
> which its meaning is most closely connected.]

> *Fragment:* Several members of Congress asked for copies of the Vice
> President's position paper. Which called for reform of the Environmental
> Protection Agency. [The clause beginning after the first period is a subordi-
> nate clause written as if it were a complete sentence.]

> *Corrected:* Several members of Congress asked for copies of the Vice
> President's position paper, which called for reform of the Environmental
> Protection Agency.

2.3   SPELLING

All of us have special spelling problems, words whose correct spelling we
have not yet committed to memory. Most writers are not as bad at spelling as
they believe themselves to be. Usually it is just a handful of words that the
individual finds troubling. The most important thing to do when confronting
your spelling problems is to be as sensitive as possible to those words with
which you know you have trouble and keep a dictionary handy. No writer
should be without a dictionary. There is no excuse for failing to look up a
questionable spelling.

When using a computer to type your paper, take advantage of the "spell
check" feature available with most word-processing software. It allows you to
check those words listed in the program's dictionary. But do not rely entirely
on your computer's spell checker. It will miss a variety of words that are properly spelled, but are improperly used variants within a particular context.
Notice that the mistakes in the following sentences would go unnoticed by a
computer's spell checker:

> Wilbur wood rather dye than admit that he had been their. When he cited
> the bare behind the would pile, he thought "Isle just lye hear until he goes
> buy."

Following are two lists of words that often give writers trouble. Read
through the lists, looking for those words which tend to give you trouble.

2.3.1   COMMONLY CONFUSED WORDS

The words in each pair listed below are often confused with each other. If you do not know the difference in a particular pair, consult your dictionary:

accept/except	know/no
advice/advise	later/latter
affect/effect	lay/lie
aisle/isle	lead/led
allusion/illusion	lessen/lesson
an/and	loose/lose
angel/angle	may be/maybe
ascent/assent	miner/minor
bare/bear	moral/morale
brake/break	of/off
breath/breathe	passed/past
buy/by	patience/patients
capital/capitol	peace/piece
choose/chose	personal/personnel
cite/sight/site	plain/plane
complement/compliment	precede/proceed
conscience/conscious	presence/presents
corps/corpse	principal/principle
council/counsel	quiet/quite
dairy/diary	rain/reign/rein
descent/dissent	raise/raze
desert/dessert	reality/realty
device/devise	respectfully/respectively
die/dye	reverend/reverent
dominant/dominate	right/rite/write
elicit/illicit	road/rode
eminent/immanent/imminent	scene/seen
envelop/envelope	sense/since
every day/everyday	stationary/stationery
fair/fare	straight/strait
formally/formerly	taught/taut
forth/fourth	than/then
hear/here	their/there/they're
heard/herd	threw/through
hole/whole	too/to/two
human/humane	track/tract
its/it's	waist/waste

waive/wave
weak/week
weather/whether
were/where

which/witch
whose/who's
your/you're

2.3.2   COMMONLY MISSPELLED WORDS

a lot
acceptable
accessible
accommodate
accompany
accustomed
acquire
against
annihilate
apparent
arguing/argument
authentic
before
begin/beginning
believe
bulletin
business
cannot
category
committee
condemn
courteous
definitely
dependent
desperate
develop
different
disappear
disappoint
easily
efficient
environment
equipped
exceed
exercise

existence
experience
fascinate
finally
foresee
forty
fulfill
gauge
guaranteed
guard
harass
hero/heroes
humorous
hurried/hurriedly
hypocrite
ideally
immediately
immense
incredible
innocuous
intercede
interrupt
irrelevant
irresistible
irritate
knowledge
license
likelihood
maintenance
manageable
meanness
mischievous
missile
necessary
nevertheless

no one

noticing/ noticeable

nuisance

occasion/occasionally

occurred/occurrences

omit/omission

opinion

opponent

parallel

parole

peaceable

performance

pertain

practical

preparation

probably

professor

prominent

pronunciation

process

psychology

publicly

pursue/pursuing

questionnaire

realize

received/receipt

recession

recommend

referring

religious

remembrance

reminisce

repetition

representative

rhythm

ridiculous

roommate

satellite

scarcity

scenery

science

secede/secession

secretary

senseless

separate

sergeant

shining

significant

sincerely

skiing

stubbornness

studying

succeed/success/successfully

susceptible

suspicious

technical

temporary

tendency

therefore

tragedy

truly

tyranny

unanimous

unconscious

undoubtedly

until

vacuum

valuable

various

vegetable

visible

without

women

writing

CHAPTER 3

FORMATS

Good order is the foundation of all things.

—Edmund Burke, 1729–1797

Order is heaven's first law.

—Alexander Pope, 1688–1784

Let all things be done decently and in order.
—St. Paul, First Letter to the Corinthians 14:40

Your format makes your paper's first impression. Justly or not, accurately or not, the format of your paper announces the level of your professional competence. A well-executed format implies that your paper is worth reading. More than that, however, a proper format brings information to your readers in a familiar form that has the effect of setting their minds at ease. Your paper's format should impress readers with your academic competence as a sociologist by following accepted professional standards. Like the style and clarity of your writing, format communicates messages that are often more readily and profoundly received than the content of the document itself.

The formats in this chapter are based on those endorsed by the American Sociological Association and published in the *ASA Style Guide* (1996). These formats, structured for use by scholars sending papers to professional journals, conform to standards generally accepted in the discipline of Sociology. Chapter 4 offers ASA-approved guidelines and models for citing and referencing sources used in a sociology paper. Unless your course instructor gives you special format instructions, follow the directions in this manual exactly.

This chapter contains format instructions for the following elements:

- General page format
- Title page
- Abstract
- Text
- Heading and subheadings
- Illustrations and figures
- Tables
- References
- Appendices

3.1   GENERAL PAGE FORMAT DIRECTIONS

Paper for typing or printing sociology assignments should be 8½-by-11-inch premium white bond, 20 lb. or heavier. Do not use any other color or size except to comply with special instructions from your instructor, and do not use an off-white or poor quality (draft) paper. Always submit to your instructor an original typed or computer (preferably laser) printed manuscript. Do not submit a photocopy! Always print a second copy for your own files in case the original is lost. If you are using a computer—and we highly recommend that you do—it's a good idea to keep an electronic file copy of your paper on the hard drive, another on a disk you can store in a safe place, and a third hard copy of the paper in case the computer crashes and the disk is lost.

Margins should be 1¼ inches from all sides of the paper. All papers should be double-spaced in a 12-point word processing font or typewriter pica type (10 cpi). Select a font that is plain and easy to read such as Helvetica, Courier, Garamond, or Times Roman. Do not use script, stylized, or elaborate fonts. Typewriter elite type may be used if other fonts are not available.

Page numbers should appear in the upper right hand corner of each page, starting immediately after the title page. No page number should appear on the title page or on the first page of the text. Page numbers should appear 1¼ inches from the right side and one-half inch from the top of the page. If you are using a computer or word processor, you may need to set the top margin at .5 inch in order to achieve this spacing. Page numbers should proceed consecutively beginning with the title page (even if the first number is not actually printed on the title page). For the pages that precede the first page of text, such as the title page, table of contents, and table of figures, you may choose to use small roman numerals (i, ii, iii, iv, v, etc.); but if you use them, they must be placed at the center of the bottom of the page, and the first page of the text becomes page 1. In special cases, as when your instructor wants no pages preceding the first page of text, the title of the paper should appear one inch from the top of the first page, followed by your name and course information. Most formats omit placing the page number on this first page of text, but some instructors may require it to be placed at the bottom center. All other page numbering should follow the aforementioned guidelines.

Do not bind your paper or enclose it within a plastic cover sheet unless instructed to do so. Place one staple in the upper left corner, or use a paper clip at the top of the paper. Note that a paper submitted to a journal for publication should not be clipped, stapled, or have any form of binding.

3.2 TITLE PAGE

This title page format differs slightly from professional ASA format in order to allow for student information. Student writers should center the following information on the title page:

- title of the paper
- name of student (author)
- course name, number, and section number
- instructor
- name of college or university
- date

A sample title page appears on page 64. The title should clearly describe the problem addressed in the paper. If the paper discusses juvenile recidivism in Muskogee County jails, for example, the title "Recidivism in the Muskogee County Juvenile Justice System" is professional, clear, and helpful to the reader. "Muskogee County," "Juvenile Justice," or "County Jails" are titles to be avoided for this particular topic—they are all too vague. Also, the title should not be "cute." A cute title may attract attention for a Broadway play, but it will detract from the credibility of a sociology paper. "Inadequate Solid Waste Disposal Facilities in Muskogee" is professional; "Down in the Dumps" is not.

3.3 ABSTRACT

An abstract is a brief summary of a paper, written primarily to allow potential readers to determine whether the paper contains information of sufficient interest for them to read. People conducting research need specific kinds of information, and they often read dozens of abstracts looking for papers that contain information relevant to their research topic. Abstracts have the title of the paper centered at the top of the page, followed by a paragraph that precisely states the paper's topic, research and analysis methods, and results and conclusions. An abstract should be written in one paragraph that does not exceed 150 words. Remember that an abstract is not an introduction; it is a very succinct summary of your paper, as demonstrated in the sample on page 65.

SAMPLE TITLE PAGE

A Comparison of the Sociological Theories
of Karl Marx and Emile Durkheim

by

Lawanda Brown

Sociological Theory
Sociology 4473, Section 5233
Professor Chelsea Blake

Middlebury College

May 12, 1998

SAMPLE ABSTRACT

Abstract

Bertrand Russell's View of Mysticism

This paper reviews Bertrand Russell's writings on religion, mysticism, and science and defines his perspective on the contribution of mysticism to scientific knowledge. Russell drew a sharp distinction between what he considered to be (1) the essence of religion and (2) dogma or assertions attached to religion by theologians and religious leaders. Although some of his writings, including "Why I Am Not a Christian," appear hostile to all aspects of religion, Russell actually asserted that religion, freed from doctrinal encumbrances, not only fulfills certain psychological needs, but evokes many of the most beneficial human impulses. He believed that religious mysticism generates an intellectual disinterestedness that may be useful to science, but that it is not a source of a special type of knowledge beyond investigation by science.

3.4   TEXT

Ask your instructor for the number of pages required for the paper you are writing. The text should follow the directions explained in Chapters 1 and 2 of this manual, and should conform to the sample below.

3.5   HEADINGS AND SUBHEADINGS

Generally, three heading levels should meet your organizational needs. Primary headings should:

    a.   be centered on the page or left-justified and
    b.   be printed in all capital letters.

Example of a Primary Heading
BASIC RISK FACTORS FOR YOUTH POPULATIONS

Note that this heading, like the other two types, should give your reader an

 SAMPLE PAGE OF TEXT

There is some evidence that the idea "you can never be too rich or too thin" (Rockett and McMinn 1990:278) has been taken to heart by many American women. Of 33,000 females responding to a survey published in *Glamour* magazine (1984:200), when asked what would make them happy, 42 percent marked losing weight as their first choice. Interestingly, in addition to overweight females, women of normal weight marked this response most often, as did many underweight women.

Dissatisfaction with body often translates into dissatisfaction with self (Freedman 1984:34). It is important to investigate the factors that lead to feelings of inferiority about the body in order to deal effectively with women who suffer the often painful consequences associated with this dilemma.

This paper examines the relationship between women's body image and the following variables: (1) age, (2) self-esteem, (3) locus of control, (4) body weight, (5) opinion of ideal female body weight, and (6) opinion of the male's view of ideal female body weight.

idea about the content of the text that follows. In other words, it is unnecessary to begin your text with the heading INTRODUCTION.

Secondary headings should:

a.   be centered or left-justified,
b.   be printed in italics, and
c.   have the first letters of all words capitalized except for prepositions, articles, and coordinating conjunctions.

Example of a Secondary Heading
Alcohol and/or Other Drug Use

Tertiary headings should:

a.   be indented at the beginning of the paragraph,
b.   be printed in italics,
c.   use standard sentence capitalization, and
d.   be followed by a period.

Example of a Tertiary Heading (Placed at the Head of a Paragraph)

Risk factors for peers. An examination of meaningful associations among members of this high risk/high use group provides several significant implications....

3.6 TABLES

Tables in the text are used to show relationships among data, to help the reader come to a conclusion or understand something. They should be numbered consecutively throughout the text and placed as close as possible to the passage in the text where the data are discussed. (Note: The *ASA Style Guide* tells scholars writing professional articles to place each table at the end of the manuscript on a separate sheet of paper and insert in the text a note indicating the proper placement of the table.) Tables should not reiterate the content of the text. They should say something new, and they should stand on their own; that is, the reader should be able to understand your table without reading the text.

Give each table a title that clearly indicates the table's function. Excluding articles, prepositions, and conjunctions, each word in the title should begin with a capital letter. Use headings to label columns and rows. Do not use abbreviations in headings. When dealing with numbers, carry decimal fractions to the thousandths place and do not use leading zeros. In other words, say .547, not 0.547 or .5472. Study the sample table on page 68.

SAMPLE TABLE

Table 1

Population Change in Ten U.S. Cities, 1980–1986

City	1986 Rank	1980 Population	1986 Population	Percentage Change, 1980–1986
New York	1	7,071,639	7,262,700	2.7
Los Angeles	2	2,968,528	3,259,300	9.8
Chicago	3	3,005,072	3,009,530	.2
Houston	4	1,611,382	1,728,910	7.3
Philadelphia	5	1,688,210	1,642,900	-2.3
Detroit	6	1,203,369	1,086,220	-9.7
San Diego	7	875,538	1,015,190	16.0
Dallas	8	904,599	1,003,520	10.9
San Antonio	9	810,353	914,350	12.8
Phoenix	10	790,183	894,070	13.1

Source: (U.S. Bureau of the Census 1988).

3.7   ILLUSTRATIONS AND FIGURES

Illustrations are not normally inserted in the text of a sociology paper, and they are not included even in the appendix unless they are necessary to explain the material in the text. Do not paste or tape photocopies of photographs or similar materials to the pages of the text, and do not include them in that manner in your appendices. If such materials are necessary, photocopy each one on a separate sheet of paper and center each illustration, along with its typed title, within the normal margins of the paper. The format of the titles of each illustration should be the same as the format for tables and figures.

Figures in the form of charts and graphs, however, may be very helpful in presenting certain types of information, as in the sample on page 69.

Sample Figure

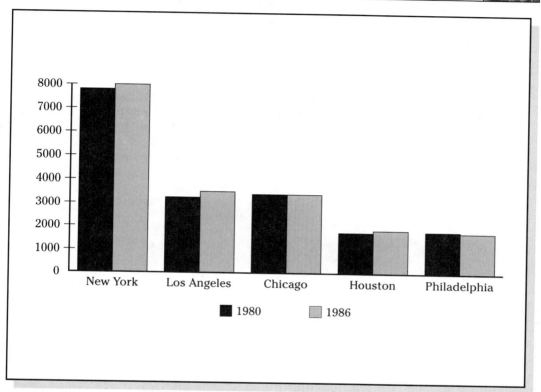

3.8 References Page

The format for referencing the sources cited in your paper is discussed in detail in Chapter 4 of this manual, along with the system used (American Sociological Association) to cite sources.

3.9 Appendices

Appendices are reference materials provided for the convenience of the reader that are not included in the text but are attached to the end of the paper. They provide information that supplements the important facts contained in the text. They may include maps, charts, tables, and selected documents necessary to the reader to fully understand the text (i.e., question-naires, computer files, etc.) Do not place in your appendix materials that are merely interesting or decorative. Add in an appendix only items that will answer questions raised by the text or necessary to explain the text. Do not append an entire government report, journal article, or other publication, but only the portions of such documents necessary to support your paper. The source of the information should always be included at the bottom of the last page of the appendix.

Follow the guidelines for formatting illustrations, tables, and figures when adding material in an appendix. If you have only one appendix, label it "Appendix" at the top center of the page and append a name:

Appendix. Violent Crime Statistics

For more than one appendix, label each with a letter:

Appendix A. Specific Items on the Questionnaire

CHAPTER 4

CITING SOURCES

You will find it a very good practice always to verify your references, sir.
—*Martin Routh, 1755–1854*

One of your most important jobs as a research writer is to document your use of source material carefully and clearly. Failure to do so will cause your reader confusion, damage the effectiveness of your paper, and perhaps make you vulnerable to a charge of plagiarism. Proper documentation is more than just good form; it is a powerful indicator of your own commitment to scholarship and the sense of authority that you bring to your writing. Good documentation demonstrates your expertise as a researcher and increases the reader's trust in you and your work; it gives credibility to what you are writing.

Unfortunately, as anybody who has ever written a research paper knows, getting the documentation right can be a frustrating, confusing job, especially for the novice writer. Positioning each element of a single reference citation accurately can require what seems an inordinate amount of time spent thumbing through the style manual. Even before you begin to work on specific citations, there are important questions of style and format to answer.

4.1 WHAT TO DOCUMENT

Direct quotes must always be credited, as must certain kinds of paraphrased material. Information that is basic—important dates, and facts or opinions universally acknowledged—need not be cited. Information that is not widely known, whether fact or opinion, should receive documentation.

What if you are unsure whether or not a certain fact is widely known? You are, after all, very probably a newcomer to the field in which you are conducting your research. If in doubt, supply the documentation. It is better to overdocument than to fail to do justice to a source.

4.2   WHICH FORMAT TO USE

While the question of which documentation style to use may be decided for you in some classes by your instructor, others may allow you a choice. There are several styles available, each designed to meet the needs of writers in particular fields. The citation and reference systems approved by the Modern Language Association (MLA) and the American Psychological Association (APA) are often used in the humanities and the social sciences.

The American Sociological Association (ASA) has its own system that is widely used by sociology students and professionals. The ASA has adopted a modification of the style elaborated in *The Chicago Manual of Style* (CMS), perhaps the most universally approved of all documentation authorities. One of the advantages of using the ASA style, which is outlined in a pamphlet entitled *ASA Style Guide* (1996), is that it is designed to guide the professional sociologist in preparing a manuscript for submission to a journal. The ASA style is required for all papers submitted to the *American Sociological Review*, the official journal of the ASA and the most influential sociology journal in publication. It is also required for all the leading journals in sociology and many of the less prestigious ones.

This chapter also includes the Student Citation System (SCS), which has been developed for use in all undergraduate college classes. The advantage of the SCS is that it may be used in any college class (English, physics, psychology, sociology, political science, journalism, economics, etc.) in which it is permitted by the instructor. In addition, it is a simple system with few rules and its punctuation is familiar to students who use the Internet. You will find the SCS described at the conclusion of the following section, which is based on the ASA citation system.

4.3   CITING SOURCES IN ASA FORMAT

A parenthetical reference or citation is a note placed within the text, near where the source material occurs. In order not to distract the reader from the argument, the citation is as brief as possible, containing just enough information to refer the reader to the full reference listing that appears in the bibliography or reference section following the text. Usually the minimum information necessary is the author's last name—meaning the name by which the source is alphabetized in the references at the end of the paper—and the year of the publication of the source. As indicated by the following models, this information can be given in a number of ways. Models of reference list bibliographical entries that correspond to these parenthetical citations are given in the next section of this chapter.

4.3.1 TEXT CITATIONS

Citations within the text should include the author's last name and the year of publication. Page numbers should be included only when quoting directly from a source or referring to specific passages. Subsequent citations of the same source should be identified the same way as the first (ASA 1996). The following examples identify the *ASA Style Guide's* (1996) citation system for a variety of possibilities.

When the author's name is *in* the text, it should be followed by the publication year in parentheses:

> Freedman (1984) postulates that when individuals ...

When the author's name is *not* in the text, the last name and publication should be enclosed in parentheses:

> ... encourage more aggressive play (Perrez 1979).

Page numbers are included only when necessary. The page number should be included when the material referred to is quoted directly, or when you wish to refer the reader to a specific page of the source text. When the page number is included, it should follow the publication year and be preceded by a colon with no space between the colon and the page number:

> Thomas (1961:741) builds on this scenario ...

When the publication has two authors, both last names should be given:

> ... establish a sense of self (Holmes and Watson 1872:114–116).

When a publication has three authors, all three last names should be cited in the first citation, with *et al.* used for subsequent citations in the text. In first citation,

> ... found the requirements very restrictive (Mollar, Querley, and McLarry 1926).

thereafter,

> ... proved to be quite difficult (Mollar et al. 1926).

For more than three authors, use *et al.* in all citations.

When citing two authors with the same last name, use a first initial to differentiate between them.

> ... the new budget cuts (K. Grady 1994).
> ... stimulate economic growth (B. Grady 1993).

When citing two works by the same author, in the same note, place a comma between the publication dates of the works.

> George (1992, 1994) argues for ...

If the two works were published in the same year, differentiate between them by adding lowercase letters to the publication dates. Be sure to add the letters to the references in the bibliography, too.

> ... the city government (Estrada 1994a, 1994b).

Direct quotes of fewer than four lines should be placed in the text with quotation marks at the beginning and end. The citation should include the page number in one of the following formats:

> The majority of these ads promote the notion that "If you are slim, you will also be beautiful and sexually desirable" (Rockett and McMinn 1990:278).
> Smith and Hill (1997) found that "women are far more likely to obsess about weight" (p. 127).

Direct quotes of *four lines or more* should be indented from both sides, single spaced, and present in a smaller font or type when possible. They should be blocked—no tab set for the first line—with no quotation marks as follows:

> According to Brown (1985):
>
> > There are few girls and women of any age or culture raised in white America, who do not have some manifestation of the concerns discussed here, i.e., distortion of body image, a sense of "out-of-control" in relationship to food, addiction to dieting, binging, or self-starvation. (P. 61)

It should be noted that in the block quote the author, date, and or page number follows the period at the end, and that the "P" for "page" is capitalized when the page number appears alone without the author and date, as in this example.

The *ASA Style Guide* only briefly discusses reference formats for works published anonymously. Section 16.40 of *The Chicago Manual of Style* (1993) indicates that if the authorship of an anonymous work is known, the name is given in brackets.

> ([Morey, Cynthia] 1994)

According to section 16.41 of *The Chicago Manual of Style*, if the name of the author of an anonymous work cannot be ascertained, the reference begins with the title of the work. The first of the following models refers to a magazine article, the second to a book. Note that in the case of the book title, the initial article *The* is moved to the end of the title.

("The Case for Prosecuting Deadbeat Dads" 1996:36–38)
(*Worst Way to Learn: The Government's War on Education, The* 1996)

Section 16.46 of *The Chicago Manual of Style* recommends that the name of an editor, compiler, or translator is used, without an abbreviation such as *ed.*, *comp.*, or *trans.*, when there is no author's name given.

Chapters, tables, appendices, etc., should be cited as follows:

... (Johnson 1995, chap. 6).

or

... (Blake 1985, table 4:34).

or

... (Shelby 1976, appendix C:177).

When citing a work reprinted from an earlier publication, give the earliest date of publication in brackets, followed immediately by the date of version you have used:

... Baldwin ([1897] 1992) interpreted this ...

When citing more than one source, separate citations by a semicolon and order them in a manner of your choice. You may arrange them in alphabetical order, date order, or order of importance to your argument, but whatever order you choose, use it consistently throughout your paper.

... are related (Harmatz 1987:48; Marble et al. 1986:909; Powers and Erickson 1986:48; Rackley et al. 1988:10; Thompson and Thompson 1986:1067).

The date should be given for dissertation and unpublished papers. When the date is not available, use *n.d.* (no date) in place of the date. Use the word *forthcoming* when materials cited are unpublished but scheduled for publication.

Studies by Barkley (forthcoming) and Jorden (n.d.) lend support ...

When citing National Archives or other archival sources, abbreviate citations:

... (NA, 266, Box 567, June 15, 1952).

When citing machine-readable data files, authorship and date should be included:

> ... (American Institute of Public Opinion 1989).

When citing classic texts, such as the Bible, standard translations of ancient Greek texts, or numbers of the Federalist Papers, you may use the systems by which they are subdivided. Since any edition of a classic text employs the standard subdivisions, this reference method has the advantage of allowing your reader to find the source passage in any published edition of the text. It is not necessary to include a citation for a classic text in the reference section.

You may cite a biblical passage by referring to the particular book, chapter, and verse, all in roman type, with the translation given after the verse number:

> "But the path of the just is as the shining light, that shineth more and more unto the perfect day" (Proverbs 4:18 King James Version).

The Federalist Papers are numbered:

> Madison addresses the problem of factions in a republic (Federalist 10).

According to *The Chicago Manual of Style* (1993, section 16.117), references to material in daily newspapers should be handled within the syntax of your sentence:

> In an August 10, 1993, editorial, the *New York Times* painted the new regime in glowing colors.

or

> An article entitled "Abuse in Metropolis," written by Harry Black and published in the *Daily Planet* on December 24, 1996, took exception to Superman's remarks.

According to *The Chicago Manual of Style* description, references to newspaper items are not usually included in the reference list or bibliography. If you wish to include newspaper references, however, there is a model of a bibliographical entry in the next section of this chapter.

When citing a public/government document or one with institutional authorship, you should supply the minimum identification:

> ... (U.S. Bureau of the Census 1993:223).

Since the *ASA Style Guide* gives formats for only two types of government publications, the following models are based not only on practices from the ASA guide but also on formats found in *The Chicago Manual of Style*, sections

15.322–411 and 16.148–79. Corresponding bibliography entries appear in the next section.

Parenthetical text references to both the *Senate Journal* and the *House Journal* start with the journal title in place of the author, the session year, and, if applicable, the page:

> (*Senate Journal* 1997:24).

Congressional debates are printed in the daily issues of the *Congressional Record*, which are bound biweekly and then collected and bound at the end of the session. Whenever possible, you should consult the bound yearly collection instead of the biweekly compilations. Your parenthetical reference should begin with the title *Congressional Record* (or *Cong. Rec.*) in place of the author's name and include the year of the congressional session, the volume and part of the *Congressional Record*, and finally the page:

> (*Cong. Rec.* 1930, 72, pt. 8:9012).

References to congressional reports and documents, which are numbered sequentially in one- or two-year periods, include the name of the body generating the material, the year, and the page:

> (U.S. Congress 1997:12).

Note that any reference that begins with *U.S. Senate* or *U.S. House* may omit the *U.S.*, if it is clear from the context that you are referring to the United States. Whichever form you use, be sure to use it *consistently*, in both the notes and the bibliography.

Bills and Resolutions   According to *The Chicago Manual of Style*, section 15.347–48, bills and resolutions, which are published in pamphlets called "slip bills," on microfiche, and in the *Congressional Record*, are not always given a parenthetical text reference and a corresponding bibliography entry. Instead, the pertinent reference information appears in the syntax of the sentence. If, however, you wish to cite such information in a text reference, the form depends on the source from which you took your information. If citing to a slip bill, use one of these forms:

> (U.S. Senate 1996)
> (*Visa Formalization Act of 1996*)

You may cite either the body that authored the bill or the title of the work itself. Whichever method you choose, remember to begin your bibliography entry with the same material. Here is a model for citing to the *Congressional Record*:

> (U.S. Senate 1996:S7658).

The number following the date and preceded by an *S* (for Senate; *H* for House) is the page in the *Congressional Record*.

As with bills and resolutions, laws (also called statutes) are not necessarily given a parenthetical text reference and a bibliography entry. Instead, the identifying material is included in the text. If you wish to make a formal reference for a statute, you must structure it according to the place where you found the law published. Initially published separately in pamphlets, as slip laws, statutes are eventually collected and incorporated, first into a set of volumes called *U.S. Statutes at Large* and later into the *United States Code*, a multivolume set that is revised every six years. You should use the latest publication. When citing to a slip law, you should either use *U.S. Public Law*, in roman type, and the number of the piece of legislation, or the title of the law:

> (U.S. Public Law 678:16-17)
> (*Library of Congress Book Preservation Act of 1997*:16–17)

When citing to the *Statutes at Large*, use this form:

> (*Statutes at Large* 1997: 466)

The following form is for citing to the *United States Code*:

> (*Library of Congress Book Preservation Act of 1997*, U.S. Code. Vol. 38, Sec. 1562)

According to *The Chicago Manual of Style*, section 15.367, references to the United States Constitution include the number of the article or amendment, the section number, and the clause, if necessary:

> (U.S. Constitution, art. 3, sec. 3)

It is not necessary to include the Constitution in the bibliography.

A reference to a report, bulletin, circular, or any other type of material issued by the Executive Department starts with the name of the agency issuing the document, although you may use the name of the author, if known:

> (Department of Labor 1984:334).

As with laws, Supreme Court decisions are rarely given their own parenthetical text reference and bibliography entry but are instead identified in the text. If you wish to use a formal reference, however, you may place within the parentheses the title of the case, in italics, followed by the source (for cases after 1875 this is the *United States Supreme Court Reports*, abbreviated *U.S.*), which is preceded by the volume number and followed by the page number. You should end the first reference to the case that appears in your paper with the date of the case, in brackets. You need not include the date in subsequent references:

> (*State of Nevada v. Goldie Warren* 324 U.S. 123 [1969])

Before 1875, Supreme Court decisions were published under the names of official court reporters. The reference below is to William Cranch, *Reports of Cases Argued and Adjudged in the Supreme Court of the United States, 1801–1815,* 9 vols. (Washington, D.C., 1804–17). The number preceding the clerk's name is the volume number; the last number is the page:

(1 Cranch 137)

For most of these parenthetical references, it is possible to move some or all of the material outside the parentheses simply by incorporating it in the text:

In 1969, in *State of Nevada v. Goldie Warren* (324 U.S. 123), the judge ruled that an observer of a traffic accident has an obligation to offer assistance to survivors.

Lower Courts   Decisions of lower federal courts are published in the *Federal Reporter*. The note should give the volume of the *Federal Reporter (F.)*, the series, if it is other than the first (2d, in the model below), the page, and, in brackets, an abbreviated reference to the specific court (the example below is to the Second Circuit Court) and the year:

(*United States v. Sizemore*, 183 F. 2d 201 [2d Cir. 1950])

According to *The Chicago Manual of Style*, section 15.368, references to bulletins, circulars, reports, and study papers that are issued by various government commissions should include the name of the commission, the date of the document, and the page:

(Securities and Exchange Commission 1985:57)

Because government documents are often credited to a corporate author with a lengthy name, you may devise an acronym or a shortened form of the name and indicate in your first reference to the source that this name will be used in later citations:

(*Bulletin of Labor Statistics* 1997, 1954; *hereafter BLS*)

The practice of using a shortened name in subsequent references to any corporate author, whether a public or private organization, is sanctioned in most journals and approved in *The Chicago Manual of Style*, section 15.252. Thus, if you refer often to the *U.N. Monthly Bulletin of Statistics*, you may, after giving the publication's full name in the first reference, use a shortened form of the title—perhaps an acronym such as *UNMBS*—in all later cites.

According to *The Chicago Manual of Style*, section 15.377, references to state and local government documents are similar to those for the corresponding national government sources:

(Oklahoma Legislature 1995:24)

The Chicago Manual of Style, section 16.178, restricts bibliographical information concerning state laws or municipal ordinances to the running text.

According to *The Chicago Manual of Style* (sections 16.127, 16.130), in the author-date system, citations to interviews should be handled by references within the text—in the syntax of a sentence—rather than in parentheses:

> In a March 1997 interview with O.J. Simpson, Barbara Walters asked questions that seemed to upset and disorient the former superstar.

For published or broadcast interviews, no parenthetical reference is necessary but there should be a complete citation under Walter's name in the bibliography.

An unpublished interview conducted by the writer of the paper should also be cited in the syntax of the sentence:

> In an interview with the author on April 23, 1993, Dr. Kennedy expressed her disappointment with the new court ruling.

If you are citing material from an interview that you conducted, identify yourself as "the author" and give the date of the interview.

4.3.2   REFERENCES

Parenthetical citations in the text point the reader to the fuller source descriptions at the end of the paper known as the references, or bibliography. This reference list, which always directly follows the text under the heading *References*, is arranged alphabetically according to the first element in each citation. As with most alphabetically arranged bibliographies, there is a kind of reverse-indentation system: After the first line of a citation, all subsequent lines are indented five spaces. The entire references section is double-spaced.

The ASA uses standard, or "headline style," capitalization for titles in the reference list. In this style, all first and last words in a title, and all other words except articles (*a, an, the*), coordinating words (*and, but, or, for, nor*), and all prepositions (*among, by, for, of, to, toward*, etc.), are capitalized.

Remember that every source cited in the text, with those exceptions noted in the examples below, must have a corresponding entry in the references section. Do not include references to any work not cited in the text of your paper.

Most of the following formats are based on those given in the *ASA Style Guide* (1996). Formats for bibliographical situations not covered by the ASA guide are taken from *The Chicago Manual of Style* (1993).

Books

ONE AUTHOR. First comes the author's name, inverted, then the date of publication, followed by the title of the book, the place of publication, and the name of the publishing house. Use first names for all authors or initials if no first name is provided. Add a space after each initial, as in the example below. For place of publication, always identify the state unless the city is New York. Use postal abbreviations to denote states (OK, MA, etc.).

Periods are used to divide most of the elements in the citation, although a colon is used between the place of publication and publisher. Custom dictates that the main title and subtitle are separated by a colon, even though a colon may not appear in the title as printed on the title page of the book.

> Northrup, A. K. 1997. *Living High off the Hog: Recent Pork Barrel Legislation in the Senate.* Cleveland, OH: Johnstown.

TWO AUTHORS. Only the name of the first author is reversed, since it is the one by which the citation is alphabetized. Note that there is no comma between the first name of the first author and the *and* following:

> Spence, Michelle and Kelly Rudd. 1996. *Hiring and the Law.* Boston, MA: Tildale.

THREE OR MORE AUTHORS. The use of *et al.* is not acceptable in the references section; list the names of all authors of a source. While the ASA style places commas between all names in the text citation—(Moore, Rice, Macrory, and Traylor 1998)—it deletes the comma separating the next-to-last and last names in the bibliographical reference. Note also that the ASA does not advocate abbreviating the word *University* in the name of a press, as indicated in the model below.

> Moore, J. B., Jeannine Macrory, Allen Rice and Natasha Traylor. 1998. *Down on the Farm: Culture and Folkways.* Norman, OK: University of Oklahoma Press.

ANONYMOUS SOURCE. Section 16.40 of *The Chicago Manual of Style* (1993), states that if you can ascertain the name of the author when that name is not given in the work itself, place the author's name in brackets:

> [Morey, Cynthia]. 1977. *How We Mate: American Dating Customs, 1900–1955.* New York: Putney.

Do not use the phrase "anonymous" to designate an author whose name cannot be determined; instead, according to section 16.41 of *The Chicago Manual of Style*, begin your citation with the title of the book, followed by the date. You may move initial articles (*a, an, the*) to the end of the title:

> *Worst Way to Learn: The Government's War on Education, The.* 1997. San Luis Obispo, CA: Blakeside.

EDITOR, COMPILER, OR TRANSLATOR AS AUTHOR. When no author is listed on the title page, begin the citation with the name of the editor, compiler, or translator:

Trakas, Dylan, comp. 1998. *Making the Road-Ways Safe: Essays on Highway Preservation and Funding.* El Paso, TX: Del Norte Press.

EDITOR, COMPILER, OR TRANSLATOR WITH AUTHOR.

Pound, Ezra. 1953. *Literary Essays.* Edited by T. S. Eliot. New York: New Directions.
Stomper, Jean. 1973. *Grapes and Rain.* Translated by John Picard. New York: Baldock.

UNTRANSLATED BOOK. If your source is in a foreign language, it is not necessary, according to section 15.118 of *The Chicago Manual of Style*, to translate the title into English. Use the capitalization format of the original language.

Picon-Salas, Mariano. 1950. *De la Conquesta a la Indipendéncia.* Mexico D. F.: Fondo de Cultura Económica.

If you wish to provide a translation of the title, do so in brackets or parentheses following the title. Set the translation in roman type, and capitalize only the first word of the title and subtitle, proper nouns, and proper adjectives:

Wharton, Edith. 1916. *Voyages au front* (Visits to the Front). Paris: Plon.

TWO OR MORE WORKS BY THE SAME AUTHOR. The author's name in all citations after the first may be replaced, if you wish, by a three-em dash (six strokes) of the hyphen:

Russell, Henry. 1978. *Famous Last Words: Notable Supreme Court Cases of the Last Five Years.* New Orleans, LA: Liberty Publications.
_____. 1988. *Great Court Battles.* Denver: Axel and Myers.

CHAPTER IN A MULTIAUTHOR COLLECTION.

Gray, Alexa North. 1998. "Foreign Policy and the Foreign Press." Pp. 188–204 in *Current Media Issues*, edited by Barbara Bonnard and Luke F. Guinness. New York: Boulanger.

The parenthetical text reference may include the page reference:

(Gray 1998, 195–97)

You *must* repeat the name if the author and the editor are the same person:

Farmer, Susan A. 1995. "Tax Shelters in the New Dispensation: How to Save Your Income." Pp. 58–73 in *Making Ends Meet: Strategies for the Nineties*, edited by Susan A. Farmer. Nashville, TN: Burkette and Hyde.

AUTHOR OF A FOREWORD OR INTRODUCTION. According to section 16.51 of *The Chicago Manual of Style*, there is no need to cite the author of a foreword or introduction in your bibliography, unless you have used material from that author's contribution to the volume. In that case, the bibliography entry is listed under the name of the author of the foreword or introduction. Place the name of the author of the work itself after the title of the work:

> Farris, Carla. 1998. Foreword to *Marital Stress among the Professoriat: A Case Study*, by Basil Givan. New York: Galapagos.

The parenthetical text reference cites the name of the author of the foreword or introduction, not the author of the book:

> (Farris 1998)

SUBSEQUENT EDITIONS. If you are using an edition of a book other than the first, you must cite the number of the edition or the status, such as *Rev. ed.* for Revised edition, if there is no edition number:

> Hales, Sarah. 1994. *The Coming Water Wars*. 2d ed. Pittsburgh, PA: Blue Skies.

MULTIVOLUME WORK. If you are citing a multivolume work in its entirety, use the following format:

> Graybosch, Charles. 1988–89. *The Rise of the Unions*. 3 vols. New York: Starkfield.

If you are citing only one of the volumes in a multivolume work, use the following format:

> Graybosch, Charles. 1988. *The Beginnings*. Vol. 1 of *The Rise of the Unions*. New York: Starkfield.

REPRINTS.

> Adams, Sterling R. [1964] 1988. *How to Win an Election: Promotional Campaign Strategies*. New York: Starkfield.

CLASSIC TEXTS. According to *The Chicago Manual of Style*, sections 15.294 and 15.298, references to classic texts such as sacred books and Greek verse and drama are usually confined to the text and not given citations in the bibliography.

Periodicals

JOURNAL ARTICLES. Journals are periodicals, usually published either monthly or quarterly, that specialize in serious scholarly articles in a particular field.

JOURNAL WITH CONTINUOUS PAGINATION. Most journals are paginated so that each issue of a volume continues the numbering of the previous issue. The reason for such pagination is that most journals are bound in libraries as complete volumes of several issues; continuous pagination makes it easier to consult these large compilations:

> Hunzecker, Joan. 1987. "Teaching the Toadies: Cronyism in Municipal Politics." *Review of Local Politics* 4:250–62.

Note that the name of the journal, which is italicized, is followed without punctuation by the volume number, which is itself followed by a colon and the page numbers. There should be no space between the colon and the page numbers, which are *inclusive*. Do not use *p.* or *pp.* to introduce the page numbers.

JOURNAL IN WHICH EACH ISSUE IS PAGINATED SEPARATELY. The issue number appears in parentheses immediately following the volume number.

> Skylock, Browning. 1991. "'Fifty-Four Forty or Fight!': Sloganeering in Early America." *American History Digest* 28 (3):25–34.

ARTICLE PUBLISHED IN MORE THAN ONE JOURNAL ISSUE.

> Crossitch, Vernelle. 1997. "Evaluating Evidence: Calibrating Ephemeral Phenomena," parts 1–4. *Epiphanic Review* 15:22–29; 16:46–58; 17:48–60.

ARTICLES PUBLISHED IN FOREIGN-LANGUAGE JOURNALS.

> Sczaflarski, Richard. "The Trumpeter in the Tower: Solidarity and Legend" (in Polish). *World Political Review* 32:79–95.

MAGAZINE ARTICLES. Magazines, which are usually published weekly, bimonthly, or monthly, appeal to the popular audience and generally have a wider circulation than journals. *Newsweek* and *Scientific American* are examples of magazines.

MONTHLY MAGAZINE.

> Stapleton, Bonnie and Ellis Peters. 1981. "How It Was: On the Trail with Og Mandino." *Lifetime Magazine*, April, pp. 23–24, 57–59.

WEEKLY OR BIMONTHLY MAGAZINE.

> Bruck, Connie. 1997. "The World of Business: A Mogul's Farewell." *The New Yorker*, October 18, pp. 12–15.

NEWSPAPER ARTICLES.

> Everett, Susan. 1996. "Beyond the Alamo: How Texans View the Past." *Carrollton Tribune*, February 16, D1, D4.

The article *The* is omitted from the newspaper's title.

Sources Stored in Archives   According to the *ASA Style Guide*, if you refer to a number of archival sources, you should group them in a separate part of the references section and name it "Archival Sources."

Clayton Fox Correspondence, Box 12. July–December 1903. File: Literary Figures 2. Letter to Edith Wharton, dated September 11.

Public Documents   Since the *ASA Style Guide* gives formats for only two types of government publications, the following bibliographical models are based not only on practices from the ASA guide but also on formats found in *The Chicago Manual of Style*, sections 15.322–411 and 16.148–79.

CONGRESSIONAL JOURNALS. References to either the *Senate Journal* or the *House Journal* begin with the journal's title and include the years of the session, the number of the Congress and session, and the month and day of the entry:

U.S. Senate Journal. 1997. 105th Cong., 1st sess., 10 December.

The ordinal numbers *second* and *third* may be represented as *d* (52d, 103d) or as *nd* and *rd*, respectively.

CONGRESSIONAL DEBATES.

Congressional Record. 1930. 71st Cong., 2d sess. Vol. 72, pt. 8.

CONGRESSIONAL REPORTS AND DOCUMENTS.

U.S. Congress. 1997. House Subcommittee on the Study of Governmental/Public Rapport. *Report on Government Efficiency As Perceived by the Public.* 105th Cong., 2d sess., pp. 11–26.

BILLS AND RESOLUTIONS.

Citing to a Slip Bill   The abbreviation *S. R.* in the first model below stands for *Senate Resolutions*, and the number following is the bill or resolution number. For references to House bills, the abbreviation is *H. R.* Notice that the second model refers the reader to the more complete first entry. The choice of formats depends upon the one you used in the parenthetical text reference.

U.S. Senate. 1996. *Visa Formalization Act of 1996.* 105th Cong. 1st sess. S. R. 1437.

or

Visa Formalization Act of 1996. See U.S. Senate. 1996.

Citing to the Congressional Record

Senate. 1997. *Visa Formalization Act of 1997.* 105th Cong., 1st sess., S. R. 1437. *Congressional Record* 135, no. 137, daily ed. (10 December): S7341.

LAWS.

Citing to a Slip Law

U.S. Public Law 678. 105th Cong., 1st sess., 4 December 1997. *Library of Congress Book Preservation Act of 1997.*

or

Library of Congress Book Preservation Act of 1997. U.S. Public Law 678. 105th Cong., 1st sess., 4 December 1997.

Citing to the Statutes at Large

Statutes at Large. 1998. Vol. 82, p. 466. *Library of Congress Book Preservation Act of 1997.*

or

Library of Congress Book Preservation Act of 1997. Statutes at Large 82:466.

Citing to the United States Code

Library of Congress Book Preservation Act, 1997. U.S. Code. Vol. 38, sec. 1562.

UNITED STATES CONSTITUTION. According to the *CMS* (16.172), the Constitution is not listed in the bibliography.

EXECUTIVE DEPARTMENT DOCUMENTS.

Department of Labor. 1998. *Report on Urban Growth Potential Projections.* Washington, D.C.: GPO.

The abbreviation for the publisher in the above model, *GPO*, stands for the *Government Printing Office*, which prints and distributes most government publications. According to the *CMS* (15.327), you may use any of the following formats to refer to the GPO:

Washington, D.C.: U.S. Government Printing Office, 1984.
Washington, D.C.: Government Printing Office, 1984.
Washington, D.C.: GPO, 1984.
Washington, 1984.
Washington 1984.

Remember to *be consistent* in using the form you choose.

LEGAL REFERENCES.

Supreme Court   According to section 16.174 of *The Chicago Manual of*

Style, Supreme Court decisions are only rarely listed in bibliographies. If you do wish to include such an entry, here is a suitable format:

> *State of Nevada v. Goldie Warren*. 1969. 324 U.S. 123.

For a case prior to 1875, use the following format:

> *Marbury v. Madison*. 1803. 1 Cranch 137.

Lower Courts

> *United States v. Sizemore*. 1950. 183 F. 2d 201 (2d Cir.).

PUBLICATIONS OF GOVERNMENT COMMISSIONS.

> U.S. Securities and Exchange Commission. 1984. *Annual Report of the Securities and Exchange Commission for the Fiscal Year*. Washington, D.C.: GPO.

PUBLICATIONS OF STATE AND LOCAL GOVERNMENTS. Remember that references for state and local government publications are modeled on those for corresponding national government documents:

> Oklahoma Legislature. 1991. Joint Committee on Public Recreation. *Final Report to the Legislature, 1995*, Regular Session, on Youth Activities. Oklahoma City.

Interviews   According to section 16.130 of *The Chicago Manual of Style*, interviews need not be included in the bibliography, but if you or your instructor wants to list such entries, here are possible formats:

PUBLISHED INTERVIEW.

Untitled Interview in a Book

> Jorgenson, Mary. 1998. Interview by Alan McAskill. Pp. 62–86 in *Hospice Pioneers*, edited by Alan McAskill. Richmond, VA: Dynasty Press.

Titled Interview in a Periodical

> Simon, John. 1997. "Picking the Patrons Apart: An Interview with John Simon," by Selena Fox. *Media Week*, March 14, pp. 40–54.

INTERVIEW ON TELEVISION.

> Snopes, Edward. 1998. Interview by Kent Gordon. *Oklahoma Politicians*. WKY Television, June 4.

UNPUBLISHED INTERVIEW.

> Kennedy, Melissa. 1997. Interview by author. Tape recording. Portland, ME, April 23.

Unpublished Sources

PERSONAL COMMUNICATIONS. According to section 16.130 of *The Chicago Manual of Style*, references to personal communications may be handled completely in the text of the paper:

> In a letter to the author, dated July 16, 1997, Mr. Bentley admitted the organizational plan was flawed.

If, however, you wish to include a reference to an unpublished communication in the bibliography, you may do so using one of the following models:

Bentley, Jacob. 1997. Letter to author, July 16.
Duberstein, Cindy. 1996. Telephone conversation with the author, June 5.
Timrod, Helen. 1997. E-mail to author, April 25.

THESES AND DISSERTATIONS.

Hochenauer, Klint. 1980. "Populism and the Free Soil Movement." Ph.D. dissertation, Department of Sociology, Lamont University, Cleveland, OH.

PAPER PRESENTED AT A MEETING.

Zelazny, Kim and Ed Gilmore. 1997. "Art for Art's Sake: Funding the NEA in the Twenty-First Century." Presented at the annual meeting of the Conference of Metropolitan Arts Boards, June 15, San Francisco, CA.

UNPUBLISHED MANUSCRIPTS.

Borges, Rita V. 1993. "Mexican-American Border Conflicts, 1915–1970." Department of History, University of Texas at El Paso, El Paso, TX. Unpublished manuscript.

WORKING AND DISCUSSION PAPERS.

Blaine, Emory and Ralph Cohn. 1995. "Analysis of Social Structure in Closed Urban Environments." Discussion Paper No. 312, Institute for Sociological Research, Deadwood College, Deadwood, SD.

Electronic Sources

CITING ON-LINE SOURCES. The need for a reliable on-line citation system continues to grow, but attempts to establish one are hampered by a number of factors. For one thing, there is no foolproof method of clearly reporting even such basic information as the site's author(s), title, or date of establishment. Occasionally authors identify themselves clearly; sometimes they place a link to their home page at the bottom of the cite. But it is not always easy to determine exactly who authored a particular cite. Likewise, it can be difficult to determine whether a site has its own title or instead exists as a subsection of a larger document with its own title. Perhaps the biggest problem facing on-line researchers is the instability of Internet sites. While some cites may remain in place for weeks or months, many either move to another cite—not always leaving a clear path for you to find it—or disappear.

The *ASA Style Guide* acknowledges that the American Sociological Association has not yet endorsed a standard referencing system for on-line sources and points the reader to the fourth edition of the *Publication Manual of the American Psychological Association* (1995:218–212). *The Chicago Manual of Style*, our supplemental guide through the last two sections of this chapter, offers little information about referencing electronic sources.

You can watch bibliographical history being made on a day-to-day basis on the Internet, where a number of researchers are working to establish viable electronic citation formats. See what you can find, for example, on the following cite on the World Wide Web:

> http://www.fis.utoronto.ca/internet/citation.htm

This site offers links to several pages where bibliographers are coming to grips with the problems of Internet referencing. Therefore, until such time as an authoritative citation system for the Internet is available, we suggest the following simple formats, based in part on the work of other researchers currently available on the Internet.

BIBLIOGRAPHICAL REFERENCE FOR A SITE ON THE WORLD WIDE WEB. Place the following information in this order, separating most of the elements with periods: Name of author (if known), reversed. Title of Document (in quotation marks). Edition, revision, or version information. Date of document. Site address, starting on the next line and enclosed in v-brackets (< and >), followed by the date upon which you last accessed the cite (in parentheses).

> Page, Melvin E. "A Brief Citation Guide for Internet Sources in History and the Humanities." Ver. 2.1. February 20, 1996. <http://www.nmmc.com/lib-web/employee/citguide.him> (April 13, 1997).

The two symbols < and > that surround the site address are not part of the address; they serve merely to differentiate the address from the rest of the citation. It is important not to break the often lengthy information string that constitutes the site address, hence the relatively short second line of the citation. Note that there is no period between the > and the access date, in parentheses.

BIBLIOGRAPHICAL REFERENCE FOR AN FTP SITE.

> Dodd, Sue A. "Bibliographic References for Computer Files in the Social Sciences: A Discussion Paper." Rev. May 1990. <ftp://ftp.msstate.edu/pub/docs/history/netuse/electronic.biblio.cite> (April 13, 1997).

Remember, the one thing that is absolutely required in order to find a site on the Internet is the site address, so make sure that you copy it accurately.

BIBLIOGRAPHICAL REFERENCE FOR A CD-ROM. A CD-ROM's publisher can usually be identified in the same way as a book's publisher. The following model is for a source with an unascertainable author. Note that it is still necessary to include, in parentheses, the latest date on which you accessed the database.

> *Dissertation Abstracts Ondisc.* 1861–1994. CD-ROM: UMI/Dissertation Abstracts Ondisc. (December 15, 1996).

BIBLIOGRAPHICAL REFERENCE FOR AN E-MAIL DOCUMENT. Due to the ephemeral nature of e-mail sources, most researchers recommend not including citations to e-mail in the bibliography. Instead, you may handle e-mail documentation within the text of the paper.

> In an e-mail dated March 22, 1997, Bennett assured the author that the negotiations would continue.

If, however, you would like to include an e-mail citation in your references section, here is a possible format:

> Bennett, Suzanne. <sbb@mtsu.socla.edu>. 15 March 1997. RE: Progress on education reform petition [Email to Courtney Cline <coline@usc.cola.edu>].

The name of the author of the e-mail message is placed first, followed by the author's e-mail address and the date of the message. Next comes a brief statement of the subject of the message, followed by the recipient's name and e-mail address, in brackets.

A sample references page is shown on page 91.

4.4   THE STUDENT CITATION SYSTEM (SCS)

As an alternative to the American Sociological Association (ASA) citation system, you may want to use the Student Citation System (SCS). Be sure to get your instructor's approval before using the SCS system. Why, you may ask, would anyone want another citation system, especially since so many disciplines already have their own (MLA, APA, etc.)? It is precisely because college students are currently required to use several different citation systems that the SCS was created. SCS was the first system specifically designed for use in all undergraduate college courses. Students can use it in their English, psychology, sociology, math, science, history, political science, and other courses.

How is the SCS different from other citation systems? In addition to its multidisciplinary applications, SCS has other distinctive features:

- ■   SCS is made for students, not academics. It is simpler, has fewer rules to learn, and is easier to type than other systems.

SAMPLE REFERENCES PAGE

References

Adams, Daniel D., Thomas C. Johnson and Steven P. Cole. 1989. "Physical Fitness, Body Image, and Locus of Control in College Freshman Men and Women." *Perceptual and Motor Skills* 68:400–402.

Blaylock, Heather S. 1996. *The Body Electric*. Cleveland, OH: Fowler.

Fallon, April E. 1985. "Sex Differences in Perceptions of Desirable Body Shape." *Journal of Abnormal Psychology* 94:102–105.

———. 1987. "Personal References: A Sexual Perspective." *Journal of Applied Psychology* 49(2):11–21.

Graves, Elliot. 1997. "Lineaments of Gratified Desire: Body English in the 1980s." Pp. 124–145 in *The Physics of Physicality*, edited by Lilly Deaver. Boston, MA: Hurstwood.

Luckinbill, Gladys. [1965] 1985. *Advertising to Win: A Manual*. New York: Dalliance.

Nestman's Encyclopedia of Advertising Agencies: 1967. 1966. New York: Holyrod.

Wortmann, Joseph. "Social Protocols, Grades 9–12." September 1996. <ftp://ftp.elp.texu/soc/libart.cite> (April 12, 1997).

Yates, John D. 1996. "The American Dream of the Self." Presented at the annual meeting of the Conference on Sociology and the Media, November 10, 1996, Austin, TX.

■   SCS uses the punctuation and syntax of a new grammar that students
    are quickly learning around the world: the universal language of the
    Internet. The Internet is rapidly becoming the foremost means of a
    wide range of research and communication activities. SCS symbols
    are familiar to anyone who has used the Internet: / @ + . They allow
    citations to be constructed with a minimum of space, effort and con-
    fusion.

4.4.1   RULES FOR NOTES

Like other citation systems, SCS requires that each source citation include (1)
a note in the text in which the reference to the source cited occurs, and (2) an
entry in a reference page. Notes in the text always appear at the end of the
sentence in which the reference is made. Study the models that accompany
the following list of rules for notes.

Rule 1   Notes in the text always contain, in this order: a forward slash
(/); a source reference numeral (1, 2, 3, etc.); a dot (.) that ends the sentence.

> Reagan waved to the convention /1.

Note that there is a space before the /, but no spaces between the / and the 1,
or between the 1 and the dot.

Rule 2   Direct quotes and references to materials on a specific page
both require a page number.

> Reagan waved to the convention /1.23.

Note that no space appears between the dots and the page number.

Rule 3   You may indicate a range of pages, or a page and a range of
pages.

> Reagan waved to the convention /1.23–25.
> Reagan waved to the convention /1.19.23–25.

Rule 4   Indicate chapters, sections, parts, and volumes in the note with
appropriate abbreviations. Note that there is no dot between the abbreviation
and the number of the chapter, section, part, or volume.

> Reagan waved to the convention /1.c3.
> Reagan waved to the convention /1.s3.
> Reagan waved to the convention /1.pt3.
> Reagan waved to the convention /1.v3.

Rule 5   You may cite more than one source in a single note. Separate sources using a /, without spaces between any of the characters.

Reagan waved to the convention 1.v3.23/4/13c6.

This note refers to source 1, volume 3, page 23; source 4; and source 13, chapter 6.

Rule 6   Once used, reference numbers always refer to the same source. They may be used again to refer to a quote or idea from that same source.

Reagan waved to the convention /1.19. Nancy, who had had a severe headache the evening before, came to join him /5/7. One source reported that they had argued about the color suit he was to wear /1.33.

The second note in this passage refers the reader to two difference sources, numbers 5 and 7. The third note is another reference to the first source used in the paper.

Rule 7   Refer to Constitutions with article and section number.

Bill Clinton fulfilled his obligation to address the state of the nation /18.3.

Rule 8   Refer to passages in the Bible, the Koran, and other ancient texts that are divided into standard verses with the verse citation in the note.

Jake forgot that "the seventh day shall be your Holy day" /6.Exodus 35.2.

This example refers to the book of Exodus, chapter 35, verse 2. The 6 indicates that this is the sixth source cited in the paper. There is a dot between the source number and the verse citation.

4.4.2   RULES FOR THE REFERENCES PAGE

General Format Rules   The reference list is usually the final element in the paper. It is entitled *References*. Its entries are arranged in the order that citations appear in the paper. The references page has standard page margins. All lines are double spaced. A sample references page is shown on page 99.

Rules of Punctuation and Abbreviation

1. Punctuation imitates the format used on the Internet.
2. No spaces appear between entry elements (author, date, and so on) or punctuation marks (/ . + @ ").
3. Dots (.) always follow entry elements with exceptions for punctuation rules 5–6.

4. The source number is always followed immediately by a dot.

5. Dots are also used to separate volume and edition numbers in journals.

6. Additional authors are denoted by a plus (+) sign.

7. Subtitles of books and articles are separated from main titles by a colon and a single space: "Crushing Doubt: Pascal's Bleak Epiphany."

8. Book chapters and periodical articles are enclosed in quotation marks (" ").

9. The following abbreviations are used:

c	chapter
comp	compiler
ed	editor
NY	New York (Use postal abbreviations for all states. Note that NY is unique in that when it is used alone it always means New York City. Cite other New York state locations in this form: "Oswego NY." Cite cities in other states similarly: "Chicago IL" "Los Angeles CA" "Boston MA.")
pt	part
s	section
sess	session
tr	translator
v	volume
S	September (Months: Ja F Mr Ap My Je Jl Au S Oc N D)
C	College
I	Institute
U	University

10. Full names instead of initials of authors are used whenever they are used in the original source. When listing publishers, you may use the commonly used names instead of full titles. For example, use "Yale" for Yale University Press; use "Holt" for Holt, Rinehart and Winston. Use Internet abbreviations when known, such as "Prenhall" for Prentice Hall. When abbreviating universities in dissertation and thesis citations, place no dot between the names of the state or city and the university. For example, use "MaIT" for the Massachusetts Institute of Technology and "UMa" for the University of Massachusetts. Always use the second letter of the state abbreviation, in lower case, to avoid the following type of confusion: "OSU" could be a university in Ohio, Oklahoma, or Oregon.

4.4.3   RULES OF ORDER

Elements are always entered in the order shown in the following list of examples. Not all elements are available for every citation. For example, authors are sometimes not provided in source documents. Also, an element may be inappropriate for a certain type of citation. Cities of publication, for instance, are not required for magazines. Carefully examine the order of elements in the examples on pages 95–98.

Books

ONE AUTHOR. Note the order of elements:

- Reference number of note (1, 2, 3, etc.), followed by a dot
- Author's name
- Year of publication
- Title of book
- Number of edition, if other than the first
- Name of publisher
- City of publication
- State of publication (not necessary for New York City)

3.Edna Applegate.1995.My Life on Earth.4th ed.Howard Press.St. Louis MO.

TWO TO THREE AUTHORS.

10.William Grimes+Joan Smith+Alice Bailey.1996.Philosophy and Fire.Harvard.Cambridge MA.

MORE THAN THREE AUTHORS.

42.Lois Mills+others.1989.Revolution in Thought.Agnew.NY.

EDITOR, COMPILER, OR TRANSLATOR AS AUTHOR. Remember that the citation for New York City does not require a state abbreviation.

1.Michael Schendler ed.1992.Kant's Cosmology.Bloom.NY.

EDITOR, COMPILER, OR TRANSLATOR WITH AUTHOR.

9.Elena White.1997.Nietzsche Was Right.Alexander Nebbs tr.Spartan.Biloxi MS.

NO AUTHOR, EDITOR, COMPILER, OR TRANSLATOR. Reverse the placement of the date and title of the book, beginning the entry with the title.

5.The Book of Universal Wisdom.1993.4th ed.Northfield Publications.Indianapolis IN.

SEPARATELY AUTHORED FOREWORD, AFTERWORD, OR PREFACE AS SOURCE.

17.Beulah Garvin.1992.Preface.Down in the Hole by James Myerson.Philosopher's Stone Press.Boston MA.

SEPARATELY AUTHORED CHAPTER, ESSAY, OR POEM AS SOURCE.

5.Jack Wittey.1994."Chickens and People."Animal Rights Anthology. 3rd ed.Gene Cayton comp.Palo Duro Press.Canyon TX.73–90.

ONE VOLUME IN A MULTIVOLUME WORK.

9.Astrid Schultz+others.1991.The Myth of the West.v3 of The Development of European Thought.8 vols.Muriel Hodgson ed.University of Rutland Press.Rutland ME.

Encyclopedias

CITATION FROM AN ENCYCLOPEDIA THAT IS REGULARLY UPDATED. The date refers to the edition of the encyclopedia. Cite the name of the article exactly as it appears in the encyclopedia.

24.Ronald Millgate.1985."Mill, John Stuart."Encyclopedia Americana.

WHEN NO NAME IS GIVEN FOR THE ARTICLE'S AUTHOR.

2."Mill, John Stuart."1946.Hargreave's Encyclopedia.

Ancient Texts

BIBLE, KORAN, ETC. Because the book, chapter, and verse numbers are given in the textual reference, it is not necessary to repeat them here. Remember to cite the traditional divisions of the work instead of the page number and publication information of the specific edition you used.

24.Holy Bible.New International Version.

Periodicals

JOURNAL ARTICLES.

Article with Author or Authors Named   This citation refers to an article published in a journal entitled *Philosopher's Stone*, volume 12, number 4, pages 213–227.

30.Ellis Michaels+Andrea Long.1996."How We Know: An Exercise in Cartesian Logic."Philosopher's Stone.12.4.213–227.

Article with No Author Named

7."Odds and Ends."1995.Philosopher's Stone.12.4.198–199.

MAGAZINE ARTICLES.

Article in a Weekly or Bi-Weekly Magazine   This citation refers to an article published in the June 6, 1994, issue of *Mental Health*.

11.Lorraine Bond.1994."The Last Epicurean."Mental Health.6Jn.34–41.

Article in a Monthly Magazine   The difference between a citation for a monthly magazine and one for a weekly or bi-weekly magazine is that the former does not include a reference to the specific day of publication.

3.Allan Hull.1996."My Secret Struggle."Pathology Digest.Mr.17–30.

NEWSPAPERS.

Article with Named Author   The word *The* is omitted from the newspaper's title.

> 10.Anne Bleaker.1995."Breakthrough in Artificial Intelligence."New York Times.10My.14.

Article with Unnamed Author

> 22."Peirce Anniversary Celebration Set."1996.Kansas City Times-Democrat.1Ap.14.

When City Is Not Named in Newspaper Title   Place the name of the city, and the abbreviation for the state if the city is not well known, in parentheses before the name of the paper.

> 13.Boyd Finnell.1996."Stoic Elected Mayor."(Eugenia TX)Daily Equivocator.30D.1.

Government Documents

AGENCY PUBLICATIONS. Note that, when no author's name is given, the government department is considered the author. Because the Government Printing Office [GPO], the government's primary publisher, is located in Washington,D.C., you need not list the city of publication.

> 28.U.S. Department of Commerce.1996.Economic Projections: 1995–2004.GPO.

LEGISLATIVE JOURNALS. The first citation below refers to the record, published in the *Senate Journal*, of the first session of the 103rd Congress, held on December 10, 1993. The second citation refers to the account of the second session [sess.2] of the 71st Congress, published in volume 72, part 8, of the *Congressional Record*.

> 31.Senate Journal.1993.103Cong.sess1.D10.
> 8.Congressional Record.71Cong.sess.2.72.8.

BILLS IN CONGRESS. This citation refers to Senate Resolution 1437, originated in the first session of the 105th Congress. Bills originating in the House of Representatives are designed by the abbreviation HR.

> 13.U.S. Senate.1997.Visa Formalization Act of 1997.105Cong.sess1.SR.1437.

LAWS. The law referred to in this citation is recorded in section 1562 of volume 38 of the *U.S. Code*.

> 17.U.S. Public Law 678.1993.Library of Congress Book Preservation Act of 1993.U.S.Code.38.1562.

Constitutions. The second citation below refers to the Missouri State Constitution.

> 31.U.S.Constitution.
> 8.MO.Constitution.

Internet Documents   The last two items in an Internet citation are always the website at which the document was found, followed by the date upon which the site was accessed by the researcher.

> 4.Akiko Kasahara and K-lab,Inc.1995.ArtScape of the Far East: Seminar on the Philosophy of Art.Shinshu.University Nagano.Japan.@http://Pckiso3.cs.Shinshu-u.ac.jp/artscape/index.html.Oct27.96.

Unpublished Materials

Interview.

> 12.Lily Frailey.1994.Interview with Clarence Parker.Santa Fe NM.10Ag.

Thesis or Dissertation.

> 21.Gregory Scott.1973.Mysticism and Politics in the Thought of Bertrand Russell.MA thesis.UVa.

Paper Presented at a Meeting. The citation includes the name of the conference and the date on which the paper was presented, and ends with the city where the conference took place.

> 5.Celia Hicks.1995."What Whitehead Would Say."Conference on the Western Imagination.14Ja.Boston MA.

Manuscript Housed in a Collection. Unpublished manuscripts are sometimes left unnamed and undated by their authors. Use any relevant information supplied by the repository catalogue to complete the citation. When a date is hypothesized, as in the above example, place a question mark after it.

> 32.Jose Sanchez.1953?–1982.Journal.Southwest Collection.Arial Library.Chisum Academy.Canyon TX.

Manuscript in the Author's Possession. The citation includes the institution with which the author is affiliated and ends with a description of the format of the work: typescript, photocopy, and so on.

> 14.Jane Fried.1996.Life in California.UTx.Photocopy.

SAMPLE REFERENCES PAGE

References

1. Amanda Collingwood.1993.Architecture and Philosophy.Carlington Press.Detroit MI.

2. Tom Barker+Betty Clay,eds.1987.Swamps of Louisiana.Holt.NY.

3. Joan Garth+Allen Sanford.1963."The Hills of Wyoming."Critical Perspectives on Landscape.Prentice Hall.Upper Saddle River NJ.49–75.

4. Hayley Trakas,ed.1994.Russell on Space.3rd ed.Harmony Press.El Paso TX.

5. Philippe Ariès.1962.Centuries of Childhood: A Social History of Family Life in the Northeastern Region of Kentucky.Robert Baldock tr.Knopf.NY.

6. Jesus Gonzolez.1995."The Making of the Federales."Mexican Stories Revisited.Jules Frank ed.Comanche Press.San Antonio TX.54–79.

7. Carla Harris.1994.Foreword.Marital Stress and the Philosophers:A Case Study by Basil Givan.Galapagos.NY.

8. Jasper Craig.1993."The Flight from the Center of the Cities."Time.10S.67–69.

9. Matthew Moen.1996."Evolving Politics of the Christian Right."PS:Political Science and Politics.29.3.461–464.

10. Patrick Swick.1996."Jumping the Gun on the Federal Reserve."New York Times.10My.78.

11. Frances Muggeridge.1993."The Truth is Nowhere."Conundrum Digest.Mr.40–54.

12. Alan McAskill.1994."Interview with Mary Jordan."Hospice Pioneers of New Mexico.Dynasty Press.Enid.OK.62–86.

13. Jane Smith.1997.Interview with Jerry Brown.San Francisco CA.15Oc.

14. Jacob Lynd.1973.Perfidy in Academe: Patterns of Rationalization in College Administrations.Ph.D. diss.UVA.

15. Holy Bible.New King James Version.

16. Paula Thomas.1970–1976.Diary.Museum of the Plains.Fabens TX.

17. U.S.Department of Labor.1931.Urban Growth and Population Projections:1930–1939.GPO.

18. Senate Journal.1993.103Cong.sess1.D10.

19. U.S.Senate.1997.Visa Formalization Act of 1997.105Cong.sess1.SR.1437.

20. Peter Bolen.1995."Creating Designs in Social Systems."The Internet Journal of Sociological Welfare.14.6.http://www.carmelpeak.com.

21. U.S.Public Law 678.1993.Library of Congress Book Preservation Act of 1993.U.S.Code.38.1562.

22. U.S.Constitution.

CHAPTER 5

ORGANIZING THE RESEARCH PROCESS

5.1 GAINING CONTROL OF THE RESEARCH PROCESS

The research paper is where all your skills as an interpreter of details, an organizer of facts and theories, and a writer of clear prose come together. Building logical arguments with facts and hypotheses is the way things get done in sociology, and the most successful social scientists are those who master the art of research.

Students new to writing research papers sometimes find themselves intimidated. After all, the research paper adds what seems to be an extra set of complexities to the writing process. As any other expository or persuasive paper does, a research paper must present an original thesis using a carefully organized and logical argument. But a research paper often investigates a topic that is outside the writer's own experience. This means that the writer must locate and evaluate information that is new to him, in effect educating himself as he explores his topic. A beginning researcher sometimes feels overwhelmed by the basic requirements of the assignment or by the authority of the source material.

In the beginning it may be difficult to establish a sense of control over the different tasks you are undertaking in your research project. You may have little notion which direction to take in searching for a thesis, or even where the most helpful sources of information might be located. If you fail to monitor your own work habits carefully, you may unwittingly abdicate responsibility for the paper's argument by borrowing it wholesale from one or more of your sources.

Who is in control of your paper? The answer must be you—not the instructor who assigned you the paper, and certainly not the published writers whose opinions you solicit. If all your paper does is paste together the opinions of others, it has little use. It is up to you to synthesize an original idea through the evaluation of your source material. At the beginning of your research project, there will be many elements of your paper about which you are unsure—you will probably not yet have a definitive thesis sentence, for example, or even much understanding of the shape of your argument. You can establish a measure of control over the process you will go through to complete the paper. And if you work regularly and systematically, keeping yourself open to new ideas as they present themselves, your sense of control will grow. The following are some suggestions to help you establish and maintain control of your paper.

5.1.1   UNDERSTAND YOUR ASSIGNMENT

A research assignment can fall short simply because the writer did not read the assignment carefully. Considering how much time and effort you are about to put into your project, it is a very good idea to make sure you have a clear understanding of what it is you are to do. Be sure to ask your instructor about any aspect of the assignment that is unclear to you—but only after you have thought about it carefully. Recopying the assignment instructions in your own handwriting is a good way to start, even though your instructor may have given them to you in writing.

5.1.2   ESTABLISH YOUR TOPIC

It may be that the assignment gives you a great deal of specific information about your topic, or that you are allowed considerable freedom in establishing one for yourself. In a social problems class in which you are studying issues affecting American society, your professor might give you a very specific assignment—for example, a paper examining the difficulties of establishing viable community policy in the wake of significant changes in the urban family structure—or she may allow you to choose for yourself the issue that your paper will address. You need to understand the terms, set up in the assignment, by which you will design your project.

5.1.3   ASCERTAIN YOUR PURPOSE

Whatever the degree of latitude you are given in the matter of your topic, pay close attention to the way in which your instructor has phrased the assignment. Is your primary job to describe a current social issue or to take a stand on it? Are you to compare social systems, and if so, to what end? Are you to classify, persuade, survey, or analyze? Look for such descriptive terms in the assignment directions to determine the purpose of the project.

5.1.4   UNDERSTAND WHO YOUR AUDIENCE IS

Your own orientation to the paper is profoundly affected by your conception of the audience for whom you are writing. Granted, your number one reader is your instructor, but who else would be interested in your paper? Are you writing for the citizens of a community? A group of professionals? A city council? A paper that describes the complex changes in the urban family may justifiably contain much more technical jargon for an audience of sociology professionals than for a citizens group made up of local business and civic leaders.

5.1.5   DETERMINE THE KIND OF RESEARCH YOU ARE DOING

In your paper you will do one or both of two kinds of research, primary and secondary. Primary research requires you to discover information firsthand, often by conducting interviews, surveys, or polls. In primary research, you are collecting and sifting through raw data—data that has not already been interpreted by researchers—which you will study, select, arrange, and speculate on. This raw data may be the opinions of experts or people on the street, historical documents, the theoretical speculations of a famous sociologist, or material collected from other researchers. It is important to carefully set up the method(s) by which you collect your data. Your aim is to gather the most accurate information possible, from which sound observations may be made later, either by you or by other writers using the material you have uncovered.

Secondary research makes use of secondary sources—that is, published accounts of primary materials. While the primary researcher might poll a community for its opinion on the outcome of a recent bond election, the secondary researcher will use the material from the poll to support a particular thesis. In other words, secondary research focuses on interpretations of raw data. Most of your college papers will be based on your use of secondary sources.

PRIMARY AND SECONDARY SOURCES

PRIMARY SOURCE	SECONDARY SOURCE
A published collection of Thurgood Marshall's letters	A journal article arguing that the volume of letters illustrates Marshall's attitude toward the media
An interview with the mayor	A character study of the mayor based on the interview
Material from a questionnaire	A paper basing its thesis on the results of the questionnaire

5.1.6 KEEP YOUR PERSPECTIVE

Whichever type of research you perform, you must keep your results in perspective. There is no way in which you, as a primary researcher, can be completely objective in your findings. It is not possible to design a questionnaire that will net you absolute truth, nor can you be sure that the opinions you gather in interviews reflect the accurate and unchanging opinions of the people you question. Likewise, if you are conducting secondary research, you must remember that the articles and journals you are reading are shaped by the aims of their writers, who are interpreting primary materials for their own ends. The farther you get from a primary source, the greater the possibility for distortion. Your job as a researcher is to be as accurate as possible, and that means keeping in view the limitations of your methods and their ends.

5.2 EFFECTIVE RESEARCH METHODS

5.2.1 PRELIMINARY CONSIDERATIONS AND GENERAL APPROACH

In any research project there will be moments of confusion, but establishing effective procedures can prevent confusion from overwhelming you. You need to design a schedule for the project that is as systematic as possible, yet flexible enough so that you do not feel trapped by it. A schedule will help keep you from running into dead ends by always showing you what to do next. At the same time, it will help you to retain the presence of mind necessary to spot new ideas and new strategies as you work.

Give yourself plenty of time. There may be reasons why you feel like putting off research: unfamiliarity with the library, the pressure of other tasks, or a deadline that seems comfortably far away. Do not allow such factors to deter you. Research takes time. Working in a library often seems to speed up the clock, so that the hour you expected it to take to find certain sources becomes two hours. You should allow yourself time not only to find material, but to read, assimilate, and set it in context with your own thoughts.

The schedule on page 104 lists the steps of a research project in the order in which they are generally accomplished. Remember that each step is dependent on the others, and that it is quite possible to revise earlier decisions in light of later discoveries. After some background reading, for example, your notion of the paper's purpose may change, which may, in turn, alter other steps. One of the strengths of a good schedule is its flexibility.

The general schedule lists tasks for both primary and secondary research; you should use only those steps that are relevant to your project.

Do background reading. Whether you are doing primary or secondary research, you need to know what kinds of work have already been done in

RESEARCH SCHEDULE

TASK	DATE OF COMPLETION
Determine topic, purpose, and audience.	_____
Do background reading in reference books.	_____
Narrow your topic; establish a tentative hypothesis.	_____
Develop a working bibliography.	_____
Consult alternative sources of information, if necessary.	_____
Read and evaluate written sources, taking notes.	_____
Determine whether to conduct interviews or surveys.	_____
Draft a thesis and outline.	_____
Write a first draft.	_____
Obtain feedback (show draft to instructor, if possible).	_____
Do more research, if necessary.	_____
Revise draft.	_____
Correct bibliographical format of paper.	_____
Prepare final draft.	_____
Proofread.	_____
Proofread again, looking for characteristic errors.	_____
Deadline date of final draft.	_____

your field of study. A good way to start is by consulting general reference works, though you do not want to overdo it (see the following paragraph). Chapter 6 lists specialized reference works focusing on topics of interest to sociologists. You might find help in such volumes even for specific, local problems, such as how to restructure a juvenile treatment program or plan an antidrug campaign aimed at area schools.

Be very careful not to rely too exclusively on material taken from general encyclopedias. You may wish to consult one for an overview of a topic with which you are unfamiliar, but students new to research are often tempted to import large sections—if not entire articles—from such volumes, and this practice is not good scholarship. One major reason that your instructor has required a research paper from you is to have you experience the kinds of books and journals in which the discourse of sociology is conducted. General reference encyclopedias, such as *Encyclopaedia Britannica* or *Colliers Encyclopedia*, are good places for instant introductions to subjects; some encyclopedias even include bibliographies of reference works at the ends of their articles. But you will need much more detailed information about your subject to write a useful paper. Once you have gotten some general background information from an encyclopedia, move on.

A primary rule of source hunting is to use your imagination. Determine which topics relevant to your study might be covered in general reference works. For example, if you are looking for introductory readings to help you with the aforementioned research paper on antidrug campaign planning, you might look into such specialized reference tools as the *Encyclopedia of Social Work*. Remember to check articles in such works for lists of references to specialized books and essays.

Narrow your topic and establish a working thesis. Before beginning to explore outside sources, it would be a good idea for you to examine what you already know or think about your topic, a job that can only be accomplished well in writing. You might wish to use one or more of the prewriting strategies described in Chapter 1. You might be surprised by what you know—or don't know—about the topic. This kind of self-questioning can help you discover a profitable direction for your research.

For a research paper on a course in social problems, Dorian Gray was given the general topic of studying grassroots attempts to legislate morality in American society. She chose the topic of textbook censorship. Here is the path her thinking took as she looked for ways to limit the topic effectively and find a thesis:

General Topic	**Textbook Censorship**
Potential topics	How a local censorship campaign gets started
	Funding censorship campaigns
	Reasons behind textbook censorship
	Results of censorship campaigns
Working thesis	It is disconcertingly easy in our part of the state to launch a textbook censorship campaign.

It is unlikely that you will come up with a satisfactory thesis at the beginning of your project. You need to guide yourself through the early stages of research toward a main idea in a way that is both useful and manageable. Having in mind a working thesis—a preliminary statement of your purpose—can help you select material that is of greatest interest to you as you examine potential sources. The working thesis will probably evolve as your research progresses, and you need to be ready to accept such change. You should not fix on a thesis too early in the research process, or you may miss opportunities to refine it.

Develop a working bibliography. As you begin your research, you will look for published sources—essays, books, interviews with experts in the field—that may help you with your project. This list of potentially useful sources is your working bibliography. There are many ways to discover items for the bibliography. You can search the cataloging system in your library, as well as the specialized published bibliographies in your field, for titles. (Some of these bibliographies are listed in Chapter 6.) The general reference works you consulted for your background reading may also list such sources, and each specialized book or essay you find will have a bibliography of sources its writer used which may be useful to you.

From your working bibliography you can select items for the final bibliography, which will appear in the final draft of your paper. Early in your research you may not know which sources will help you and which will not. It is important to keep an accurate description of each entry in your working bibliography to tell clearly which items you have investigated, which you will need to consult again, and which you will discard. Building the working bibliography also allows you to practice using the required bibliographical format for the final draft. As you list potential sources, include all the information about each source needed for your format, and place the information in the correct order, using the proper punctuation.

The American Sociological Association's (ASA) bibliographical format—the one most often required for sociology papers—is described in detail in Chapter 4 of this manual.

Consult alternative sources of information. In the course of your research you may need to consult a source that is not immediately available to you. For example, while working on the antidrug campaign paper, you might find that a packet of potentially useful information is available from a government agency or a public interest group at the state or federal level. Maybe an essential book is not held by your university library or by any other local library. Or perhaps a successful antidrug program has been implemented in the school system of a city comparable in size to yours but located in another state. In such situations, it may be tempting to disregard potential sources because of the difficulty of obtaining them. If you ignore the existence of material important to your project, however, you are not doing your job.

It is vital that you take steps to acquire the needed material. In the first situation, you can simply write to the state or federal agency; in the second, you may use your library's interlibrary loan procedure to obtain a copy of the book; in the third, you can track down the council that manages the antidrug campaign, by E-mail, mail, or phone to ask for information. Remember that many businesses and government agencies want to share their information with interested citizens; some even have employees or entire departments whose job is to facilitate communication with the public. Be as specific as possible when asking for information by mail. It is a good idea to briefly outline your project—in no more than a few sentences—in order to help the respondent determine the type of information you need. Also, be sure to begin the job of locating and acquiring long-distance source material as soon as possible, to allow for the various delays that often occur while conducting a search at a distance.

Read and evaluate written sources, taking notes. Few research experiences are more frustrating than half-remembering something worth using from a source that you can no longer identify. Establish an efficient method of examining and evaluating the sources listed in your working bibliography that will leave you with an accurate written record of your examination. The following are some suggestions for using written sources.

Determine quickly the potential usefulness of a source. For books, you can read through the prefatory material (the introduction, foreword, and preface), looking for the author's thesis; you can also examine chapter headings, dust jackets, and indexes. A journal article should announce its intention in its abstract or introduction, which in most cases will be a page or less in length. This preliminary examination should tell you whether a more intensive examination is worthwhile. Note that whatever you decide about the source, you should copy the title page of the book or journal article on a photocopy machine, making sure that all important publication information (including title, date, author, volume number, and page numbers) is included. Write on the photocopied page any necessary information that is not printed there. Without such a record, later on in your research you might forget that you had looked at that text, and you may find yourself examining it again.

When you have determined that a potential source is worth closer inspection, explore it carefully. If it is a book, determine whether you should invest the time it will take to read it in its entirety. Whatever the source, make sure you understand not only its overall thesis, but also each part of the argument that the writer sets up to illustrate or prove the thesis. Get a feel for the shape of the writer's argument, how the subtopics mesh to form a logical defense of her main point. What do you think of her logic? Her examples? Coming to an accurate appraisal may take more than one reading.

As you read, try to get a feel for the larger argument in which this source takes its place. References to other writers will give you an indication of where else to look for source material, as well as indicate the general shape of scholarly opinion concerning your subject. If you can see the article you are reading as only one element of an ongoing dialogue instead of an attempt to have the last word on the subject, then you can place the argument of the paper in perspective. The same goes for book-length treatments.

Use photocopies. Periodicals and most reference works cannot be checked out of the library. Before the widespread placement of photocopy machines, students could use these materials only by sitting in the library, reading sources, and jotting down information on note cards. While there are advantages to using the note card method, photocopying saves you time in the library and allows you to take the source information in its original shape home with you, where you can decide how to use it at your convenience, perhaps shaping the material at your computer keyboard.

If you decide to make copies of source material, you should do the following:

■   Follow all copyright laws.
■   Have the exact change for the photocopy machines.
■   Record all necessary bibliographical information on the photocopy. If you forget to do this, you may find yourself making an extra trip to the library just to get an accurate date of publication or set of page numbers.

Remember that photocopying a source is not the same thing as examining it. You will still have to spend time going over the material, assimilating it in order to use it accurately. It is not enough merely to have the information close to hand or even to read it through once or twice. You should understand it thoroughly. Be sure to give yourself time for this kind of evaluation.

Determine whether to conduct interviews or surveys. If your project calls for primary research, you may need to interview experts on your topic or to conduct a survey of opinions among a select group using a questionnaire. Be sure to prepare yourself as thoroughly as possible for any primary research. Following are some tips for conducting an interview.

Establish a purpose for each interview, bearing in mind the requirements of your working thesis. In what ways might your discussion with the subject benefit your paper? Write down your formulation of the interview's purpose. Estimate the length of time you expect the interview to take and inform your subject. Arrive for your scheduled interview on time and dressed appropriately. Be courteous.

Learn as much as possible about your topic by researching published sources. Use this research to design your questions. If possible, learn something about the people you interview. This knowledge may help you establish rapport with your subjects and will also help you tailor your questions. Take a list of prepared questions to the interview. However, be ready to depart from your list of questions to follow any potentially useful direction that the interview takes.

Take notes during the interview and bring along extra pens. The use of a tape recorder may inhibit some interviewees. If you wish to use audiotape, ask for permission from your subject. Follow up your interview with a thank you letter and, if feasible, a copy of the published paper in which the interview is used.

5.2.2   DESIGNING AND CONDUCTING A SURVEY OR QUESTIONNAIRE

If your research requires a survey or questionnaire, see Chapter 12 for instructions on designing and conducting surveys, polls, and questionnaires.

5.3   ETHICAL USE OF SOURCE MATERIAL

Your goal is to integrate the source material skillfully into the flow of your written argument, using it as effectively as possible. This means that sometimes you will need to quote from a source directly, while at other times you should recast (paraphrase) source information into your own words.

5.3.1   QUOTING

When should you quote? You should directly quote from a source when the original language is distinctive enough to enhance your argument, or when rewording the passage would lessen its impact. You should also quote a passage to which your paper will take exception. In the interest of fairness, it is important to let a writer taking an opposing view state his case in his own words. Rarely, however, should you quote a source at great length (longer than two or three paragraphs). Nor should your paper, or any lengthy section of it, be merely a string of quoted passages. The more quotations you take from others, the more disruptive they are to the rhetorical flow of your own language. Too much quoting creates a "cut and paste" paper, a choppy patchwork of varying styles and borrowed purposes in which the sense of your own control over the material is lost.

Acknowledge quotations carefully. Failing to signal the presence of a quotation skillfully can lead to confusion or choppiness:

> The U.S. Secretary of Labor believes that worker retraining programs have failed because of a lack of trust within the American business culture. "The American business community does not visualize the need to invest in its workers" (Winn 1992:11).

The phrasing of the first sentence in this passage seems to suggest that the quote following it comes from the Secretary of Labor. Note how this revision clarifies the attribution:

> According to reporter Fred Winn (1992), the U.S. Secretary of Labor believes that worker retraining programs have failed because of a lack of trust within the American business culture. Summarizing the Secretary's view, Winn writes, "The American business community does not visualize the need to invest in its workers" (p. 11).

The origin of each quote must be signaled (citation) within your text at the point where the quote occurs, as well as in the list of works cited (references) which follows the text. Chapter 4 describes documentation formats set forth by the American Sociological Association (ASA) and *The Chicago Manual of Style*, along with the alternative Student Citation System (SCS).

Quote accurately. If your quotation introduces careless variants of any kind, you are misrepresenting your source. Proofread your quotations very carefully, paying close attention to such surface features as spelling, capitalization, italics, and the use of numerals. Occasionally, either to make a quotation fit smoothly into a passage, to clarify a reference, or to delete unnecessary material from a quotation, you may need to change the original wording slightly. You must signal any such change to your reader by using brackets:

> "Several times in the course of his speech, the attorney general said that his stand [on gun control] remains unchanged" (McAffrey 1995:2).

Ellipses may be used to indicate that words have been left out of a quote:

> "The last time voters refused to endorse one of the senator's policies ... was back in 1982" (Laws 1992:143).

When you integrate quoted material with your own prose, it is unnecessary to begin the quote with ellipses:

> Benton raised eyebrows with his claim that "nobody in the mayor's office knows how to tie a shoe, let alone balance a budget" (Williams 1990:12).

5.3.2   PARAPHRASING

Your writing has its own rhetorical attributes, its own rhythms and structural coherence. Inserting too many quotations into a section of your paper can disrupt the patterns you establish in your prose and diminish the effectiveness of your own language. Paraphrasing, or recasting source material in your own words, is one way of avoiding the risk of creating a choppy hodgepodge of quotations. Paraphrasing allows you to communicate ideas and facts from a source in your own prose, thereby keeping intact the rhetorical characteristics that distinguish your writing.

Remember that the salient fact about a paraphrase is that its language is yours. It is not a near copy of the source writer's language. Merely changing a few words of the original does justice to no one's prose and frequently produces stilted passages. This sort of borrowing is actually a form of plagiarism. To fully integrate the material you wish to use into your writing, use your own language. Paraphrasing may actually increase your comprehension of source material; recasting a passage requires you to think carefully about its meaning—more carefully, perhaps, than you might if you merely copied it word for word.

5.3.3   AVOIDING PLAGIARISM

Paraphrases require the same sort of documentation that direct quotes do. The words of a paraphrase may be yours, but the idea is someone else's. Failure to give that person credit, in the form of references within the text and in the bibliography, may make you vulnerable to a charge of plagiarism.

What kind of paraphrased material must be acknowledged? Basic material that you find in several sources need not be acknowledged by a reference. For example, it is unnecessary to cite a source for the information that Franklin Delano Roosevelt was elected to a fourth term as President of the United States shortly before his death, because this is a commonly known fact. However, Professor Smith's opinion, published in a recent article, that Roosevelt's winning of a fourth term hastened his death is not a fact, but a theory based on Smith's research and defended by her. If you wish to make use of Smith's opinion in a paraphrase, you need to give her credit for it, as you should the judgments and claims of any other source. Any information that is not widely known, whether factual or open to dispute, should be documented. This includes statistics, graphs, tables, and charts taken from a source other than your own primary research.

Plagiarism is the using of someone else's words or ideas without giving that person credit. While some plagiarism is deliberate, produced by writers who understand that they are guilty of a kind of academic thievery, much of it is unconscious, committed by writers who are not aware of the varieties of plagiarism or who are careless in recording their borrowings from sources. Plagiarism includes:

- quoting directly without acknowledging the source.
- paraphrasing without acknowledging the source.
- constructing a paraphrase that closely resembles the original in language and syntax.

One way to guard against plagiarism is to keep careful records in your notes of when you have quoted source material directly and when you have paraphrased—making sure that the wording of the paraphrase is yours. Make sure that all direct quotes in your final draft are properly set off from your own prose, either with quotation marks or in indented blocks.

CHAPTER 6

THE LIBRARY AND OTHER SOURCES OF INFORMATION

The resources of civilization are not yet exhausted.
—William E. Gladstone, 1809–1898

Where we get our information is extremely important. The ability to locate valid and reliable information efficiently is vitally important when you are writing papers in sociology. For most papers written in college, the library is the place to find most—if not all—of the information needed. Mastering effective information gathering will help you to be more productive in your research and writing. Further, effective library research skills enable you to practice lifelong learning using information sources available at most libraries.

This chapter highlights methods of information retrieval for major sources in sociology. To give a specific example, let's assume you have been assigned a paper or want information on the traditional American family. With the materials introduced in this chapter, you should be able to find a concise definition of "traditional family," lists of articles and books written about the topic, theories about its impact upon American society, reviews of books to provide a balanced coverage, and government and other statistical sources that help document historical change of the American family—while associating it with a variety of variables, such as age, geographic region, race and socioeconomic status.

In some cases, someone in a public agency or private organization has probably already conducted significant research on your topic. If you can find the right person, you may be able to secure much more information in much less time than you can by looking in the local library by yourself.

Did you know, for example, that the members of the U.S. Senate and House of Representatives constantly use the services of the Congressional

Research Service (CRS), and that upon request to your congressperson or senator, materials from the CRS may be sent to you on the topic of your choice? Further, every agency of government on the local, state, and national levels employs people who are responsible primarily for the purpose of gathering information that is needed to help their managers make decisions. Much of the research that is done by these employees is available upon request.

This chapter is divided into sections, each describing a type of reference tool. The sections are arranged so that you can become familiar with the nature and uses of general reference works first, and then with the nature and uses of specialized studies. Bibliographic examples were selected according to the following criteria: All are available in English, most are available in college libraries, and all are examples of sources potentially useful to sociology students. Publications that may seem unusually dated often represent the inaugural issue of the document or publication being described.

6.1   LEVELS OF ACADEMIC WRITING

Researchers who study the written work of college students find that several patterns of effort and expertise emerge. Morgan (1981:5–6) refers to these patterns as levels of academic writing, and believes they appear in nearly every college class and that they refer to graduate and undergraduate students alike. While writing quality increases with grade level, many students—no matter what their grade level—have trouble using words effectively.

6.1.1   LEVEL ONE: THE FACT-GATHERING LEVEL

Students at this level have little more to offer in their writing than opinions that they have heard others state or that they found in a newspaper or periodical. If asked, "What is Social Security?" a level-one student might answer, "Social Security is welfare for the elderly or disabled" or, "Social Security is a liberal program." Students who are stranded at level one or below are unable to advance much further than a fact or two to support their statements. This is the lowest level of scholarship. The level-one student, when assigned a report, will simply go to the library and assemble facts and opinions incoherently and return with a paper. At best, this is a very simple presentation of "What is?" However, mastery of level one is a necessary learning experience.

6.1.2   LEVEL TWO: THE INFORMATIONAL LEVEL

At this level, students learn to clarify facts and understand them more completely through the process of comparison. When asked the question, "What is Social Security?" the student writing at level two might draw on what she has learned of political science and economics to suggest different ideological perspectives, each with its own facts. A level-two answer shows greater depth of knowledge than a level one answer; the student has advanced beyond a recitation of facts, taking the initial steps toward analysis.

6.1.3   LEVEL THREE: THE ANALYTICAL LEVEL

At this level, the student becomes familiar with and somewhat proficient in completing various types of sociological analysis. Using the same example, "What is Social Security?" some students might present their facts in numerical terms, using formulas, mathematical curves, statistical tests, or tables to express relationships among variables. Other students might reduce their data to common prose, utilizing different theories to analyze and explain the same phenomena.

6.1.4   LEVEL FOUR: THE CREATIVE LEVEL

This is the highest and most difficult level of academic writing. The student is able to use facts, theories, and analytical ability to reach levels of creativity. At the creative level, the student is essentially alone, trying to discover something new, perhaps an insight that colleagues can't appreciate initially.

To the question, "What is Social Security?" the creative sociologist, utilizing the sociological imagination described in Chapter 1, might employ both historical analysis and creative forecasting to discover new information. The creative level is where knowledge is advanced, its frontiers pushed inevitably outward.

It is the purpose of this book to help you advance, from whatever level at which you presently find yourself, to the full professional expression of level four—creative and insightful writing in sociology. In the remainder of this chapter, we provide a sample of the many types of resources available to help you reach your sociology writing goals.

6.2   GUIDES TO THE LITERATURE

Guides to the literature are books or articles that identify sources that enable students to search for information on individual topics. Some guides focus exclusively on the two principal categories of reference works: finding aids, such as bibliographies and periodical indexes; and content reference works, such as handbooks, yearbooks, subject dictionaries, and subject encyclopedias.

Some guides include discussions of various types of research materials, such as government publications, while others include lists of important book-length studies on topics in a subject field. Students can identify sociological reference publications by consulting a guide that covers a wide spectrum of fields related to their areas of interest. There are several general guides that can be of great benefit. The following are three examples of such guidebooks.

BRAY, R., ED. 1996. *GUIDE TO REFERENCE BOOKS*. CHICAGO, IL: AMERICAN LIBRARY ASSOCIATION. Bray and his associates have compiled one of the most complete guides to reference sources in sociology and other areas. Many of the works listed throughout this chapter were obtained from the *Guide*. One of its strengths is its classification of works into many areas that fall under the umbrella of sociology—such as general sociology, social conditions/social welfare, social work, aging, alcoholism and drug abuse, childhood and adolescence, death and dying, homelessness and the homeless, marriage and the family, population planning, poverty and the poor, sex and sexual behavior, urbanization, ethnic groups, and women. Bray's guide further classifies the type of reference work within each of these areas—such as guides, bibliographies, periodicals, indexes, encyclopedias, dictionaries, book reviews, directories, atlases, chronologies, biographies, terminology, quotations, handbooks, and statistics. We believe that this guide is probably the best on the market for the serious sociology student.

SHEEHY, E. P., ED. 1986. *GUIDE TO REFERENCE BOOKS*. 10TH ED. CHICAGO, IL: AMERICAN LIBRARY ASSOCIATION. Like Bray's *Guide*, the primary purpose of this volume is to list and evaluate reference sources. Individual books are grouped under these headings: general reference works, humanities, social sciences, history and area studies, and pure and applied sciences. Within each group, titles are subdivided by subject, then by specific type of material (encyclopedia, dictionary, bibliography, etc.).

THE NEW YORK PUBLIC LIBRARY DESK REFERENCE. 1993. NEW YORK: STONESONG PRESS. This reference book includes commonly needed material on a vast range of topics—some of interest to social science students, such as the addresses of national, state, county, and city government consumer protection agencies; spoken and written forms of addressing government and military personnel; brief accounts of events in world history; and descriptions of international organizations. There is an index.

For most academic disciplines, there are specialized guides to the literature. Given an unfamiliar topic in sociology or a related field, a student can consult a guide that focuses on the social sciences for titles of content reference works containing information on the topic. The following are two examples:

ABY, S. H., 1987. *SOCIOLOGY: A GUIDE TO REFERENCE AND INFORMATION SOURCES*. LITTLETON, CO: LIBRARIES UNLIMITED. Part of the *Reference Sources in the Social Sciences Series* (No. 1), this excellent guide is divided into three sections: (1) works of use to all social sciences, (2) individual social science resources of use to sociologists, and (3) sociological sources, including general works and a section on resources especially useful in twenty-two subdivisions of sociology.

WHITE, C. 1973. *SOURCES OF INFORMATION IN THE SOCIAL SCIENCES*. 2D ED. CHICAGO, IL: AMERICAN LIBRARY ASSOCIATION. This one-volume guide covers eight social sciences, each in a separate chapter. The first part of each chapter introduces important monographs on the development, organization, and content of a discipline and its subfields; the second part lists and annotates major reference works in the discipline by type (dictionaries, encyclopedias, handbooks, etc.). There is an inclusive author-title-subject index.

Sometimes there are guides that reference all available information on a given subject or constellation of subjects. The following is an example of such a guidebook.

SELTH, J. P. 1985. *ALTERNATIVE LIFESTYLES: A GUIDE TO RESEARCH COLLECTIONS ON INTENTIONAL COMMUNITIES, NUDISM, AND SEXUAL FREEDOM*. WESTPORT, CT: GREENWOOD. This book describes thirty research collections on intentional communities, nudism, and sexual freedom in the United States, which total 120,000 volumes, 15,000 periodicals, 125,000 audiovisual items, over 3 million photographs, and many ephemeral materials.

6.2.1   HANDBOOKS

A handbook is a compact fact book designed for quick reference. It usually deals with one broad subject area, and emphasizes generally accepted data rather than recent findings. In the latter respect, handbooks differ from yearbooks, although these reference tools overlap in the way they are used and the information they include. Two types of handbooks useful to sociologists are: (1) statistical handbooks, which provide data about a number of demographic and social characteristics, and (2) subject handbooks, which offer a comprehensive summary of research findings and theoretical propositions for broad substantive areas in a discipline.

Statistical Handbooks   Containing data gathered from numerous sources, statistical handbooks provide students with information necessary for the description and analysis of social trends and phenomena. Among the many statistical handbooks useful to sociologists are the following:

U.S. BUREAU OF THE CENSUS. 1949. *COUNTY AND CITY DATA BOOK*. WASHINGTON, DC: GOVERNMENT PRINTING OFFICE. This handbook contains statistics on population, housing, income, education, and employment for counties, standard metropolitan statistical areas, cities, urbanized areas, and unincorporated places. Since there is no subject index, the only subject access to the tables is through the "Outline of Tabular Subject Content" located in the front of the volume. This handbook is published irregularly.

HISTORICAL STATISTICS OF THE UNITED STATES: COLONIAL TIMES TO 1970. 1971. WASHINGTON, DC: GOVERNMENT PRINTING OFFICE. This two-volume work contains statistics on a wide spectrum of social and economic developments from the colonial period to 1970. The tables are accompanied by explanatory notes and references to additional sources of statistical information. To use this work effectively, you may turn to the table of contents, which provides a broad subject access; the subject index, which offers a more narrow topical approach to the data; or the time period index, which provides access to statistics on major topics for individual decades.

HURDLE, ANGELA AND ANDREA YURASITS, EDS. 1996. *DEMOGRAPHICS USA: COUNTY ADDITION*. NEW YORK: BILL COMMUNICATIONS. The information in this guide is organized within a geographic hierarchy by region, state, metropolitan area, and county. Summaries are provided for each geographic area. You will find information dealing with the area's total population, its percentage of the U.S. total, and listings by age, sex, number of households, number of persons in household, and so on.

SIMON MARKET RESEARCH BUREAU. 1992. *THE NEW AMERICAN FAMILY: SIGNIFICANT AND DIVERSIFIED LIFESTYLES*. NEW YORK. This book draws from government sources and from the publisher's study of media and markets. It provides tables, charts, and figures on income, shopping habits, marital status, mobility, and so on, for groups such as new mothers, singles, baby boomers, empty nesters, and teens.

Students may also want to consult the following statistical guides:

- Horton, C. P. and J. C. Smith, eds. 1990. *Statistical Record of Black America*. Detroit, MI: Gale.

- Gall, S. B. and T. L. Gall, eds. 1993. *Statistical Record of Asian Americans*. Detroit, MI: Gale.

- *Statistical Record of Native North Americans*. 1993. Detroit, MI: Gale.

- Reddy, M. A., ed. 1993. *Statistical Record of Hispanic Americans*. Detroit, MI: Gale.

- Darnay, A. J., ed. 1994. *Statistical Record of Older Americans*. Detroit, MI: Gale.

- Schick, F. L. and R. Schick, eds. 1994. *Statistical Handbook on Aging Americans*. Phoenix, AZ: Oryx.

- Ficke, R. C. 1992. *Digest of Data on Persons with Disabilities*. Washington, DC: National Institute on Disability and Rehabilitation Research.

Subject Handbooks   Subject handbooks in sociology provide a summary and a synthesis of concepts, research, and theoretical approaches of specific topical areas within the discipline—such as formal organizations, socialization, and social psychology. Students who want a brief overview of well-established information or an explanation of major concepts in one substantive area—such as women's studies—will find that the following subject handbook is a convenient source.

ZOPHY, A. H. AND F. M. KARENIK, EDS. 1990. HANDBOOK OF AMERICAN WOMEN'S HISTORY. NEW YORK: GARLAND. This book is the result of networking among women's history and women's studies colleagues. It offers introductory and fundamental information necessary for a general understanding of the field. It was designed to assist both students and teachers who wanted to research basic information regarding sources and materials.

Other subject handbooks available to sociology students include the following:

- Bart P. and L. Frankel. 1986. *The Student Sociologist's Handbook*, 4th ed. New York: Random House.
- Rebach, H. M. and J. G. Bruhn, eds. 1991. *Handbook of Clinical Sociology*. New York: Plenum Press.
- Smelser, N. J., ed. 1988. *Handbook of Sociology*. Newbury Park, CA: Sage.
- Binstock, R. H. and L. K. George, eds. 1990. *Handbook of Aging and the Social Sciences*. San Diego, CA: Academic Press.
- Sussman, M. B. and S. K. Steinmetz, eds. 1987. *Handbook of Marriage and the Family*. New York: Plenum Press.
- Hawes, J. M. and E. I. Nybakken, eds. 1991. *American Families: A Research Guide and Historical Handbook*. New York: Greenwood.
- Adler, L. L., ed. 1993. *International Handbook on Gender Roles*. Westport, CT: Greenwood.
- Woods, G. 1993. *Drug Abuse in Society: A Reference Handbook*. Santa Barbara, CA: ABC-Clio.
- Hurrelmann, K., ed. 1994. *International Handbook of Adolescence*. Westport, CT: Greenwood.

6.2.2 YEARBOOKS

While in many cases they contain a good deal of background information, yearbooks are fact books that focus on the developments and events of a given year. Unlike handbooks, they emphasize current information. Like handbooks, there are two types of yearbooks most useful for sociology students: (1) statistical yearbooks, which provide the most recent data on social and demographic characteristics, and (2) subject yearbooks, which review current theory and research.

Statistical Yearbooks You can turn to the most recent yearbook for the latest data available on topics such as population composition, fertility, and economic activity, and you can also use back issues to collect data for previous time periods. This is especially true in cases where no handbook presents data for a specific geographical or topical area. Among the general statistical yearbooks often used by sociologists are the following:

STATISTICAL YEARBOOK. NEW YORK: UNITED NATIONS/STATISTICAL OFFICE. This annual publication is prepared by the Statistical Office of the United Nations. Tables cover population, workforce, agriculture, production, mining construction, consumption, transportation, external trade, wages and prices, national income, finance, social statistics, education, and culture. Normally, a ten to twenty year span is given for each series. The table of contents is the only subject access to this book. Sources are cited. Textual material, including indexes, is in French and English.

STATISTICAL YEARBOOK. PARIS: UNESCO. The statistical charts in this annual publication are printed in three languages, and cover aspects of education, science, and culture in 200 member nations of UNESCO. The data is generated from questionnaires given to a wide variety of respondents. There is no index.

GOVERNMENT FINANCE STATISTICS YEARBOOK. WASHINGTON, DC: INTERNATIONAL MONETARY FUND. This annual reference volume publishes tables that document revenues and spending by governments around the world. There is no index.

VITAL STATISTICS OF THE UNITED STATES. 2 VOLS. HYATTVILLE, MD: U.S. DEPARTMENT OF HEALTH AND HUMAN SERVICES. This yearly series is published annually. Volume 1 presents the year's birth statistics at the national and local levels, and volume 2 covers death statistics.

STANLEY, H. W. AND R. G. NIEMI, EDS. *VITAL STATISTICS ON AMERICAN POLITICS 1993*, 5TH ED. WASHINGTON, DC: CONGRESSIONAL QUARTERLY. The charts and tables in this guide cover a wide range of topics related to American politics, including the media (newspaper endorsements of presidential candidates from 1932 to 1988 are graphed), interest groups, and the geographical and ethnic composition of political bodies. An index is included.

YEARBOOK OF LABOUR STATISTICS. GENEVA: INTERNATIONAL LABOUR OFFICE. This book publishes statistical tables on the economic development of countries around the world. There is an index of countries.

O'LEARY, K., ED. *STATE RANKINGS 1995: A STATISTICAL VIEW OF THE 50 UNITED STATES*, 6TH ED. LAWRENCE, KS: MQ. This book features a huge collection of up-to-date statistical information about the 50 states. Tables (546 in all) compare states in a wide variety of areas: agriculture, crime, defense, economy, government finance, health, housing, population, social welfare, and transportation.

Other valuable sources for statistical information include the following:

- *Digest of Educational Statistics*
- *Historical Statistics of the United States*
- *State and Metropolitan Area Data Book*

- *Statistical Abstract of the United States*
- *County and City Data Book*

Statistical yearbooks focusing on a special subject are often useful to sociologists interested in specific problems. Two yearbooks focusing on specific subjects are the following:

DEMOGRAPHIC YEARBOOK. NEW YORK: UNITED NATIONS/STATISTICAL OFFICE. This annual contains demographic statistics for over 200 separate geographic areas. Population and vital statistics appear in each annual volume, but the subject matter of the other statistical compilations varies from year to year. Each volume includes an introduction that defines terms and describes the tables. The table of contents lists tables by broad categories. A cumulative index in each volume identifies the annual volumes in which statistics on individual topics are to be found and indicates the time span of the statistics in individual volumes.

U.S. FEDERAL BUREAU OF INVESTIGATION UNIFORM CRIME REPORTS FOR THE UNITED STATES. WASHINGTON, DC: GOVERNMENT PRINTING OFFICE. This annual report contains statistics on crimes, offenders, and law enforcement personnel. Tables include statistics by type of offenses, geographical divisions, age groups, trends, and police employment. The table of contents provides the only subject access to the tables.

Subject Yearbooks   The subject yearbook (also known as the annual review) is particularly useful because it contains articles that give a brief overview of recent major developments in the field. These articles, based on the latest published research, allow a student beginning a research project to define and clarify the subject matter. The bibliographies appended to the articles can provide useful leads for further reading. The subject yearbook for sociology is the following:

ANNUAL REVIEW OF SOCIOLOGY. PALO ALTO, CA: ANNUAL REVIEWS. New developments in the field of sociology are discussed in approximately sixteen essays covering ten broad subject areas in this annual. Areas covered include formal organizations, social processes, urban sociology, and institutions. The essays average twenty-five to thirty pages in length and include extensive bibliographies. Each volume, beginning with the second, contains cumulative indexes that list essays by author and broad subject area.

6.2.3   SUBJECT DICTIONARIES AND ENCYCLOPEDIAS

Subject Dictionaries   The primary purpose of a dictionary is to supply meanings and give accurate spellings of words. The words that are included, and the exhaustiveness of their definitions, depend on the type of dictionary. This discussion focuses on subject dictionaries.

Virtually all academic disciplines have their own specialized language. The function of a subject dictionary is to explain briefly the words—whether terms or names—that make up a particular subject's specialized jargon. Such a source lists terms unfamiliar in common usage, as well as rather ordinary terms that have taken on specialized and technical meanings within the context of a subject discipline.

Sociology is a broad field encompassing every aspect of human social behavior. Many concepts or terms that have a common usage take on a specialized meaning in sociology. The term *norm* is an example. In common usage the word refers to something common or "normal." In sociology, however, *norm* refers to the rules or sets of expectations that guide social behavior.

In addition to defining concepts, subject dictionaries are also useful for locating brief descriptions of methodological techniques or tests and definitions of major theories. When students are unsure of the exact meaning of a concept or theory, or of the function of a specific methodological technique, they can consult a sociology dictionary or a broader dictionary of the social sciences. The following are examples:

THEODORSON, G. A. AND A. G. THEODORSON. 1969. *A MODERN DICTIONARY OF SOCIOLOGY.* NEW YORK: BARNES & NOBLE. This comprehensive dictionary, prepared for the student sociologist, contains extensive definitions of words as they are used by sociologists—especially those linked with the related fields of social psychology, demography, and political sociology.

GOULD J. AND W. L. KOLB. 1964. *A DICTIONARY OF THE SOCIAL SCIENCES.* NEW YORK: FREE PRESS. This excellent dictionary includes approximately 1,000 terms used in the social sciences. Selections were made from a study of the literature in political science, social anthropology, economics, social psychology, and sociology.

Other examples of dictionaries in sociology, some of which are designed for specific areas within the discipline of sociology, include the following:

- Boudon, R. and F. Bourricaud. 1989. *A Critical Dictionary of Sociology.* Chicago: University of Chicago Press.
- Jary, D. and J. Jary. 1991. *HarperCollins Dictionary of Sociology.* New York: HarperPerennial.
- Harris, D. K. 1988. *Dictionary of Gerontology.* New York: Greenwood.
- Abel, E. L. 1984. *A Dictionary of Drug Abuse Terms and Terminology.* Westport, CT: Greenwood.
- Lindsey, M. P. 1989. *Dictionary of Mental Handicap.* New York: Routledge.
- Richter, A. 1993. *Dictionary of Sexual Slang.* New York: Wiley.
- Mills, J. 1992. *Womanwords: A Dictionary of Words about Women.* New York: Free Press.

Encyclopedias   While dictionaries contain brief definitions of terms, encyclopedias include summary essays about individual topics. There are two types of encyclopedias: general encyclopedias, which are wide-ranging in topical coverage, and subject encyclopedias, which focus on topics within an individual subject discipline or a group of related disciplines. This discussion focuses on subject encyclopedias.

The essays in subject encyclopedias are often written by recognized scholars. They include bibliographies listing major topical studies and cross references listing other essays that may contain useful additional information. You can use a subject encyclopedia in several ways—as an introduction to a topic, as a means of viewing a topic in a wider context, or as the starting point for research. You may find an essay on the topic helpful for clarification and definition of your research project, and the bibliography can provide valuable leads for further reading. The following three subject encyclopedias are especially useful to sociology majors.

1968. *INTERNATIONAL ENCYCLOPEDIA OF THE SOCIAL SCIENCES*. NEW YORK: MACMILLAN. This seventeen-volume set contains articles covering the subject matter of the following fields, as well as some of the most important contributors in their development: anthropology, economics, geography, history, law, political science, psychiatry, psychology, sociology, and statistics. The treatment of individual topics is often divided into more than one essay, each approaching the topic from the perspective of a different social science. Although the encyclopedia is arranged alphabetically by subject, the articles are lengthy and cover broad areas. To find a specific topic, you should consult the index in the last volume. There is also a useful "Classification of Articles" section in the last volume. The essays themselves are carefully cross-referenced, and the bibliographies accompanying the articles—some of which are extensive although dated—remain useful.

TIERNEY, H., ED. 1989–1991. *WOMEN'S STUDIES ENCYCLOPEDIA: VIEWS FROM THE INSIDE*. NEW YORK: GREENWOOD. This is an excellent resource for students interested in this area. The major focus of this three-volume work is on the American experience. There is no single feminist perspective informing the entries. Contributors had the widest possible latitude in developing their articles.

BORGATTA, E. F. AND M. L. BORGATTA, EDS. 1992. *ENCYCLOPEDIA OF SOCIOLOGY*. NEW YORK: MACMILLAN. This four-volume set is a comprehensive general sociology encyclopedia intended for a broad audience. It contains 370 lengthy, articles written by 339 sociologists, each two to eighteen pages in length, which conclude with bibliographies.

Among others, the *Encyclopedia of Philosophy*, the *Encyclopedia of Psychology*, and the *Encyclopedia of Religion* can also be very helpful referencing tools for sociology students. The following is a list of encyclopedias covering specific areas within sociology:

- DiCanio, M. 1993. *The Encyclopedia of Violence: Origins, Attitudes, Consequences.* New York: Facts on File.
- Maddox, G. L., ed. 1987. *The Encyclopedia of Aging.* New York: Springer.
- Roy, F. H. and C. Russell, eds. 1992. *The Encyclopedia of Aging and the Elderly.* New York: Facts on File.
- Evans, G., R. O'Brien and S. Cohen, eds. 1991. *The Encyclopedia of Drug Abuse.* New York: Facts on File.
- O'Brien, R. and M. Chafetz, eds. 1991. *The Encyclopedia of Alcoholism.* New York: Facts on File.
- Clark, R. E. and J. F. Clark, eds. 1989. *The Encyclopedia of Child Abuse.* New York: Facts on File.
- Lerner, R., A. C. Petersen and J. Brooks-Gunn, eds. 1991. *Encyclopedia of Adolescence* (2 vols.). New York: Garland.

6.2.4   INDEXES AND ABSTRACTS

Indexes contain lists of citations of articles printed in journals, magazines, and other periodicals. The standard citation for articles in indexes includes the author's name, the date of the issue in which the article appears, the article title, the name of the journal, the volume and/or issue number, and page numbers. Abstracts contain short summaries of articles or books. Indexes and abstracts are important because the articles in scholarly journals often update information found in books, or in some cases constitute the only published treatments of certain topics.

Computer On-Line Database Systems   Specialized indexes and abstracts list articles published in scholarly journals by subject and author. Most are now retrievable through computer on-line database systems located in the library. These CD-ROM networks index thousands of professional and popular articles in most academic areas. The most useful databases for sociology are stored in Sociofile, which indexes over 1,900 international journals in sociology and related fields that are stored in two print indexes titled *Sociological Abstracts* (1974–present) and *Social Sciences Index* (1983–present). *Social Sciences Index* indexes journals in most of the social sciences, including anthropology, area studies, economics, environmental science, geography, law, and political science.

Other databases that offer potential sources for your sociology studies are the following:

- ERIC, an education database (1966–present) consisting of the *Resources in Education* file and the *Current Index to Journals in Education* file, compiling journal article citations with abstracts from over 750 professional journals.
- Psyclit, a psychology database (1974–present) that compiles summaries for literature in psychology and related disciplines and corresponds to *Psychological Abstracts*, which indexes about 1,300 professional journals in twenty-seven languages.

■ *Readers' Guide to Periodical Literature*, a popular and general interest database (1983–present) that provides citations from more than 900 journals and magazines in the popular press.

■ *United States Government Periodical Index*, a government periodicals database (November 1994–present) that indexes approximately 180 U.S. government sources covering a wide variety of subjects. The reference department in many libraries also allows you to access over forty other databases on *FIRSTSEARCH*.

Discipline Indexes   Discipline indexes identify articles in journals by the discipline or group of related disciplines (such as social sciences) rather than by the topic, while others identify journal articles according to broad topical areas without a discipline focus. An example of a discipline index that indexes by subject articles in social science, economics, and anthropology journals as well as those in sociology is the following:

SOCIAL SCIENCES INDEX. 1974/75. NEW YORK: H. W. WILSON. A quarterly publication with annual cumulations, this index organizes—by subject and author—articles in over 260 journals in anthropology, sociology, law, and criminology. A helpful feature is the separate "Book Reviews" index at the back of each issue.

Topical Indexes   An important topic often becomes the focus of an index, which is generated to make all articles relevant to that topic available to researchers—regardless of field or discipline. Examples of topical indexes frequently used by sociologists are the following:

POPULATION INDEX. 1935. PRINCETON, NJ: OFFICE OF POPULATION RESEARCH, PRINCETON UNIVERSITY AND POPULATION ASSOCIATION OF AMERICA. This quarterly indexes books, journals, and government publications. The annotated entries are arranged by broad subjects—such as mortality, internal migration, and spatial distribution. Each issue also contains several articles on topics of current interest. Geographical, author, and statistical indexes cumulate annually.

STATISTICAL REFERENCE INDEX ANNUAL ABSTRACTS. BETHESDA, MD: CONGRESSIONAL INFORMATION SERVICE. This annual volume is a guide to American statistical publications produced by private organizations and state governments. Contents are organized by the type of organization publishing the reports, each of which is briefly described. An accompanying volume includes four indexes: subject and name, category, issuing sources, and title.

Other topical indexes of interest to sociology students are the following:

■ *Inventory of Marriage and Family Literature*. 1973. St. Paul, MN: National Council on Family Relations.

■ *The Kaiser Index to Black Resources, 1948–1986*. 1992. Brooklyn, NY: Carlson.

- *Newman R. Black Index: Afro-Americana in Selected Periodical, 1907–1949.* 1981. New York: Garland.
- *Women's Studies Index.* 1991. Boston: G. K. Hall Citation Indexes.

Citation Indexes   A third type of index, the citation index, lists articles that have referred to previous research by a particular author. When a researcher knows of one article—or author of articles—on a particular topic, newer related materials can be found by locating articles that cite the original work or author. Thus you can find articles without depending on any subject classification system. This type of index is useful for determining the quality of a specific key research paper, or for tracing the developments in theory and methods that were stimulated by this key paper. A student can determine the number of times a key article has been used, as well as the names of the sociologists who have cited it. A citation index useful to sociologists is:

SOCIAL SCIENCES CITATION INDEX. 1972. PHILADELPHIA, PA: INSTITUTE FOR SCIENTIFIC INFORMATION. This service enables the user to identify recent articles that refer to earlier works. Each issue is divided into three parts. This Citation Index, arranged alphabetically by cited author, lists articles in which a particular work was cited. The Source Index lists alphabetically the authors who are citing the original work and gives bibliographic information for each article that cites the original work. The Permaterm Subject Index lists articles by all the significant words in the titles. The index is issued three times a year and cumulates annually.

General Abstracts   Like indexes, abstracts provide a complete citation for each article, and include a brief summary of its contents. Abstracts enable researchers to determine whether an article is useful without having to locate and read it. This can be important when students are working in a library with a small periodical collection and must depend on interlibrary loans to acquire articles. A general abstract covering topics in the field of sociology is the following:

SOCIOLOGICAL ABSTRACTS. 1952. NEW YORK: SOCIOLOGICAL ABSTRACTS. This source indexes and summarizes over 6,000 books and journal articles each year. Within broad subject areas—such as group interaction, social differentiation, and feminist studies—abstracts are arranged alphabetically by author. The last issue of each year contains cumulative author and subject indexes. The abstract is currently issued five times a year.

Specialized Abstracts   A specialized abstract covers a particular topic in greater detail than general abstracts and cites research that is published outside the field of sociology. A particularly useful one to sociologists is the following:

CRIMINAL JUSTICE ABSTRACTS. 1968. HACKENSACK, NJ: NATIONAL COUNCIL ON CRIME AND DELINQUENCY. This quarterly (entitled *Crime and Delinquency Literature through 1976*) abstracts books and journals in the area of crime and delinquency. Abstracts are arranged under broad subject areas, such as correction and law enforcement. There is a detailed subject index. Each issue also contains a review of current developments in one area, such as aid to victims, employee theft, and delinquency prevention.

Examples of other specialized abstracts within the broader discipline of sociology include the following:

- *Abstracts in Social Gerontology.* 1990. Newbury Park, CA: Sage.
- *Child Development Abstracts and Bibliography.* 1928. Chicago: University of Chicago Press.
- *Sage Family Studies Abstracts.* 1979. Beverly Hills, CA: Sage.
- *Sage Race Relations Abstracts.* 1975. Beverly Hills, CA: Sage.
- *Women's Studies Abstracts.* 1972. New York: Rush.

6.2.5   BIBLIOGRAPHIES

Bibliographies constitute a particularly important category of finding aids. An individual bibliography might list any or all of the following: books, periodicals, periodical articles, published documents, unpublished documents, or unpublished manuscripts. Our focus is on bibliographies as finding aids for articles and for books other than reference books. Whenever you use a bibliography that does not list journal articles, you must also consult a periodical index or abstract in order to compile a thorough reading list on the topic.

Some bibliographies provide only citations for the books and articles they list; others provide annotations as well. Standard bibliographic citation form for journal articles includes author, title, journal name, volume and sometimes number, and date of publication. Usually, the information is sufficiently complete to locate the item. Annotated bibliographies provide more information, helping you decide if an individual title might be useful. An annotation is a brief summary of the article or book's content along with a comment on its quality.

Bibliographies come in two formats: Some are short and are appended to articles or books, and others are book length.

Appended Bibliographies   Appended bibliographies identify titles that are either cited in the article or book or are relevant to the topic being discussed. You can use a bibliography appended to a reliable book or article as a guide to your readings on the topic. To identify appended bibliographies on a particular topic, you may consult the following:

BIBLIOGRAPHIC INDEX. 1937. NEW YORK: H. W. WILSON. Published in April and August and in a cumulated annual volume in December, this work lists, by subject, bibliographies with fifty or more entries that are published separately or as parts of books or periodicals in English and West European languages. Citations specify whether the bibliographies are annotated. Each volume begins with a prefatory note that briefly explains the forms used in the entries.

Book-Length Bibliographies   Bibliographic indexes also identify book-length bibliographies. Their scope is ordinarily wider than that of appended bibliographies. Some book-length bibliographies are published only once and are retrospective in nature. An example of this type is the *International Bibliography of Research in Marriage and the Family*. St. Paul, MN: Family Social Science, University of Minnesota.

Others are published periodically, sometimes annually, and are called current bibliographies. Each new edition lists titles that have appeared since the previous edition. However, most current bibliographies have a one- to two-year lag time between the publication of a book and its citation.

Some useful current bibliographies cover a particular academic discipline, such as sociology, or a group of related disciplines, such as social sciences. Generally, the coverage includes articles as well as books, and the scope is international. The following is an example:

INTERNATIONAL BIBLIOGRAPHY OF SOCIOLOGY. 1955. LONDON: TAVISTOCK. One of a set entitled *International Bibliography of the Social Sciences*, this volume attempts to provide comprehensive coverage of scholarly publications in the field, regardless of country of origin, language, or type. Three to five thousand citations are arranged in a detailed classification scheme, with author and subject indexes providing complete access. Citations are not annotated. All information is given in French and English. Although the volume is published each year, there is a one- to two-year lag time.

National libraries, such as the British Library or the Library of Congress, have copies of most of the important books on all subjects that are available in that country. Therefore, the subject catalogue of the Library of Congress, available in most college and university libraries, can be used as a reasonably comprehensive current bibliography on most topics.

U.S. LIBRARY OF CONGRESS. 1950. SUBJECT CATALOG: A CUMULATIVE LIST OF WORKS REPRESENTED BY LIBRARY OF CONGRESS PRINTED CARDS. WASHINGTON, DC: LIBRARY OF CONGRESS. Published in quarterly, yearly, and five-year cumulative editions since 1950, the *Subject Catalog* lists books cataloged by the Library of Congress and other major libraries in the United States. Each edition offers the single most comprehensive bibliography of works on every subject (excluding works of fiction), and from all parts of the world, that have become available during the period it covers. Subject headings are cross-referenced.

The following bibliographies contain materials with potential use for students of sociology:

- Berndt, J. 1986. *Rural Sociology: A Bibliography of Bibliographies*. Metuchen, NJ: Scarecrow.
- Bruhn, J. G., B. U. Philips and P. L. Levine. 1985. *Medical Sociology: An Annotated Bibliography*. New York: Garland.
- Ghorayshi, P. 1990. *The Sociology of Work: A Critical Annotated Bibliography*. New York: Garland.

- Kinlock, G. C. 1987. *Social Stratification: An Annotated Bibliography.* New York: Garland.
- Aday, R. H. 1988. *Crime and the Elderly: An Annotated Bibliography.* New York: Greenwood.
- Nordquest, J. 1991. *The Elderly in America: A Bibliography.* Santa Cruz, CA: Reference and Research Services.
- Nordquest, J. 1988. *Substance Abuse I: Drug Abuse: A Bibliography.* Santa Cruz, CA: Reference and Research Services.
- Nordquest, J. 1990. *Substance Abuse II: Alcohol Abuse: A Bibliography.* Santa Cruz, CA: Reference and Research Services.
- Nordquest, J. 1988. *The Homeless in America: A Bibliography.* Santa Cruz, CA: Reference and Research Services.
- De Young, M. 1987. *Child Molestation: An Annotated Bibliography.* Jefferson, NC: McFarland.
- Dabney, M. C. 1984. *Incest: An Annotated Bibliography.* Jefferson, NC: McFarland.
- Engeldinger, E. A. 1986. *Spouse Abuse: An Annotated Bibliography of Violence Between Mates.* Metuchen, NJ: Scarecrow.
- Soliday, G. L., ed. 1980. *History of the Family and Kinship: A Select International Bibliography.* Millwood, NY: Kraus International Publ.

6.2.6   GENERAL PERIODICALS AND NEWSPAPERS

General Periodicals   General periodicals contain articles on a range of topics intended to attract general readers with varied interests. News magazines, hobby or recreational magazines, and a host of publications such as the *Saturday Review* and the *New Yorker* are all classified as general periodicals. A student can find information on specific topics covered in general periodicals by consulting the *Readers' Guide to Periodical Literature* in printed format on the library shelf, going back for several decades, or on the CD-ROM Database Network back to 1983.

In addition to broadening a student's knowledge and outlook, general periodicals can also serve a legitimate research function for sociologists. Many general periodicals include regular features on important social problems (such as poverty, unemployment, or busing) and public opinion (attitudes toward marijuana smoking, abortion, etc.). Among the major general periodicals that are nonsociological but that emphasize social and political affairs are the *New York Times Magazine, Atlantic Monthly, Newsweek, U.S. News and World Report, Time,* and *Harper's.* General periodicals reporting current events and issues of interest to the sociologist usually do not analyze them from a sociological perspective. However, one general periodical that does is the following:

SOCIETY (FORMERLY *TRANSACTION: SOCIAL SCIENCE AND MODERN SOCIETY*). 1967. NEW BRUNSWICK, NJ: RUTGERS. Written for the layperson by well-known sociologists and other social scientists, this periodical covers a wide variety of topics in the areas of government, housing, welfare, law, race relations, and education. It is issued monthly.

Other examples of similar utility are *Business Week, Psychology Today,* and *Library Journal.* These periodicals cover professional news, trends, developments, and other events for the professions. Articles are often written by professionals in the field.

Newspapers   Newspapers are regularly issued publications (daily, weekly, semiweekly) that report events and discuss topics of current interest. The types of information that sociologists may find useful are: news items comprising factual reporting of events; editorials, representing the editor's thinking on current issues; feature articles, presenting an investigation of a topic; and columns, including comments or reports on current events or issues by journalists. In newspapers you can find factual information on topics such as crime or intergroup conflict. Also, you can identify attitudes of people toward important social issues.

Newspapers distinguished for the extensive coverage they give to national affairs are the *Washington Post* and the *New York Times.* You can find articles that cover specific topics in the *New York Times* by consulting its index:

NEW YORK TIMES INDEX. 1913. NEW YORK: NEW YORK TIMES. The *New York Times Index* provides subject access to *New York Times* news stories, editorials, and other features. Published every two weeks, it is cumulated annually. Each entry begins with a subject, followed by references to other sections in the index (if there are any). Then the article is summarized. For the sake of brevity, the citation identifies each month by one or two letters, followed by the date, a roman numeral for a section, an Arabic page number, and sometimes a column number, prefaced by a colon. The year is always identified on the cover and title page and is essential information to record when copying citations. One important item to note in using this index is that the cross-references that directly follow the subject in each entry must be checked in the index to obtain a complete citation. You cannot identify the exact location of the articles noted in this section without doing so.

The following major newspapers have indexes available either in print or on microfilm:

- *The Chicago Tribune*
- *The Houston Post*
- *The Los Angeles Times*
- *The National Observer*
- *The New Orleans Times-Picayune*
- *The New York Times*
- *The Times of London*
- *The Wall Street Journal*
- *The Washington Post*

You may need coverage of an important topic from a number of different perspectives. In such a research project, a local newspaper or the *New York Times* would not suit your needs. For example, you may want to compare the coverage of right-to-work laws presented in a southwestern newspaper to those presented in a northern newspaper. For that type of project you should consult the following:

NewsBank: Urban Affairs Library. 1975. Greenwich, CT: Office of Urban Affairs. This publication not only indexes articles on subjects from over 150 daily and weekly urban newspapers but also includes the articles themselves on microfiche. The index is divided into thirteen subject sections—Business and Economic Development, Consumer Affairs, Government Structure, Social Relations, Welfare and Poverty, Housing and Urban Renewal, Law and Order, Education, Political Development, Health, Transportation, Environment, and Employment—each contained in a separate binder. The microfiche copies of the articles are located in the back of each binder. Note that there is a separate binder containing an Introduction, Guide to the Index, and an overall Name Index. The Guide to the Index section is designed as an aid to determine in which of the thirteen major subject categories a particular topic is covered. A cumulative subject index for each topical area is provided annually.

6.2.7   ACADEMIC JOURNALS

Articles in scholarly journals, written by specialists and critically evaluated by other scholars prior to being accepted for publication, represent the most recent additions to an academic discipline's shared store of knowledge or to its debate on a particular topic. Students interested in compiling a well-rounded and up-to-date reading list on a topic should always consult the scholarly journals.

Most journals contain a book review section in which scholars in the field present critiques of recently published books. These reviews usually give an accurate assessment of the book's quality from the field's standpoint. When faced with a choice of several books, you can save time by reading book reviews to select the most useful, authoritative sources.

Sociologists publish numerous journals, some rather general in scope, and some devoted to a particular subfield within the discipline, such as family studies. As a sociology student, you should be familiar with the following journals:

American Journal of Sociology. 1895. Chicago: University of Chicago Press. This bimonthly journal reports research and fieldwork on a variety of topics in sociology. The articles range from twelve to fifty pages, though the average length is approximately twenty-seven pages. Short papers that summarize recent empirical research are included in the Research Notes section. Each issue also contains a comprehensive book review section with evaluative reviews.

AMERICAN SOCIOLOGICAL REVIEW. 1936. WASHINGTON, DC: AMERICAN SOCIOLOGICAL ASSOCIATION. The official journal of the American Sociological Association, this bimonthly publication contains articles that cover all areas of sociology. The average length of articles is twelve pages. The journal also reports the activities of the Association and contains a section for comments and discussions of previous articles.

SOCIAL FORCES. 1922. CHAPEL HILL, NC: UNIVERSITY OF NORTH CAROLINA PRESS. This quarterly, which contains articles averaging twenty pages in length, includes papers on all aspects of sociology. The journal is international in scope, but articles about the United States predominate. Each issue contains a number of authored book reviews. Special issues, in which all the articles focus on a specific topic, appear at least once a year.

These major sociology journals represent a small fraction of the scholarly periodicals published by sociologists. Students can find a brief description of other scholarly journals within sociology and other academic disciplines by consulting:

KATZ, W. 1978. *MAGAZINES FOR LIBRARIES.* 3D ED. NEW YORK: BOWKER. This work contains publication information and descriptive and evaluative annotations for over 6,500 periodicals and newspapers. Titles are organized into approximately 100 subject areas, such as: Aeronautics Space Science, Africa, Business Education, General Magazines, Government Magazines, History, Newspapers, and Opinion Magazines. Because of this topical organization, the volume's index is particularly useful for locating individual titles.

6.2.8   PROFESSIONAL JOURNALS

The following is a list of professional journals of interest to sociologists, political scientists, and other social scientists. Some are refereed—that is, the articles they contain are sent out to scholars for review before publication—while others are not. But all contain articles with potential use for sociology students.

- Addiction
- Addictive Behaviors
- Administration
- Administration and Society
- Administration in Social Work
- Administrative Science Quarterly
- Adolescence
- Africa Quarterly
- African Affairs
- African Studies

- Age and Aging
- Aging and Society
- AIDS and Public Policy Journal
- Alcohol Health and Research World
- Alcoholism Treatment Quarterly
- Alternatives: A Journal of World Policy
- American Anthropologist
- American Behavioral Scientist
- American Demographics
- American Economic Review

- American Educational Research Journal
- American Ethnologist
- American Indian Culture and Research Journal
- American Journal of Community Psychology
- American Journal of Drug and Alcohol Abuse
- American Journal of Economics and Sociology
- American Journal of Education
- American Journal of Family Therapy
- American Journal of Human Genetics
- American Journal of International Law
- American Journal of Orthopsychiatry
- American Journal of Philology
- American Journal of Physical Anthropology
- American Journal of Political Science
- American Journal of Psychiatry
- American Journal of Psychoanalysis
- American Journal of Psychology
- American Journal of Psychotherapy
- American Journal of Public Health
- American Journal of Sociology
- American Political Science Review
- American Politics Quarterly
- American Prospect
- American Psychologist
- American Scholar
- American Scientist
- American Society for Information Science Journal
- American Sociologican Review
- American Sociologist
- American Statistician
- Annals of the American Academy of Political and Social Science
- Annual Review of Anthropology
- Annual Review of Psychology
- Annual Review of Sociology
- Anthropological Quarterly
- Antioch Review

- Applied Psycholinguistics
- Archive of Sexual Behavior
- Argumentation and Advocacy
- Armed Forces and Society
- Asian Affairs
- Asian Quarterly
- Asian Survey
- Atlantic Community Quarterly
- Australian and New Zealand Journal of Sociology
- Australian Journal of Anthropology
- Australian Journal of Politics and History
- Australian Journal of Public Administration
- Australian Journal of Social Issues
- Behavior Research and Therapy
- Behavior Research Methods, Instruments, and Computer
- Behavior Science Research
- Behavior Therapy
- Behavioral Health Management
- Behavioral Neuroscience
- Behavioral Science
- Black Politician
- Black Scholar
- Brain
- British Journal of Clinical Psychology
- British Journal of Criminology
- British Journal of Educational Psychology
- British Journal of Educational Studies
- British Journal of International Studies
- British Journal of Law and Society
- British Journal of Political Science
- British Journal of Psychology
- British Journal of Social Psychology
- British Journal of Sociology
- Bulletin of the Association for Business Communication
- Bureaucrat
- Business
- Business and Society

- Cambridge Journal of Education
- Campaign and Elections
- Canadian Journal of Behavioral Science
- Canadian Journal of Criminology
- Canadian Journal of Economics
- Canadian Journal of Experimental Psychology
- Canadian Journal of Nursing Research
- Canadian Journal of Political Science
- Canadian Journal of Psychiatry
- Canadian Journal of Psychology
- Canadian Psychologist
- Canadian Psychology
- Canadian Public Administration
- Canadian Public Policy
- Canadian Review of Sociology and Anthropology
- Change
- Child Abuse and Neglect
- Child and Adolescent Social Work Journal
- Child Development
- Child Psychiatry and Human Development
- Child Study Journal
- Child Welfare
- Children's Literature in Education
- China Quarterly
- Church History
- Clinical Social Work Journal
- Cognition
- Cognitive Psychology
- Communication Quarterly
- Communication Reports
- Communication Research
- Communication Theory
- Communist Affairs
- Communist and Post-Communist Studies
- Communities
- Community Development Journal
- Community Mental Health Journal
- Comparative Education Review

- Comparative Political Studies
- Comparative Politics
- Comparative Strategy
- Comparative Studies in Society and History
- Computers and the Humanities
- Conflict
- Conflict Bulletin
- Conflict Management and Peace Science
- Conflict Studies
- Congress and the Presidency
- Contemporary China
- Contemporary Drug Problems
- Contemporary Economic Policy
- Contemporary Education
- Contemporary Sociology
- Cooperation and Conflict
- Corrections Today
- Counseling Psychologist
- Crime and Delinquency
- Criminal Justice and Behavior
- Criminal Justice Ethics
- Criminal Justice Review
- Criminology
- Crisis
- Critical Quarterly
- Critical Review
- Critical Studies in Mass Communication
- Crossroads
- Cultural Anthropology
- Current Sociology
- Current World Leaders
- Daedalus
- Day Care and Early Education
- Death Studies
- Democracy
- Demography
- Development and Change
- Developmental Psychology
- Diplomatic History
- Dissent

- Dissertation Abstracts International, A: The Humanities and Social Sciences
- Dissertation Abstracts International, B: Sciences and Engineering
- Drugs and Society
- East European Politics and Societies
- East European Quarterly
- Economic Development and Cultural Change
- Economic History Review
- Economic Inquiry
- Economic Journal
- Economic Outlook USA
- Economica
- Economist
- Economy and Society
- Education
- Education and Urban Society
- Educational and Psychological Measurement
- Educational Gerontology
- Educational Horizons
- Educational Psychology Review
- Educational Review
- Educational Studies
- Educational Theory
- Electoral Studies
- Environment and Behavior
- Environmental Ethics
- Environmental Policy and Law
- Environmental Politics
- Ethics
- Ethnic and Racial Studies
- Ethnic Groups
- Ethnohistory
- Ethnology
- Ethnology and Sociobiology
- European Economic Review
- European Journal of Political Research
- European Journal of Political Science
- European Studies Review
- Experimental Study of Politics
- Families in Society

- Family and Community Health
- Family Economics Review
- Family Planning Perspectives
- Family Process
- Family Relations
- FBI Law Enforcement Bulletin
- Federal Probation
- Feminist Issues
- Feminist Studies
- Foreign Affairs
- Foreign Policy
- Forum of Applied Research and Public Policy
- Free Inquiry in Creative Sociology
- Futurist
- Gender and Society
- General Systems
- Generations
- Geographical Journal
- Geographical Review
- George Washington Law Review
- Georgia Review
- German Life and Letters
- German Political Studies
- German Quarterly
- Gerontologist
- Global Political Assessment
- Global Risk Assessment: Issues, Concepts and Applications
- Governance: An International Journal of Policy and Administration
- Government and Opposition
- Government Finance
- Growth and Change
- Harvard Educational Review
- Harvard Journal on Legislation
- Health and Social Work
- Health Values
- Higher Education Quarterly
- Hispania
- Hispanic Journal of Behavioral Sciences
- History and Political Economy

- History and Theory
- History of Political Thought
- History of the Human Sciences
- Hudson Review
- Human Biology
- Human Communication Research
- Human Ecology
- Human Ecology Forum
- Human Organization
- Human Relations
- Human Rights
- Human Rights Quarterly
- Human Rights Review
- Humanist
- Identities
- Impact of Science in Society
- In the Public Interest
- Indian Journal of Political Science
- Indian Journal of Public Administration
- Indian Political Science Review
- Individual Psychology
- Industrial and Labor Relations Review
- Industrial Relations
- Information Sciences
- Innovation Higher Education
- Inter-American Economic Affairs
- Interchange
- Interfaces
- International Affairs
- International Criminal Justice Review
- International Development Review
- International Economic Review
- International Interactions
- International Journal of Aging and Human Development
- International Journal of Comparative Sociology
- International Journal of Eating Disorders
- International Journal of Group Psychotherapy
- International Journal of Health Services
- International Journal of Middle East Studies

- International Journal of Offender Therapy and Comparative Criminology
- International Journal of Political Education
- International Journal of Public Administration
- International Journal of Social Psychiatry
- International Journal of Sociology of Law
- International Journal of Sociology of the Family
- International Journal of Urban and Regional Research
- International Labour Review
- International Migration Review
- International Organization
- International Political Science Review
- International Relations
- International Review of Education
- International Review of Social History
- International Security
- International Social Science Journal
- International Social Science Review
- International Social Work
- International Studies
- International Studies Quarterly
- Interpretation: Journal of Political Philosophy
- Japan Quarterly
- Jerusalem Journal of International Relations
- Journal for the Scientific Study of Religion
- Journal of Abnormal Child Psychology
- Journal of Abnormal Psychology
- Journal of Addictive Diseases
- Journal of Adolescence
- Journal of Adolescent Chemical Dependency
- Journal of Adolescent Health
- Journal of Adolescent Research
- Journal of Advertising
- Journal of African Studies
- Journal of Aging and Social Policy

- Journal of Aging Studies
- Journal of American History
- Journal of American Indian Education
- Journal of Anthropological Research
- Journal of Applied Behavior Analysis
- Journal of Applied Behavioral Science
- Journal of Applied Communication Research
- Journal of Applied Gerontology
- Journal of Applied Psychology
- Journal of Applied Social Psychology
- Journal of Asian and African Studies
- Journal of Asian Studies
- Journal of Behavior Therapy and Experimental Psychiatry
- Journal of Black Psychology
- Journal of Black Studies
- Journal of Business Communication
- Journal of Child and Family Studies
- Journal of Child Psychology and Psychiatry and Allied Disciplines
- Journal of Clinical Child Psychology
- Journal of Clinical Psychology
- Journal of Common Market Studies
- Journal of Commonwealth and Comparative Politics
- Journal of Communication
- Journal of Community Health
- Journal of Comparative and Physiological Psychology
- Journal of Comparative Economics
- Journal of Comparative Family Studies
- Journal of Comparative Psychology
- Journal of Conflict Resolution
- Journal of Constitutional and Parliamentary Studies
- Journal of Consumer Research
- Journal of Contemporary Ethnography
- Journal of Contemporary History
- Journal of Counseling Psychology
- Journal of Creative Behavior
- Journal of Criminal Justice
- Journal of Criminal Law and Criminology

- Journal of Cross-Cultural Psychology
- Journal of Democracy
- Journal of Developing Areas
- Journal of Development Economics
- Journal of Development Studies
- Journal of Divorce and Remarriage
- Journal of Drug Education
- Journal of Drug Issues
- Journal of Econometrics
- Journal of Economic History
- Journal of Economic Issues
- Journal of Economic Literature
- Journal of Economic Perspectives
- Journal of Economic Theory
- Journal of Education
- Journal of Educational Measurement
- Journal of Educational Research
- Journal of Elder Abuse and Neglect
- Journal of Environmental Economics and Management
- Journal of Environmental Management
- Journal of Ethnic Studies
- Journal of European Integration
- Journal of Experimental Child Psychology
- Journal of Experimental Education
- Journal of Experimental Social Psychology
- Journal of Extension
- Journal of Family History
- Journal of Family Issues
- Journal of Family Law
- Journal of Family Psychology
- Journal of Family Violence
- Journal of Fluency Disorders
- Journal of Gambling Studies
- Journal of General Education
- Journal of General Psychology
- Journal of Genetic Psychology
- Journal of Gerontological Social Work
- Journal of Gerontology
- Journal of Group Psychotherapy, Psychodrama and Sociometry

- Journal of Health and Social Behavior
- Journal of Health Politics, Policy and Law
- Journal of Homosexuality
- Journal of Housing
- Journal of Housing and Community Development
- Journal of Human Resources
- Journal of Humanistic Psychology
- Journal of InterAmerican Studies and World Affairs
- Journal of Interdisciplinary History
- Journal of Interdisciplinary Studies
- Journal of International Affairs
- Journal of Interpersonal Violence
- Journal of Japanese Studies
- Journal of Labor Research
- Journal of Latin American Studies
- Journal of Law and Economics
- Journal of Law and Politics
- Journal of Learning Disabilities
- Journal of Legal Studies
- Journal of Leisure Research
- Journal of Libertarian Studies
- Journal of Management
- Journal of Management Studies
- Journal of Marital and Family Therapy
- Journal of Marriage and the Family
- Journal of Medical Ethics
- Journal of Memory and Language
- Journal of Modern African Studies
- Journal of Modern History
- Journal of Near Eastern Studies
- Journal of Negro Education
- Journal of Nonverbal Behavior
- Journal of Offender Rehabilitation
- Journal of Parapsychology
- Journal of Peace Research
- Journal of Peace Science
- Journal of Peasant Studies
- Journal of Pediatric Psychology
- Journal of Personal Assessment

- Journal of Personality
- Journal of Personality and Social Psychology
- Journal of Police Science and Administration
- Journal of Policy Analysis and Management
- Journal of Policy Modeling
- Journal of Political and Military Sociology
- Journal of Political Economy
- Journal of Political Science
- Journal of Politics
- Journal of Popular Culture
- Journal of Primary Prevention
- Journal of Psychiatric Research
- Journal of Psychohistory
- Journal of Psychology
- Journal of Psychosomatic Research
- Journal of Public Administration Research and Theory
- Journal of Public Policy
- Journal of Reading Behavior
- Journal of Rehabilitation
- Journal of Research and Development in Education
- Journal of Research in Crime and Delinquency
- Journal of School Psychology
- Journal of Sex Research
- Journal of Social History
- Journal of Social Issues
- Journal of Social Policy
- Journal of Social, Political and Economic Studies
- Journal of Social Psychology
- Journal of Social Work Education
- Journal of Special Education
- Journal of Specialists in Group Work
- Journal of Sport and Social Issues
- Journal of State Government
- Journal of Strategic Studies
- Journal of Studies on Alcohol
- Journal of Substance Abuse Treatment

- Journal of the American Academy of Child and Adolescent Psychiatry
- Journal of the American Geriatrics Society
- Journal of the American Oriental Society
- Journal of the American Planning Association
- Journal of the American Society for Information Science
- Journal of the Experimental Analysis of Behavior
- Journal of the History of Ideas
- Journal of the History of the Behavioral Sciences
- Journal of the Philosophy of Sport
- Journal of the Royal Anthropological Institute
- Journal of the Royal Society of Health
- Journal of Theoretical Politics
- Journal of Third World Studies
- Journal of Traumatic Stress
- Journal of Urban Affairs
- Journal of Urban Analysis
- Journal of Urban History
- Journal of Verbal Learning and Verbal Behavior
- Journal of Youth and Adolescence
- Journalism Quarterly
- Journals of Gerontology
- Journals of Gerontology (series B: psychological and social sciences)
- Landscape
- Language
- Language Learning
- Latin American Perspectives
- Latin American Research Review
- Law and Contemporary Problems
- Law and Philosophy
- Law and Policy Quarterly
- Law and Society Review
- Learning and Motivation
- Legislative Studies Quarterly
- Linguistic Inquiry
- Linguistics and Education

- Literature and Psychology
- Magazine of History
- Man
- Man-Environment Systems
- Management Communication Quarterly
- Management Science
- Mankind
- Marriage and Family Review
- Massachusetts Review
- Mathematical Social Sciences
- Meaning
- Media, Culture and Society
- Memory and Cognition
- Merill-Palmer Quarterly
- Micropolitics
- Mid-American Review of Sociology
- Middle East Journal
- Middle East Report
- Middle Eastern Studies
- Midwest Quarterly
- Millennium
- Mind
- Mississippi Quarterly
- Modern Asian Studies
- Modern China
- Modern Language Journal
- Modern Language Notes
- Modern Philology
- Monographs for the Society for Research in Child Development
- Monthly Labor Review
- Monthly Review
- Multivariate Behavioral Research
- National Interests
- New England Journal of Medicine
- New Literacy History
- New Perspectives
- New Political Science
- New Politics
- New Statesmen
- New Statesmen and Society
- Omega

- Orbis: A Journal of World Affairs
- Oxford Economic Papers
- Pacific Affairs
- Pacific Philosophical Quarterly
- Papers on Language and Literature
- Parliamentarian
- Parliamentary Affairs
- Parliaments, Estates and Representation
- Partisan Review
- Past and Present
- Peace and Change
- Peace Research
- Perception and Psychophysics
- Personality and Social Psychology Bulletin
- Perspectives
- Perspectives on Political Science
- Philological Quarterly
- Philosophical Quarterly
- Philosophical Review
- Philosophy and Phenomenological Research
- Philosophy and Public Affairs
- Philosophy and Rhetoric
- Philosophy and Science
- Philosophy of the Social Sciences
- Phylon
- Planning and Administration
- Police Chief
- Policy Analysis
- Policy and Politics
- Policy Review
- Policy Sciences
- Policy Studies
- Policy Studies Journal
- Policy Studies Review
- Political Anthropology
- Political Behavior
- Political Communication
- Political Communication and Persuasion
- Political Geography Quarterly
- Political Psychology

- Political Quarterly
- Political Research Quarterly
- Political Science
- Political Science Quarterly
- Political Science Review
- Political Science Reviewer
- Political Studies
- Political Theory
- Politics
- Politics and Society
- Politics and the Life Sciences
- Polity
- Population and Development Review
- Population Bulletin
- Presidential Studies Quarterly
- Proceedings of the Academy of Political Science
- Professional Psychology, Research and Practice
- Psychiatric Quarterly
- Psychiatry
- Psychoanalytic Review
- Psychobiology
- Psychological Assessment
- Psychological Bulletin
- Psychological Record
- Psychological Reports
- Psychological Science
- Psychology and Aging
- Psychology in the Schools
- Psychology of Women Quarterly
- Psychology Today
- Psychophysiology
- Psychosomatic Medicine
- Public Administration
- Public Administration (Australia)
- Public Administration Review
- Public Choice
- Public Finance
- Public Finance Quarterly
- Public Health Reports
- Public Interest

- Public Law
- Public Management
- Public Opinion
- Public Opinion Quarterly
- Public Policy
- Public Relations Quarterly
- Public Relations Review
- Public Welfare
- Publius: The Journal of Federalism
- Quarterly Journal of Administration
- Quarterly Journal of Economics
- Quarterly Journal of Speech
- Quarterly Review of Doublespeak
- Race and Class
- Radical America
- Radical History Review
- Ratio
- Reading Research Quarterly
- Regional Studies
- Research in Education
- Research in Higher Education
- Research in Nursing and Health
- Research on Aging
- Review of Black Political Economy
- Review of Economic Studies
- Review of Economics and Statistics
- Review of Educational Research
- Review of International Studies
- Review of Law and Social Change
- Review of Metaphysics
- Review of Politics
- Revolutionary World
- Romance Philology
- Romance Quarterly
- Round Table
- Rural Sociology
- Russian Review
- Sage
- Sais Review
- Scandinavian Political Studies
- Science

- Science and Public Affairs
- Science and Public Policy
- Science and Society
- Sciences, The
- Sex Roles
- Signs
- Simulation
- Simulation and Games
- Simulation and Gaming
- Skeptical Inquirer
- Slavic Review
- Slavonic and East European Review
- Small Group Research
- Social Action
- Social and Economic Studies
- Social Behavior and Personality
- Social Biology
- Social Casework
- Social Forces
- Social History
- Social Indicators Research
- Social Justice
- Social Philosophy and Policy
- Social Policy
- Social Praxis
- Social Problems
- Social Psychology Quarterly
- Social Research
- Social Science and Medicine
- Social Science Information
- Social Science Journal
- Social Science Quarterly
- Social Science Research
- Social Science Review
- Social Theory and Practice
- Social Work
- Social Work Education
- Social Work with Groups
- Socialism and Democracy
- Socialists Review
- Society

- Sociological Analysis and Theory
- Sociological Inquiry
- Sociological Methods and Research
- Sociological Quarterly
- Sociological Perspectives
- Sociological Review
- Sociology
- Sociology and Social Research
- Sociology of Education
- Sociology of Religion
- Sociology of Sport Journal
- Soundings
- Southern Economic Journal
- Southern Exposure
- Southern Quarterly
- Soviet Review
- Soviet Studies
- Soviet Union
- Spectrum
- State Government
- Strategic Review
- Studies in Comparative Communism
- Studies in Comparative International Development
- Studies in Conflict and Terrorism
- Studies in Family Planning
- Studies in Philosophy and Education
- Suicide and Life-Threatening Behavior
- Survey
- Survival
- Symposium
- Talking Politics
- Technological Forecasting and Social Change
- Technology and Culture
- Terrorism
- Theory and Decision
- Theory and Society
- Third World

- Trial
- UN Chronicle
- Urban Affairs Quarterly
- Urban Affairs Review
- Urban and Social Change Review
- Urban Anthropologist
- Urban Anthropology and Studies of Cultural Systems and World Economic Development
- Urban Education
- Urban Life
- Urban Review
- Urban Studies
- Victimology
- Violence and Victims
- Volta Review
- War and Society
- Washington Quarterly: A Review of Strategic and International Studies
- West European Politics
- Western Journal of Communications
- Western Political Quarterly
- Wilson Quarterly
- Women and Environments
- Women and Health
- Women and Politics: A Quarterly Journal of Research and Policy Studies
- Women and Work
- Women's Studies International Forum
- Women's Studies Quarterly
- World Affairs
- World Development
- World Marxist Review
- World Policy Journal
- World Politics
- World Today
- World Watch
- Young Children
- Youth and Society

6.3   RESEARCHING BOOKS

Academic books, along with articles from professional journals, will usually form the greater part of the sociology student's reading list on an individual research topic. If the sources of information used in book research are unreliable, the results will be unsatisfactory. There are two principal paths for a student to take in evaluating a book-length study: Rely on book reviews, or examine the bibliographic character of the book itself.

6.3.1   BOOK REVIEW SOURCES

Since 1975, reviews appearing in most of the major sociology journals have been indexed in the book review section of the *Social Sciences Index* (see previous section on indexes). The reviews are indexed by the name of the author of the book; the journal, volume, and date; and the page of the review. There is a time lag, however—sometimes more than a year—between a book's publication and the appearance of a review in a scholarly journal. The need for more current reviews led to a new type of journal, consisting entirely of scholarly book reviews. The journal for sociologists is the following:

CONTEMPORARY SOCIOLOGY: A JOURNAL OF REVIEWS. 1971. WASHINGTON, DC: AMERICAN SOCIOLOGICAL ASSOCIATION. This journal reviews books published in every area of sociology, plus many in related fields, such as education. Each issue also contains feature essays that review several books on related topics or the works of one major author. The reviews are arranged by broad subject areas, and each issue also contains a list of new publications.

For reviews of books on the popular market, along with many very academic selections, the *New York Review of Books* (1976–present) and the *New York Times Book Review* (1923–present) are two reliable sources.

6.3.2   BIBLIOGRAPHIC CHARACTER OF THE WORK

By examining a book closely, you can usually assess the quality of information presented. The preface and introduction give clues to who the author is, why the work was written, and what methodology and research tools were used in the book's preparation. If the author is an acknowledged authority in the field, this fact will often be mentioned in the preface or the foreword.

The footnotes, in-text references, and the extent and quality of the bibliography—or in some cases, the lack of one—can also serve as clues about the reliability of the work. If few or no original documents have been used, or if major works in the field have not been cited and evaluated, you have reason to question the quality of the book.

Finally, the reputation of the publisher or organization that sponsors a particular book says something about its value. Some publishers have rigid standards of scholarship and others do not. For example, the requirements of university presses are generally very high, and the major ones—such as Cambridge, Chicago, Michigan, and Harvard—are discriminating publishers of studies in sociology.

6.4   U.S. GOVERNMENT PUBLICATIONS

6.4.1   GENERAL PUBLICATIONS

U.S. government publications comprise all the printed public documents of the federal government. The materials include, for example, the official records of the meetings of Congress; the text of laws, court decisions, and public hearings and rulings of administrative and regulatory agencies; studies of economic and social issues commissioned by official agencies; and the compilation of statistics on a number of social and demographic characteristics of the U.S. population.

Federal publications provide sociologists with material for research in many subfields in sociology. You can find government publications that cover such topics as the educational attainment of minorities, sex discrimination, drug abuse, and a number of other social issues. However, the fact that a document is "official" is no automatic guarantee of the accuracy of the information or data it might contain; accuracy depends on the methods of information and data collection the agency used. Therefore, the use of these publications—like the use of any other source material—requires good judgment. You can identify relevant late nineteenth- and twentieth-century federal government publications by consulting the following:

U.S. SUPERINTENDENT OF DOCUMENTS. 1885. *MONTHLY CATALOG OF UNITED STATES GOVERNMENT PUBLICATIONS.* WASHINGTON, DC: GOVERNMENT PRINTING OFFICE. This is the most complete catalog of federal documents available. The detailed indexes—subject, author/agency, and title—identify individual items by entry number. Entries identify individual author (if any), pagination, date, illustration notes, series title, serial number, and include reference to any other publication superseded by this item, and the Superintendent of Documents number. (U.S. documents are catalogued by this number in many libraries—especially those that are depositories.)

CUMULATIVE SUBJECT INDEX TO THE MONTHLY CATALOG OF UNITED STATES GOVERNMENT PUBLICATIONS, 1900–1971. 1973. WASHINGTON, DC: CARROLLTON PRESS. This is a comprehensive subject index to more than 1 million publications listed in the Monthly Catalog from 1900 through 1971. To discover what has been published on a given subject, one first finds the topic and then goes to the appropriate subheading. This will be followed by one or more years in parentheses, each followed by one or more entry numbers, such as "(65) 14901." Then researchers must turn to the Monthly Catalog for the specified year (in this case, 1965) and locate the entry number (in this case, 14901) to find a complete citation for the publication.

The most useful list and discussion of finding aids for U.S. government publications in the social sciences is the following:

LU, J. K. *U.S. GOVERNMENT PUBLICATIONS RELATING TO THE SOCIAL SCIENCES.* BEVERLY HILLS, CA: SAGE PUBLICATIONS. An awareness of the factors that influence the U.S. government's policies toward various social issues—such as crime, welfare, minority rights—is essential to sociologists. Political policy is formulated by political officials and influenced by citizens or groups of citizens, all of whom are concerned about a specific issue. For this reason, the records of congressional hearings are valuable sources of information to the sociology student. These records provide important policy-related information: They reveal the political stands that various citizens or groups take on a specific issue, and they demonstrate the influence these people have on the formulation.

6.4.2   U.S. CENSUS PUBLICATIONS

U.S. Census Bureau publications are important resources. They allow sociology students to summarize social and demographic characteristics of various population groups in the United States by using descriptive statistics. We frequently think of the Census Bureau as a government agency that collects census data every ten years. There are actually ten categories of censuses, and data are collected and reported at different intervals. In addition to collecting data on national and state populations, the Census Bureau studies subpopulations that are of special interest. These studies are generally published in *Current Population Reports*. Recent reports, for example, have focused on the characteristics of blacks, persons of Hispanic origin, and poverty-level families.

Because the Census Bureau analyzes and publishes data, sociology students can locate relevant census materials by consulting guides and indexes to statistical reports published by the government. The following comprehensive volume indexes statistical studies by all government agencies. It can be used to locate a variety of statistics on a given topic:

AMERICAN STATISTICS INDEX. 1973. WASHINGTON, DC: CONGRESSIONAL INFORMATION SERVICE. This commercially produced abstract has become an important source for identifying statistical publications of the U.S. government. It indexes and abstracts statistics on numerous topics from the publications of many government agencies, describes these publications, and has the material available on microfiche. This source is issued monthly in two sections—indexes and abstracts—and is cumulated annually. The index volume contains four separate indexes that list the publications by subject and name; by geographic, economic, and demographic categories; by title; and by agency report numbers. The abstract volume gives brief descriptions of the publications and their content.

The Census Bureau publishes an index to its own publications. If you require information on a topic that is routinely studied by the Census Bureau, you should consult the following:

U.S. BUREAU OF THE CENSUS. 1790. *BUREAU OF THE CENSUS CATALOG.* WASHINGTON, DC: GOVERNMENT PRINTING OFFICE. An indispensable guide to materials issued by the Bureau of the Census and publications from other agencies that contain statistics, this catalog is published quarterly, updated with monthly supplements, and has annual cumulations. The basic volume is retrospective, covering the years 1790–1945 in part I, and 1946–1972 in part II. The arrangement differs in each part. The material includes annotated lists of census publications for the years covered, followed by subject and geographical indexes. The annual cumulation lists and annotates only those publications issued during that year.

A number of reports or volumes published by the Census Bureau are useful to sociology students doing research. Several of these publications— *County and City Data Book, Statistical Abstracts of the United States*, and *Historical Statistics of the United States*—have been discussed previously under other subheadings. These publications summarize many of the important findings of past censuses, as well as more recent ones.

In addition to the population census, the Bureau also conducts surveys of housing, business, and manufacturing. A student who wants information about the structural or industrial characteristics of the United States can use these decade censuses to find past and current statistics. These censuses have the advantages and disadvantages discussed earlier.

Census publications provide, at little cost to the researcher, much descriptive information on various components of the American population. However, you should be aware of some serious problems with census data. Because most data are compiled every five or ten years, often a researcher must either find more current information or use the somewhat dated statistics published by the Census Bureau. Also, the design of the census survey does not always include the type of questions or issues that are of interest to sociology students. For example, a student comparing the educational or employment status of blacks with that of persons of Hispanic origin for a period between 1970–1990 would not be able use 1970 census data because the 1970 Census of Population did not ask persons of Hispanic origin to identify their racial or ethnic background. Another disadvantage of census publications is that they use only descriptive statistics to summarize the data. Their analysis does not indicate the relevance or meaning of trends. You can determine social and demographic differences within populations, but must look elsewhere for the causes of these differences.

CHAPTER 7

SOCIOLOGY
ON THE WORLD WIDE WEB

7.1 A WHIRLWIND INTRODUCTORY TOUR OF THE INTERNET

To understand the Internet and how to use it, we need to begin with the basics. Follow along on our whirlwind tour. Let's let this symbol 🖳 represent a computer. Two or more computers linked together by a telephone line, fiber optic line, radio wave or satellite beam, compose a network:

Let's call this dot (.) a symbol for a network composed of 10,000 computers, and place a dot on a map of the world for every 10,000 computers.

The map represents, very imperfectly, the Internet. The Internet is a network of thousands of smaller computer networks linked together by communications lines that use a common computer language to communicate with one another. The Internet was conceived in the late 1960s when the Advanced Research Projects Agency of the U.S. Department of Defense began to develop a military communications systems capable of surviving a nuclear war. They produced a network of computers called the ARPANET, which at first included military research labs and universities, but which later added many more related computer systems.

Two decades later, the National Science Foundation initiated a project called NSFNET, the purpose of which was to connect American supercomputer centers so that they could communicate with each other. Throughout the world similar networks were being established, and by the late 1980s, connections among these networks came to be known as the Internet, which is now growing at a phenomenal rate. In 1991, there were only about 700,000 people using the Internet. In 1996, that number is approaching 40 million, with 160,000 new users each month.

The World Wide Web (WWW) is an organized system for accessing the information on the Internet. Tim Berners-Lee of CERN, the European Laboratory for Particle Physics in Geneva, Switzerland, launched the WWW when he created a method for using a single means of access to the networks on the Internet. The WWW is now the primary vehicle for access to information on the Internet.

7.2   HOW TO ACCESS THE INTERNET AND THE WORLD WIDE WEB

The best way to access the Internet is to obtain access to a new computer with the latest communications software and follow the directions included in the software. Before long, you will be "surfing the Net" to your heart's content. In the pages that follow, we will examine briefly each stage of the process by which you may gain access to the Internet. To access the WWW on the Internet, you need four things:

- a computer
- a modem
- a service provider
- a browser

First, you need two pieces of hardware: a computer and a modem. We will assume that you know what a computer is, but you may not be aware that your local magazine stand or bookstore carries a wide variety of periodicals that review and rate computers. When the time comes for you to purchase one, you will make a much more informed choice if you read the articles in such magazines as *Consumer Reports* and the *Computer Shopper*. It is very important to buy a computer with the largest memory and hard drive disk capacity that you can afford. The Internet is getting more sophisticated every day, and many of the materials that you will want to "download" (transmit material electronically from a computer or computer system to another computer) from the Internet to your computer will require substantial space on your computer's hard drive.

A modem is a device that connects your computer to a telephone line or other line of communication. Because it can take time to download files, and because many Internet access programs charge their customers for the time they spend hooked up to the Internet, it is important that your modem be capable of running at a fast rate of speed. Both computers and modems require software containing operating instructions.

Next, you will need an Internet service provider, a commercial business that connects you to the Internet and charges you a monthly fee that varies with the service and the amount of time you spend using it. Some of the most popular Internet service providers, with telephone numbers you can use to contact them, are:

- America Online 1-800-827-3338
- Compuserve 1-800-848-8990
- Earthlink Network 1-213-644-9500
- Global Network Navigator (GNN) 1-800-819-6112
- Microsoft Network (MSN) 1-800-386-5550
- Prodigy 1-800-776-3449

Many smaller companies also provide Internet service, and you may be able to find rates more suited to your own pattern of Internet use from them. You will find these services listed in the yellow pages of your phone book. If you buy a new computer from a major manufacturer, you may find Internet service product brochures and software included with your computer. In addition to connecting you to the World Wide Web, some services also provide you with news, communications, and other services.

Finally, you need a browser, a software program that allows you to search for information on the Internet. In 1993, the National Center for Supercomputing Applications (NCSA) introduced Mosaic, a browser that greatly facilitated searching for information on the WWW and encouraged many people to gain access to the Internet, but since that time other commercial browsers have become more popular. At the time this book is being written, Netscape Navigator is the most popular browser, but Microsoft's Internet Explorer is challenging Navigator's dominance with some success. If you contract with MSN for Internet service, you will be able to download Internet Explorer for free, and from time to time Netscape makes a special offer of its Navigator for free.

You will experience a browser as a window, or dialog box, on your computer screen that assists you in finding information on the Internet. Once you have opened the home page (the starting page for a web site) of your browser, you will notice that it offers you a number of search engines, which are programs that allow you to search the Internet using key words or phrases. Your browser will also provide a space in which you can type Internet addresses to access search engines and other Internet sites. Some of the most commonly used search engines, and their Internet addresses, are the following:

- AltaVista: http://altavista.digital.com
- EXCITE: http://www.excite.com
- LYCOS: http://www.lycos.com
- Webcrawler: http://webcrawler.com
- YAHOO: http://www.yahoo.com

Let's suppose you use the Yahoo search engine. In the search engine's dialog box you type in the word *sociology*. The search engine will then make several clickable links appear on the screen. A clickable link is an icon or line of text that is highlighted and programmed so that when you use your mouse button to click on it you immediately go to a new Internet address. One of the clickable links that your Yahoo search engine will provide for you when you search under the topic of sociology is *organizations*. Here you will find more clickable links, one of which will be entitled *ASA*, for American Sociological Association. This is a good place to begin your search for information in sociology.

7.3 SOCIOLOGY RESOURCES ON THE INTERNET

The ASA's link entitled *Departments* provides links to home pages of sociology departments at universities around the country and the world. But this is only the beginning. If you click on the browser's "back" key, you can return to the Yahoo menu that lists sources of sociology information. There you will encounter a wide variety of other resources, including many sociology home pages that are wonderful resources for finding further information. The Yahoo sociology link page includes a sociology search engine, appearing as a box in which you can type a key word, such as *welfare*. The search engine will then present a list of Internet sites that are connected in some way with the word *welfare*. The Yahoo sociology link page also includes the following links (the number of sites for each link is included in parentheses):

- Courses (5)
- Criminal Justice (71)
- Institutes (102)
- Journals (13)

■   Organizations (13)

■   Papers (12)

■   Social Psychology@ (The sites with an *at* [@] symbol are gopher sites, which have their own specialized search engines for getting information on certain topics.)

■   Urban Studies@

The Yahoo sociology search page then provides a list of specialized Internet sites, with a brief description of each site:

■   Bibliography on Organizational Computer-Mediated Communication: a dynamic (in other words, growing, audience-participation-based) bibliography of scholarly work on the organizational roles and impacts of computer-mediated communication. It is part of the *Journal of Computer-Mediated Communication*.

■   Consumer Culture: a collection of resources, bibliographies, contacts, and links for scholars in the fields of consumer culture, leisure, and critical social theories.

■   Cultural Studies Central: information, interactive commentary, and analysis focusing on popular culture.

■   From Whence These Rumblings?: Toward an Understanding of the Structural Pre-Conditions of Anti-Systemic Mobilization.

■   Lessico Multimediale di Sociologia: an Italian sociology multimedia index.

■   Norwegian Social Science Data Services (NSD): a service that develops data bases and relevant software to secure easy access to empirical data. NSD was formally established in 1971 by the Norwegian Research Council for Science and the Humanities (NAVF), and is today part of The Research Council of Norway.

■   Paths: a site focusing on issues relating to sociology and cyberspace.

■   Pleasure Watch: gambling research provided by Sytze Kingma (in Dutch).

■   Progressive Sociology Network: a mailing list of sociologists from all over the world.

■   Psychological and Sociological Technologies: a forum for researchers and other interested parties in the "Sociology of High Technology."

■   Race, Sex, and Religion: A Discussion of Humanity: a site dedicated to creating an open and honest discussion of issues that face humanity, specifically, issues of race, sex, and religion.

■   Research Engines for the Social Sciences: a central jumping off point for literature and data searching for sociologists and serious students in related disciplines. This site was developed in a graduate research design seminar at Carleton University in Ottawa.

■   Resources for Social Researchers: links for publications, data information, research organizations, graduate student information, and graduate institutions.

■   Sharing Understandings of the HIV Experience: a participatory action research project involving HIV-positive gay men.

- Sociology Corner, The: sources for sociology, post-modernism, and the Internet.
- Sociology of Knowledge: abstracts, course information, and book reviews.
- SocioWeb
- Soziologie im Internet/Sociology on the Internet: Verzeichnis soziologischer Quellen im Internet.

Each page on the Internet has an address known as a URL (Universal Resource Locator), which will appear in a form something like this: http://www.yahoo.com. When you find a page on the Internet that provides information you would like to return to, you can enter a bookmark on your browser. A bookmark is an URL that has been entered into a special location on your browser so that you can find the URL and access its content quickly and easily. Your browser will provide directions for entering bookmarks.

The number of sociology sources on the Internet is bewildering. One good place to start looking is SocioWeb (http://www.socioweb.com/~markbl/socioweb/.). SocioWeb is one of several sites that gather and present lists of sociology resources. The SocioWeb Home page features several clickable links that lead to the following general categories of resources:

- What's New
- Hot Resources
- University Departments
- Sociological Associations
- Calendar of Events
- Calls for Papers
- General Research
- Social Discourse
- Topical Research
- SocioWeb 101

If you click on the Hot Resources button, you will find the following list of sites with a short description for each:

- *Sociological Cases Database*. The goal of the Sociology Cases Database project is to create a database of sociological case studies available for all. This project could be the beginning of a very useful resource. Try to visit them and see if there are any "cases" you can contribute.
- *Corporate Governance*. The Corporate Governance site is designed to provide a springboard for explorations and discussions concerning the movement to enhance wealth by creating more democratic forms of corporate governance.
- *The Durkheim Pages*. This Web site packs the core essentials for an introduction to Emile Durkheim, who established the site (and is therefore called the site's *master*).

■ *Consumer Culture Home Page.* A new collection of resources and links for scholars in the fields of consumer culture, leisure, and related topics, this site provides bibliographies and names of researchers and other potential contacts.

■ *Sociology for Very Short Attention Spans.* This humorous guide explores the core essentials in sociology.

■ *The International Studies Association.* This association of scholars from a variety of fields focuses on international issues.

Another good Internet site to explore when looking for sociological information is Research Engines for Social Scientists (http://www.carleton.ca/~cmckie/research.html), which lists the following types of tools and resources:

■ General Resource Searchers
■ Reference Materials
■ The WWW Social Sciences Virtual Library at Coombs
■ Aggressive Pattern Searchers
■ Content to Browse
■ Social Science Data Archives
■ Sociology and Anthropology Sources
■ News and Journalism Sources
■ Psychology and Psychopathology Sources
■ Law, Law Enforcement, and Policing Sources
■ Demographic Sources
■ Political Science Sources
■ Economics Sources
■ Miscellaneous Information Sources
■ Site Information and Comments

We shall briefly describe the contents of the first three entries of the preceding list. If we click on the first item on the list, "General Resource Searchers," we find the following list:

■ Social Science Information Gateway (SOSIG) at the University of Bristol in the UK
■ NTU Electronic Library Resources for the Social Sciences
■ PRAXIS: Resources for Social and Economic Development
■ Socionet: the web site of the Sociometrics Corporation, including Social Science Links, arranged by discipline
■ Central Reference and Referral Point at the University of Michigan Library
■ Online Computer Library Center—InterCAT: an accumulating catalog of Web materials using the MARC cataloging system (Note: for the time being, this is an onward link from the Internic.)

- BUBL Composite Gopher and WWW Subject Tree arranged by discipline
- SOSIG Resources Search Engine and NUKOP Online: a web database of new official UK publications online for government and policy researchers
- Public Policy Research Links
- SOSIG subject guides to networked resources in education, law, politics, and governments, social welfare, sociology, accounting, and economics, in .doc and .rtf formats
- Social Science Data Collection at the University of California San Diego
- Atlas for the World Wide Web, a Classified Content Index on the Web
- Social Science Web Sites at the University of Washington

The second section, "Reference Materials" features dozens of entries, including The Internet for Social Scientists. The third section contains Social Sciences WWW Virtual Library at Coombs in Australia. Here you will find the following:

- What's New in WWW Social Sciences
- Archives of What's New—Social Sciences
- ANU-SocSci-WWW-Gopher-News-L dbase
- Social Sciences WWW Virtual Library
- Coombs Demography Web Page, including a worldwide list of resources
- Clearinghouse for Social Sciences Subject-Oriented Bibliographies
- Register of Social Sciences Electronic Journals
- Migration and Ethnic Relations Component in the Netherlands
- WWW Virtual Library: Sociology Section at Seton Hall
- Indigenous Studies Component of the WWW Virtual Library

It is impossible to explain the Internet or to give an adequate description of it in words. To understand it, you have to use it. The preceding lists are only the tip of the Internet sociology resources iceberg. The purpose of this chapter is to pique your curiosity and help you get started on your exploration of the Internet. Once you have begun, you will discover thousands of cites and dozens of types of information that were not mentioned in this chapter. Some of the things you will find will include:

- Mailing Lists. You can join a mailing list and receive by E-mail or in printed form publications from a wide variety of organizations.
- Bibliographies. Numerous extensive bibliographies of sociological information already appear on the Net.
- Publishers and Bookstores. You will find publishers offering to sell you virtually any title in sociology, and you will find bookstores that offer not only new books, but old, out-of-print, and rare editions of many texts.

- Sociology Projects. Many sociology research and discussion projects have home pages on the Net, and sometimes you can join in the research and discussions.
- Sociology Resource Guides. Guides to all these resources and more are on the Net, with clickable links that take you directly to the sources they cite.
- News Groups. News groups are Internet pages in which people exchange information on current events.

CHAPTER 8

CONDUCTING QUANTITATIVE RESEARCH

Social analysis is the systematic attempt to explain social events by placing them within a series of meaningful contexts. We call this activity *social science*, and we conduct it using methods that are often quantitative in nature. These quantitative methods of research are much the same in social science as they are in any other scientific field. To understand them, we should begin with a brief look at what we mean by the terms *science* and *scientific method*.

8.1 THINKING SCIENTIFICALLY

We tend to use the word science too loosely, referring to things that are not strictly science. Hoover and Donovan (1995: 4–5) describe three common uses of the term science that divert our understanding from what science really is. First, people often—and wrongly—think of science as technology. In fact, technology is a product of science. Technology results from the application of science to different tasks. For instance, the technology involved in sending people to the moon came into existence, over time, as people decided how to use discoveries they made through the application of scientific principles. While the lunar module that landed in the Sea of Tranquillity is definitely a "piece of technology," it is not "science."

A second misconception is that science is a specific body of knowledge that discloses to us the rules by which the natural world works. To say that "science tells us" something is misleading. For example, it is not science that "tells" us smoking is dangerous to our health. It is people, who, investigating the effects of smoking tobacco on a variety of human pathologies, conclude that smoking is a very harmful practice. The body of knowledge these people produce is evidence, accumulated through scientific inquiry, of the effects of smoking. It is important not to mistake the body of knowledge for the mode of inquiry that helps researchers to produce it.

Finally, Hoover and Donovan point out that it is also misleading to think of science as an activity conducted only by a specialized group of researchers called "scientists." This notion implies that some people use the scientific approach to understanding reality while others do not. In fact, all people use some form of scientific thinking to aid them in their struggle to deal with the uncertainties of life. Sometimes the thinking process is a bit crude, as when we decide what to eat by determining through trial and error what tastes good. But it is scientific thinking nonetheless.

So if science is not simply technology or a body of knowledge available only to people we call scientists, then what is it? Let us define science as a method of inquiry, a process of thinking and asking questions by which we arrive at an understanding of the world around us. Conceived of in this way, science does not exist in machines or in books or even in the natural phenomena around us, but in the mind. More specifically, science is a way of formulating questions and investigating answers—a set of rules for inquiry created to help achieve valid and reliable answers.

Historically, the scientific approach to knowledge has not done well when competing with other approaches. This is largely because, throughout the centuries, knowledge acquired through scientific investigation often threatened established values, norms, and institutions by which those in power maintained control of their world—values and institutions founded on such approaches to knowledge as myth, dogma, and superstition. Those who used science to understand and predict events were often viewed negatively by the powerful. Galileo was censured by both church and state when he used the scientific method to arrive at conclusions that challenged existing beliefs about the center of the universe. Using science to support the conclusion that the sun was in fact the center around which all things revolved, his outcome flew in the face of the Roman Catholic dogma that held the earth to be the center.

So it is safe to say that science is never practiced in a social vacuum. Today, leaders in western countries tend to rely on science, rather than superstition or dogma, to establish credibility for what they say and do. But the scientific approach to seizing and maintaining power is very new in the history of the world.

8.2   THE SCIENTIFIC METHOD

The goal of science is to explain reality. The scientific method attempts to explain reality through the development and testing of theories, which are general explanations for the existence or cause of certain classes of phenomena. For example, two centuries before Christ, Ptolemy constructed a theory to explain the movement of the stars in the sky. His theory suggested that the sun and planets all revolve around Earth. Ptolemy's theory, which described the general relationship of the planets and stars to Earth, explained much of what could be observed in the sky at night. More precise observations, however, later began to cast doubt on Ptolemy's theory.

Once they are constructed, theories must be tested to see if they actually explain the phenomena that they are intended to explain. We test theories in a two-step process:

1. We create specific statements that should be true if the theory is correct.

2. We then devise tests of these statements. A statement devised to test a theory is known as a hypothesis. A substantial part of what social science does is to test research hypotheses.

The development of this two-step scientific method was a historical and cultural breakthrough. Accomplished slowly at the end of the Middle Ages by brilliant thinkers in different European countries, it stands as one of the watershed events that differentiate the ancient world from the modern. We will now briefly examine the elements of the scientific method.

8.2.1   FORMULATING AND TESTING RESEARCH HYPOTHESES

A research hypothesis is an educated guess. It is a declarative sentence stating that a specific relationship exists between two or more phenomena. Consider the following example of a research hypothesis: "When a person's anxiety rises, his or her intolerance of others increases." This hypothesis states that there is a specific relationship between two variables: (1) a person's anxiety, and (2) the person's tolerance of other people. In addition, the hypothesis states the nature of the relationship between the two variables: an increase in the first is associated with an increase in the second.

A researcher constructs a hypothesis for the sole purpose of testing whether it is "true"—that is, whether a certain relationship exists between two phenomena that the formulator of the hypothesis is investigating. Hypotheses help define the question that our research is trying to answer. Suppose that we want to know if family relationships are affected by economic conditions. Eventually, we would like to develop a theory that will help explain how different economic conditions lead to different ways in which family members relate to one another. But before we can understand general patterns of relationships and create a theory to explain these patterns, we must become much more specific in our inquiry. Hypotheses help us to select specific aspects of a problem or question and explore them one at a time.

For instance, in our example of the economy and family relationships, we might propose the following hypothesis: "When the economy is strong, the divorce rate decreases, and when the economy is weak, the divorce rate increases." We notice, however, that there will be difficulties in testing this hypothesis. For example, what are "strong" and "weak" economies? Our hypothesis will need to be more specific. We will perhaps find that a combination of selected economic indicators, such as the rate of unemployment or the amount of manufacturing production, will help us to define strong and weak in economic terms. The problem has now become more, rather than less complicated. How will we know if family relationships are influenced by only one of these factors and not others? What if only certain combinations of these factors, and not other combinations, might have an effect upon relationships? To answer these questions, we need to start with one simple hypothesis, then test others in a careful, systematic way. Our first hypothesis might be: "When the national unemployment rate is greater than 7 percent, the divorce rate will remain above 50 percent."

Two types of hypotheses are commonly used in social science. The first may be called causal, the second relational. *Causal hypotheses* attempt to show that one phenomenon causes another. *Relational hypotheses*, on the other hand, attempt to indicate whether two phenomena are related to each other in a specific way, without demonstrating that one causes the other. Testing our hypothesis ("When the national unemployment rate is greater than 7 percent, the divorce rate will remain above 50 percent") will indicate only whether a relationship exists between unemployment and divorce, not whether unemployment causes divorce. Relations between hypotheses may be either positive or negative. A positive relation exists when an increase in one variable is associated with an increase in another. A negative relation exists when the presence of one variable coincides with the lack of another variable.

After hypotheses are constructed, we test them by observing the behavior of the variables that they contain. For example, let us phrase our hypothesis like this: "Extended periods of unemployment increase the likelihood of divorce."

8.2.2   VARIABLES

The phenomena being observed are designated as different types of variables. The *dependent variable* is the phenomenon that is in some way affected by other variables. In our example, divorce is the dependent variable.

The *independent variable* is the phenomenon that may have some effect on the dependent variable. In our example, the time period in which a person is unemployed is the independent variable and divorce is the dependent variable.

Antecedent variables are phenomena that act on or relate to independent variables. In our example, if we hypothesized that "extended periods of unemployment occur in states with fewer high-tech industries," then the number of high-tech industries in a state would be an antecedent variable.

Intervening variables are variables other than the independent variable that affect the dependent variable directly. In our example, if we said that "divorce rates decrease when it rains," then rain would be an intervening variable.

Identifying the dependent, independent, antecedent, and intervening variables is very important in conducting research because it helps you to carefully define the relationships that you are examining.

Hypotheses are constructed to find out what relationship, if any, exists between the independent and dependent variables. To test a hypothesis, therefore, you need to measure the amount of change in the dependent variable as you observe change in the independent variable. To do this, you must complete two tasks.

The first task is to find accurate measurements of the dependent and independent variables as they vary over time or in different circumstances. For measurements to be accurate, they must be both valid and reliable. *Valid measurements* measure the effects they are supposed to measure instead of measuring something else. *Reliable measurements* are those that can be made under different conditions and still yield the same result.

The second task is to determine the effects of antecedent and intervening variables on the dependent variable so that you will know how much effect the independent variable has had. For example, if the voter turnout is greater in one community than another, and the communities have different registration time periods, you must determine how much of the difference in turnout was due to the registration periods as opposed to other factors, such as the percentage of independent voters or the occurrence of rain.

Conducting a study that is reliable and valid requires an analysis that utilizes accepted statistical methods. The instructor for your course in social science research methods will help you determine the correct methods for your analysis.

8.2.3   PROBLEMS FOR THE SCIENTIFIC STUDY OF SOCIETY

A hypothesis can often be difficult to test. When attempting to test hypotheses in social science, we often encounter three general problems:

Data Insufficiency or Incongruity   After we have stated our hypothesis, we may discover through investigation that sufficient data are not available. Sometimes the records that we need have not been kept consistently or accurately, or have been compiled according to different systems or categories. If we want to compare divorce rates in the United States and Italy, for example, we may find that the American and Italian governments have different reporting requirements and that the procedures used to validate data may be much more reliable in one country than in another.

Multiplicity and Ambiguity of Variables   It is often difficult to cope with the sheer number of variables that may affect the result of our study; likewise it can be difficult to isolate the effects of one variable from those of others. If we want to find out what decreases the divorce rate, for example, we may need to try to sort out the competing effects of family histories, customs, religious beliefs, and economic factors.

Methodological Uncertainty   The third problem with the scientific study of society originates in epistemology—that is, the study of the nature of knowledge itself. Testing hypotheses, an approach fundamental to the scientific method, is an inductive process. One requirement of induction is the examination of numerous specific cases in hopes of finding general principles that help explain or predict behavior. For example, if all known cases of oak trees have acorns, one may conclude that all oak trees have acorns. But there may be a flaw in this sort of reasoning. In his book *The Logic of Scientific Discovery* (1959), Karl Popper pointed out that to show that some examples of a certain phenomenon behave in a certain manner is not to demonstrate that others will also. Even if all known examples of a phenomenon behave in a certain way, there may be examples in the future that will deviate from the pattern. Thus, the fact that all known oak trees have acorns does not mean that an oak tree without acorns will never be found.

Furthermore, said Popper, scientific observation is always selective. We must choose to observe before the actual observation takes place, and when we do observe, our observation will always take place within a particular context. This fact suggests that hypotheses are observations not of reality, but merely of one context, one view of reality. Hypotheses, therefore, are not genuine observations, but only bold guesses. Since we can never say with certainty that a hypothesis is true, Popper explains that the only time we *can* be sure of a hypothesis is when it is disproved. Scientific progress is thus made not by verifying hypotheses, but by refuting them. Because of Popper's works and those of others, this is indeed the way research often proceeds: by working not to prove hypotheses but to refute them.

A hypothesis established precisely for the purpose of being refuted is called a *null hypothesis*. Returning to a previous example, if we wanted to prove that extended registration periods increase voter turnout, we would begin by testing a null hypothesis: "Extended registration periods do not increase voter turnout." If we can find a case in which an extended registration period does increase voter turnout, we will have disproved the null hypothesis. We will not have proven that extended registration periods always increase voter turnout, but we will at least have taken the first step by showing that extended registration periods *can* increase voter turnout. Science thus proceeds by disproving successively specific null hypotheses.

No matter how we decide to treat hypotheses, there is still a question about how useful they are when it comes to major scientific discoveries. According to Thomas Kuhn (1970), even the refutation of null hypotheses is not a viable strategy if one wants to achieve the occasional new perspective that revolutionizes science. When Copernicus proposed his heliocentric theory of astronomy, the Ptolemaic model of the solar system was well entrenched in the scientific community. Kuhn calls established patterns of scientific inquiry *paradigms* and says that they are essential to the progress of science. A paradigm establishes the foundations of knowledge in a particular discipline until the paradigm is displaced by a new one.

Discrepancies in the Ptolemaic paradigm were met by increasingly complicated explanations devised to make observation conform to the theory. Copernicus' system was so different from Ptolemy's that it became a new scientific paradigm. At first, Copernicus' theory had little evidence from observation to support it. Kuhn argues that Copernicus did not come up with his new theory by disputing the Ptolemaic system. Instead of gradually and successively refuting hypotheses, Copernicus had a flash of intuition. A paradigm, for Kuhn, is never refuted by evidence; it can only be overturned when another one takes its place.

Social science, says Kuhn, needs a paradigm to establish its identity, its mission. Not having one, social science winds its way endlessly through a series of disagreements over methods and goals. Therefore, while the scientific method remains the normal way of adding to our common store of knowledge about society, the great breakthroughs of the future may as likely come from exceptional moments of human creativity as from the steady testing of statements within our normal range of exploration.

8.2.4   THE STAGES OF SOCIAL RESEARCH

How do those who practice scientific inquiry go about "doing" social research? What are the steps involved in approaching a research problem scientifically? Actually, as we have stated previously, thinking scientifically and using science to help us make decisions is a part of our everyday life. However, if we wish to use this approach to aid in the investigation of problems that are germane to sociology, the scientific method is more structured and stepwise. Whether researchers are pursuing a problem in sociology, political science, criminal justice, psychology, or any area that relies on the scientific method, they use the following steps:

- Define a research problem.
- Formulate a meaningful hypothesis.
- Conduct a literature review to determine what is known about the research problem.
- Identify dependent, independent, and intervening variables.
- Formulate a research design.
- Conduct the study.
- Analyze and interpret the results.

8.3   COMMON QUANTITATIVE RESEARCH DESIGNS

Because sociologists investigate a wide variety of issues and problems, their quantitative research can take many forms. Four of the most common quantitative research designs are:

- surveys
- experiments
- scientific observation
- content analysis

You will find detailed instructions for conducting a survey in Chapter 12 of this manual, and therefore, we will not discuss surveys further here. Because the processes of conducting experiments, performing scientific observation, and making content analysis studies require extensive additional knowledge and are normally undertaken by students only at the graduate level, we have not devoted individual chapters to them. However, it is important for you as a student of sociology to have some basic knowledge about these processes, and we therefore provide a brief introduction to them here.

8.3.1   EXPERIMENTS

Experimentation is the fundamental method of acquiring knowledge in the physical sciences. As a research method, it has one primary and substantial benefit: Experiments allow the researcher to control the variables, making it easier than it might otherwise be to determine the effect of the independent variable on the dependent variable. Experiments are more difficult to conduct in the social sciences than in the physical sciences because the research subjects are human beings and the number of variables is normally large. In spite of these difficulties, however, political scientists are now successfully conducting more experiments than they have in the past.

Experiments in the social sciences are set up according to several different basic designs. The first is the simple *post-test measurement*. For example, a lecture on the social consequences of using marijuana may be followed by a test of knowledge of the participants who heard the lecture. The *test-retest method* is more accurate. A researcher using this method might measure the effects of a lecture on the attitudes of the people in an audience by first having the members of the audience complete a survey, then listen to the lecture and, finally, complete the survey again. The researcher could then measure the differences in opinion registered before and after the survey. Without the first survey, the researcher cannot be sure of the respondents' attitudes before the test was given, and the effects of the lecture, then, are less certain.

The *alternative-form* type of experiment uses two different measures of the same concept. In a research project concerning the effects of peer pressure on adolescents, for example, the analyst could measure subjects' propensity to conform in one test and then measure their desire for acceptance in another test. The *split-halves* device is similar to the alternative-form measurement, except that two measures of the concept under study are applied at the same time.

All experiment designs confront the following problems:

- *Control of Variables:* Can the environment be controlled to rule out other factors?

- *Time Passage:* People get tired, or for some other reason take a different attitude.

- *Varying Acts of Measurement:* Poll takers may record responses differently.

- *Statistical Regression:* Someone who is on the high end of a test score range may register a high score only temporarily.

- *Experimental Mortality:* Subjects drop out.

- *Instrument Decay:* The instrument may not be used as carefully the second time.

- *Selection Error:* Control and experimental groups may not be equivalent.

Researchers have developed a number of complex methodologies to overcome these problems. *Multigroup designs*, for example, test multiple independent variables against the same dependent variable. *Factorial designs* may test the effects of several independent variables in different combinations. A simple "2 x 2" factorial design, for example, might test combinations of four possible results from two different actions a researcher might take to test the social acceptability of her actions.

Let's suppose that the researcher made an identical presentation of information on the health hazards of smoking to four different high school health classes and later had the groups fill in a questionnaire that would indicate their acceptance of her presentation. Normally the researcher would wear a traditional business suit when addressing a group, but the experiment's goal is to study how socially acceptable her appearance is to her audiences, so she decides to alter her customary appearance in each group setting, using a straw hat and a pink leotard. The following table illustrates the four possible variations in her appearance.

	WEAR PINK LEOTARD	DO NOT WEAR PINK LEOTARD
WEAR A STRAW HAT	(1) both hat and leotard	(2) hat but no leotard
DO NOT WEAR A STRAW HAT	(3) leotard but not hat	(4) neither hat nor leotard

A factorial design based on the choices set forth in the table would test the results of presentation participant acceptance according to each of the four situations.

Researchers conduct dozens of different types of experimental designs, using different combinations of strategies. The preceding factorial design is intended to be used as a part of a *field experiment*, an experiment conducted within a natural setting, which in our example would be four regular high school health classes.

In the following example, the groups who participate in the experiment have not been left in their natural setting but have been preselected by the researcher. Some researchers claim that this type of interference with subjects creates a quasi-experimental design. Let us suppose that we will design an experiment to test this research hypothesis: "Students who are anxious because they believe their instructor will have access to their evaluations of the instructor's effectiveness before the assignment of the student's final grade will give the instructor a higher evaluation than if they had no such anxiety."

For our experiment, the teacher will use two course sections of his Introduction to Sociology class, the sections being similar in size and student makeup. Section 1, the control group, will be given the teacher evaluation form in the usual manner. The teacher will leave the room while a monitor—a student in the class—dispenses the forms, reads the instructions, gathers the forms after they have been completed, seals them in an envelope, then leaves the room, supposedly to take them where they will be kept from the teacher until final grades have been assigned to transcripts. As part of the instruction, the teacher emphasizes the fact that he does not have access to the results until final grades have been recorded.

Section 2, the experimental group, will follow the same procedure, with one exception. The monitor—again a student in the class—will first disclose information she has been given about teachers being allowed to look at the evaluations prior to final grade assignment. She will state that this is something she has heard from several reliable sources, but that she is unwilling to disclose those sources. Everything else in the evaluation process will be carefully controlled to emulate the procedure used with the control group.

The evaluations are then tallied to determine if the experimental group's perception that the teacher has access to their evaluation before the final grade is assigned caused them to give their teacher significantly higher evaluations than the control group did. Experiments in sociology like this one encounter certain difficulties. See if you can answer the following questions:

- What is the dependent variable of the experiment?
- What is the independent variable?
- What are the important antecedent and intervening variables?
- What else would need to be done to control the antecedent and intervening variables?
- What ethical issues might preclude running an experiment of this kind?

8.3.2   DIRECT OBSERVATION

A number of techniques are used for data collection. *Direct observation* of political phenomena is conducted by trained observers who carefully record selected behaviors. Observation may be structured; that is, a definite list of phenomena is compiled and studied, including such items as number of social contacts or religious allusions in a speech. Or observation may be unstructured, in which case observation attempts to take in every action in a certain setting that may possibly be significant. In either case, successful observation for purposes of social science research always follows clear guidelines and standard procedures.

Direct scientific observation is difficult to conduct for several reasons. First, researchers usually consider observation data to be qualitative, and therefore subjective in nature. Although much of the data can be quantified, qualitative considerations are hard to avoid. Another problem is that social events can be difficult, time consuming, and expensive to observe, and an entire event such as an election may require several observers whose activities are highly coordinated and regulated.

8.3.3   CONTENT ANALYSIS

Content analysis is a method of analyzing written documents that allows researchers to transform nonquantitative data into quantitative data by counting and categorizing certain variables within the data. Content analysts look for certain types of words or references in the texts, then categorize them or count them. A content analyst of news articles on women, for example, might count the number of times the authors of the articles portray women in a positive manner.

Content analysts of "events data" focus on a particular event or a series of events over time. A number of content analysts have examined the major wars of this century and have attempted to identify factors that are common in situations of war. Compilations of events data, such as the *World Handbook of Political and Social Indicators*, provide a listing of the important political events (such as elections, coups, and wars) for most countries of the world. These listings help to compare trends in selected types of events from one country to another.

Press reports, statistics, televised and radio media reports, personal records, newspapers, and magazines provide inexhaustible mines of data for content analysts. Government documents are an especially rich source of material for political scientists. Different types of government documents include: presidential papers; the Code of Federal Regulations; the Congressional Record; federal, state, and local election returns; historical records; judicial decisions; and legal records. The data analyzed in content analysis is most often the words contained in books, journals, magazines, newspapers, films, and radio or television broadcasts. But content analysis may also be conducted on photographs, cartoons, or music.

An example of content analysis design is found in the research of Levin, Arluke, and Mody-Desbareau (1986), who coded 311 celebrity and noncelebrity profiles that appeared in the four most widely circulated gossip magazines—*The National Enquirer, The Star, The Globe*, and *The National Examiner*—from February through July of 1983. The researchers concluded that while the profiles of noncelebrities mostly emphasized extraordinary acts of heroism, strength, or charity, celebrities were usually featured for some mundane or minor event, such as a shopping spree or quarrel with a spouse or lover. The researchers found a hidden message in the articles they reviewed: The ordinary, "little" person in the world should be content with his or her collective place in life (Levin and Fox, 1997).

CHAPTER 9

BOOK REVIEWS

9.1 THE OBJECTIVE OF A BOOK REVIEW

Successful book reviewers answer two questions for their readers: What is the book trying to do? and How well is it doing it? People who read a book review want to know if a particular book is worth reading, for their own particular purposes, before buying or beginning to read it. These potential book readers want to know what a book is about, and the book's strengths and weaknesses, and they want to gain this information as easily and quickly as possible.

Your goal in writing a book review, therefore, is to help people decide efficiently whether to buy or read a book. Your immediate objectives may be to please your instructor and get a good grade, but these objectives are most likely to be met if you focus on a book review's audience: people who want help in selecting books to read. In the process of writing a review according to the guidelines given in this chapter, you will also learn about the following:

- the book you are reviewing and its content
- professional standards for book reviews in sociology
- the essential steps to reviewing books that apply in any academic discipline

This final objective, learning to review a book properly, has more applications than you may at first imagine. First, it helps you to focus quickly on the essential elements of a book, to draw from a book its informational value for yourself and others. Some of the most successful professional and business people speed-read many books. They read these books less for enjoyment than to assimilate knowledge quickly. These readers then apply this knowledge to substantial advantage in their professions. It is normally not wise to speed-read a book you are reviewing because you are unlikely to gain from such a fast reading enough information to evaluate the book's qualities fairly. However, writing book reviews helps you to become proficient in quickly locating the book's most valuable information and paring away material that is of secondary importance. The ability to make such discriminations is of fundamental importance to academic and professional success.

In addition, writing book reviews for publication allows you to participate in the discussions of the broader intellectual and professional community of which you are a part. People in law, medicine, teaching, engineering, administration, and other fields are frequently asked to write reviews of books to help others in their profession assess the value of newly released publications.

9.2   TWO SAMPLE BOOK REVIEWS

Before reading the specific directions for writing a book review that are contained in this chapter, read the two sample book reviews on pages 169–173. Both were selected because they represent recent, typical, academic reviews of books of interest to sociologists. The first is University of Wisconsin Professor Brenda Reimer's review of Judith Lorber's *Paradoxes of Gender* for the 1996 edition of the *Sociology of Sport Journal* (vol. 13). The second book review, Texas A & M Professor Edward Murguia's review of Isabel Valle's ethnography, *Fields of Toil: A Migrant Family's Journey*, was published in *Rural Sociology* (vol. 60) in 1995. In the instructions for writing book reviews that immediately follow in this chapter, we shall refer to both reviews, pointing out some of the positive attributes and some of the features that might be improved.

9.3   ELEMENTS OF A BOOK REVIEW

Book reviews in the social sciences contain the same essential elements of all book reviews. Since social science is nonfiction, book reviews within the disciplines focus less on writing style and more on content and method than reviews of works of fiction. Your book review should generally contain four basic elements, though not always in this order:

1. enticement
2. examination
3. elucidation
4. evaluation

SAMPLE BOOK REVIEW

Brenda Reimer's Review

of Judith Lorber's

Paradoxes of Gender

Judith Lorber offers a new paradigm of gender in her book. Instead of analyzing gender from the perception of the individual, she strives to create it as a social institution that has a history as long as human culture. Furthermore, she aims "to challenge the validity, permanence, and necessity of gender" (5).

In Chapters 1 through 5, Lorber discusses how society produces gender. She begins Chapter 1 by discussing how gender is an accepted part of everyone's life. She argues that people do not think about how gendered their lives are, but automatically "do" gender. This process of gendering is legitimized by institutions such as religion, law, and science. In order to understand the process of gender and how it is institutionalized, Lorber discusses the differences between animal behavior and human behavior, stresses the difference between sex and gender, and relates how the number of genders in a society varies. For example, most Americans would define two genders, whereas some societies have three (the berdache, for example, as a third gender). The first chapter becomes the passageway for the rest of the book, illustrating how gender is used to keep women subordinate to men.

In her chapter on biology as ideology, Lorber discusses women in sport. Lorber emphasizes how social practices transform the body. For example, men are equated with strength and power; women are equated with fragility. This is emphasized in the domain of sport in which women athletes are not treated with the same respect and admiration as male athletes.

SAMPLE BOOK REVIEW, CONT.

The masculine is approved, but only for men. This may not be an eye opener for sport sociologists, but reading about our sport literature within this context has two effects. First, it shows how our research in sport sociology transcends the sport environment, and second, it places our research within a new paradigm.

Part II of the book focuses on gender in practice. Specifically, the evolution of gender is discussed. The topics of parenting, domestic labor, and salary are discussed as examples of how gender is constructed through specific practices in society. Lorber traces the evolution of technology with the decline in women's status throughout history. This decline in status can be observed in the ways in which domestic labor is assumed to be feminine and by the negative responses of many in the United States to the issue of mothers working outside the home. For example, when compared to Sweden's policy of child care benefits, the United States' policies have the effect of gendering the work force by creating a system whereby women's work is perceived as secondary to men's. Lorber argues that this is especially true if the comparative jobs are between working parents (e.g., it is typically mothers who take time off from work to care for a sick child).

The final portion of the book discusses politics of gender. For example, the phenomenon of the glass ceiling for women and the glass elevator for men is discussed, relative to how the institution of gender is used to keep white men in positions of power. The conclusion of Lorber's book discusses how to deconstruct gender in society and offers a glimpse at what life might be like without the social constructions of gender, race, and class.

In conclusion, Lorber's paradigm of the social construction of gender is compelling. Her insights on the social construction of gender are thought provoking and would be of interest to anyone who is interested in the intersections of race, class, and gender. This book would be an excellent source for graduate students, but might prove too difficult to all but select senior seminar courses.

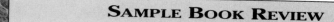

SAMPLE BOOK REVIEW

Edward Murguia's Review

of Isabel Valle's

Fields of Toil: A Migrant Family's Journey

Fields of Toil covers a year in the life of a Mexican American migrant family through Texas, Washington State, and Oregon. It shows that honest, hardworking people performing valuable work nevertheless remain in extremely marginal economic circumstances.

Much credit should go to an enlightened newspaper in the Pacific Northwest, the *Walla Walla Union Bulletin*, for initiating this project in which Valle, a reporter, spent a year (July 1991–July 1992) living with a migrant family. In essence, she became a participant observer, documenting a litany of problems faced by migrant farm workers: low pay, long hours, often oppressive working conditions, lack of jobs, lack of adequate housing, lack of medical care, and lack of education.

Raul and Maria Elena Martinez and their children, who come to symbolize the thousands of migrant workers who harvest crops throughout the United States, emerge as hardworking, decent, and intelligent human beings living a respectable but difficult life, made arduous by low wages, constant moving, and the problem of constantly having to obtain jobs and housing. Migrants are among the working poor and, in my opinion, the concept of individuals working but in poverty is a social injustice which should become as anachronistic as the concept of slavery. It's ironic that the Martinez family harvests food yet has to obtain food stamps and visit food banks for its own sustenance. It appears that Adam Smith's model of self-interest that promotes, as if by an invisible hand, the general well-being of all, breaks down here. The power differential between agribusi-

SAMPLE BOOK REVIEW, CONT.

ness and migrant farm workers is clear. Another model fits better here—one of exploitation of the powerless by the powerful.

There are programs in place to help farm workers, such as job training centers, housing provided by counties or nonprofit organizations, and school programs in some areas tailored for migrant children needs, and Valle documents the good that they do. But until the fundamental issue of low wages for agricultural workers is addressed, all of these programs probably will continue to be over-burdened, will smack of paternalism, and may continue to stigmatize. Migrant farm workers are doing an important task and they should be paid accordingly. Mechanisms to do this include either raising the minimum wage to a level where individuals earning this wage can live decent lives, a negative income tax system to raise income above the poverty level for individuals who are working but whose earnings are below poverty, or some combination of the two.

In the book, it becomes clear that illicit drugs have a corrosive effect on the migrant population. The temptation to make large amounts of money quickly by transporting drugs is very great. Drug dealing in south Texas is a serious problem because few jobs are available and jobs that do exist tend to be low paying and physically demanding. For example, Valle tells us that drugs constitute the single most serious problem in the town of La Grulla, the south Texas town from which the Martinez family originates. La Grulla is in the poorest precinct in the poorest county, Starr County, in the United States. The unemployment rate in Starr County is 48 percent and 17,000 migrants reside in the county, Valle says. The pay for transporting a single truckload of marijuana from southern Texas to northern U.S. cities can be as much as $1.4 million. In contrast, the pay for six weeks of the physically demanding work of bending over with a field box and cutting asparagus in Washington State is $4,000. It appears that those who deal in drugs and who are successful demoralize hardworking individuals who do not break the law; those who deal in drugs and get caught become entangled with the law and spend time in prison. The "choice" given to the very poor in south Texas seems to be either a life of hard work in poverty or a life largely in prison.

Although Valle should be given credit for spending much time with a migrant family and interviewing numerous directors of programs estab-

SAMPLE BOOK REVIEW, CONT.

lished to assist migrants, her writing is not sophisticated and often lacks depth. This limits the readability and usefulness of the book. Although there is an abundance of description, there is very little analysis and no theory. Perhaps Valle should not be faulted for this because her writings originally were intended as a series of newspaper articles and only later were compiled into book form. Nevertheless, the lack of a theoretical perspective even if only in a concluding chapter and the lack of analytical depth make the book less valuable. The book, though, does provide a current detailed view of the lives of Mexican-origin migrant workers, and those interested in agricultural labor should find this book of interest.

9.3.1   ENTICEMENT

The first sentence should entice people to read your review. Social studies do not have to be dull. Start your review with a sentence that both sums up the objective of the book, and catches the reader's eye. Professor Reimer's opening sentence, for example—"Judith Lorber offers a new paradigm of gender in her book"—makes it very difficult for the reader to resist reading more of her review. Be sure, however, that your opening statement, like Professor Reimer's, is an accurate a portrayal of the book as well as an enticement to the reader.

9.3.2   EXAMINATION

Your book review should encourage the reader to join you in examining the book. Tell the reader what the book is about. One of the greatest strengths of Professor Reimer's review is that her first paragraph immediately reinforces her enticing first sentence with a concise summary of the content of Lorber's book.

When you review a book, write about what is actually in the book, not what you think is probably there or what ought to be there. Do not tell how you would have written the book, but tell instead how the author wrote it. Describe the book in clear, objective terms. Include enough about the content to identify for the reader the major points that the author is trying to make.

9.3.3   ELUCIDATION

Elucidate, or clarify, the book's value and contribution to sociology by defining (1) what the author is attempting to do, and (2) how the author's work fits within current similar efforts in the discipline of sociology or scholarly inquiry in general. Notice how Reimer describes what Lorber's book is attempting to do. Reimer follows her definition of Lorber's purpose by placing the book within the context of similar concepts of "how society produces gender," noting that Reimer's discussion includes analyses of "the process of gendering," "gendering the work force," and "the glass ceiling for women and the glass elevator for men."

The elucidation portion of book reviews often provides additional information about the author. Reimer has not included information about Lorber in her review, but it would be helpful to know, for example, if the author has written other books or articles on the same subject, has developed a reputation for exceptional expertise in a certain subject, or is known to have a particular ideological bias. How would your understanding of a book be changed, for example, if you knew that its author is a leader in the feminist movement? Include in your book review information about the author that helps the reader understand how this book fits within the broader concerns of social science.

9.3.4   EVALUATION

After your reader understands what the book is attempting to do, she or he will want to know the extent to which the book has succeeded. To effectively evaluate a book, you should establish evaluation criteria and then compare the book's content to those criteria. You do not need to define your criteria specifically in your review, but they should be evident to the reader. The criteria will vary according to the book you are reviewing, and you may discuss them in any order that is helpful to the reader. Consider including the following among the criteria that you establish for your book review:

- How important is the subject matter to the study of culture and society?

- How complete and thorough is the author's coverage of her or his subject?

- How carefully is the author's analysis constructed?

- What are the strengths and limitations of the author's methodology?

- What is the quality of the writing in the book? Is the writing clear, precise, and interesting?

- How does this book compare with other books written on the same subject?

- What contribution does this book make to sociology?

- Who will enjoy or benefit from this book?

When giving your evaluation according to these criteria, be specific. If you write "This is a good book; I liked it very much," you have told the reader nothing of interest or value. But if you say, for example, "Smith's book provides descriptions of most the major sociological theories, but it fails to describe the full extent of Weber's concept of bureaucracy," then you have given your reader some concrete information.

Adequate though it is in many ways, Professor Murguia's review of Valle's book suffers from a lack of economy in both phrasing and content—weaknesses that are, unfortunately, common to much social science writing. Notice how loose and rambling Murguia's structure is compared with the tightness of Reimer's constructions. In several places throughout Murguia's review, the reader is forced to wonder, "Whose opinion is this?" Not only phrases, but ideas are repeated in Murguia's review that cannot be identified as Valle's. Also, he complains that Valle's book fails to offer satisfactory analytical content, and yet acknowledges that she writes as a journalist. Is this unfair criticism? (Journalists are rarely called upon for in-depth analytical writing.) Considering the criteria we have described in this chapter, what other comments would you make about these two book reviews?

9.3.5   REFLECTIVE OR ANALYTICAL BOOK REVIEWS

Two types of book reviews are normally assigned by instructors in the humanities and social sciences: the reflective and the analytical. Ask your instructor which type of book review she or he wants you to write. The purpose of a reflective book review is for the student reviewer to exercise creative analytical judgment without being influenced by the reviews of others. Reflective book reviews contain all the elements covered in this chapter—enticement, examination, elucidation, and evaluation—but they do not include the views of others who have also read the book.

Analytical book reviews contain all the information provided by reflective book reviews but add an analysis of the comments of other reviewers. The purpose is to review not only the book itself but also its reception in the professional community. To write an analytical book review, insert a review analysis section immediately after your summary of the book. To prepare this review analysis section, use the *Book Review Digest* and *Book Review Index* in the library to locate other reviews of the book that have been published in journals and other periodicals. As you read these reviews, use the following four steps:

1. List the criticisms (strengths and weaknesses) of the book found in these reviews.
2. Develop a concise summary of these criticisms, indicate the overall positive or negative tone of the reviews, and discuss some of the most frequent comments.
3. Evaluate the criticisms of the book found in these reviews. Are they basically accurate in their assessment of the book?
4. Write a review analysis of two pages or less that states and evaluates steps 2 and 3, and place it in your book review immediately after your summary of the book.

9.4   FORMAT AND LENGTH OF A BOOK REVIEW

The directions for writing papers provided in Part 2 of this manual apply to book reviews as well. Unless your instructor gives you other specifications, a reflective book review should be three to five pages in length, and an analytical book review should be from five to seven pages. In either case, a brief, specific, concise book review is almost always preferred over one of greater length.

CHAPTER 10

SOCIAL ISSUE ANALYSIS PAPERS

10.1 INTRODUCTORY SOCIAL ISSUE ANALYSIS PAPERS

In 1956, sociologist C. Wright Mills published *The Power Elite*, a social and political analysis of American society. According to Mills, America is controlled by a "power elite" composed of influential business, government, and military leaders who interact with each other socially and professionally.

> The power elite is not an aristocracy, which is to say that it is not a political ruling group based upon a nobility of hereditary origin. It has no compact basis in a small circle of great families whose members can and do consistently occupy the top positions in the several higher circles which overlap as the power elite. But such nobility is only one possible basis of common origin. That it does not exist for the American elite does not mean that members of this elite derive socially from the full range of strata composing American society. They derive in substantial proportions from the upper classes, both new and old, of local society and the metropolitan 400. The bulk of the very rich, the corporate executives, the political outsiders, the high military, derive from, at most, the upper third of the income and occupational pyramids. Their fathers were at least of the professional and business strata, and very frequently higher than that. They are native-born Americans of native parents, primarily from urban areas, and, with the expectations of the politicians among them, overwhelmingly from the East. They are mainly Protestants, especially Episcopalian or Presbyterian. In general, the higher the position, the greater the proportion of men within it who have derived from and who maintain connections with the upper classes. The generally similar origins of the members of the power elite are underlined and carried further by the fact of their increasingly common educational routine. Overwhelmingly college graduates, substantial proportions have attended Ivy League colleges, although the education of the higher military, of course, differs from that of other members of the power elite.... The inner core of the power elite consists, first, of those who inter-

change commanding roles at the top of one dominant institutional order with those in another: the admiral who is also a banker and a lawyer and who heads up an important federal commission; the corporation executive whose company was one of the two or three leading war material producers who is now the Secretary of Defense; the wartime general who dons civilian clothes to sit on the political directorate and then becomes a member of the board of directors of a leading economic corporation. Although the executive who becomes a general, the general who becomes a statesman, the statesman who becomes a banker, see much more than ordinary men in their ordinary environments, still the perspectives of even such men often remain tied to their dominant locales. In their very career, however, they interchange roles within the big three and thus readily transcend the particularity of interest in any one of these institutional milieux. By their very careers and activities, they lace the three types of milieux together. They are, accordingly, the core members of the power elite. (Mills, 1956: 269–297)

The Power Elite brought to social and political analysis a new perspective on social relationships and how they define the structures of political power in society. The idea that segments of society form ruling elites has a history reaching back in history to before Plato and Aristotle. Mills, however, explained how power elites operate in society in general, and he painted a graphic and detailed portrait of the American power structure as it existed in the 1950s.

While Mills examined many social and political issues, his major objective was to explore the social and political forces that make things happen in society. As a sociology student, your attempts to analyze social issues and events will probably not be as all-encompassing or far-reaching as Mills'. However, your social analysis paper will have the same general goal that Mills' study had: to help readers understand social processes. Furthermore, your paper will have a more specific primary objective: to apply the techniques of sociological analysis to a specific social issue or problem.

10.1.1   DETERMINING YOUR AUDIENCE

Before writing your paper, consider your audience. For whom are you writing? When you write a social issue paper, your audience consists of the following:

- the instructor of the course, who wants you to analyze carefully and insightfully and write well
- college students and others who study sociology, who want to improve their chances of success in their careers, or who simply want to better understand the social and political process in order to affect events or teach sociology to others
- yourself

Keep all three audiences in mind as you write. It is sometimes difficult to determine how much background material you should include in an analysis or how much basic discussion of an important but tangential subject. What would one of your classmates need to know about your topic to understand your thesis? A clear understanding of your paper's purpose will help you to pinpoint your audience and tailor your material accordingly.

10.1.2   BASIC STEPS TO WRITING A SOCIAL ISSUE ANALYSIS PAPER

There are four basic steps in writing a good social issue analysis paper. These steps are recursive, meaning that although they must all be undertaken, they need not necessarily be taken consecutively, and some of them will be taken repeatedly.

1. Select a social issue to study.
2. Narrow the focus of your study.
3. Conduct your research.
4. Write the paper.

Selecting an Issue to Study   In most cases, your teacher will ask you to select an issue that is germane to the course. For example, in a course on the family as a social institution, you might choose to write on a topic like one of these:

- The Future of "Traditional Families" in America
- Problems of Two-Paycheck Families
- Current Challenges for African-American Families
- Special Needs of Single-Parent Families

In a course in majority-minority relations you might write on one of the following topics:

- Racism in America
- Assimilating Native Americans
- Racial Discrimination in the Media
- Sexual Harassment in the Workplace
- Women of Color in the Feminist Movement

While it is not a requirement, sometimes personal experience or interest can help you decide which issue to write about. For example, you may want to do a paper on some issue related to your vocational aspirations. If you are planning to be a teacher, you could investigate the quality of public education in America or, more specifically, in your state or district. An aspiring athlete could study a particular aspect of U.S. Olympic policy or the "gloried self" problem faced by superstar athletes described by Patricia and Peter Adler (1989). A future physician may want to look at problems in medical reimbursement or the trend toward socialized medicine. Since government policy affects every vocational interest to some degree, you may find a topic by asking yourself, "What are my career goals and interests? In what way does government affect me?" Many college students, for example, are affected by government student loan policies and the issue of an income tax deduction for college tuition.

Where you have been and what you have done in your life are important, and if you are or have been personally involved with your topic, you gain more than knowledge. Your paper becomes an experiential tool; it expands your vision and increases the options available to you. By writing a good paper on some "personal" issue, you not only contribute to your success in the class and the available knowledge on the topic, you broaden your under- standing of the life *you* are living.

Another general approach to finding a topic is to select a current event. Newspapers, popular magazines, and television and radio reports continually present actual problems that are meaningful issues for sociology students to investigate. Issues related to drugs, gang violence, poverty, quality of educa- tion, abortion, and religious practices are to be found in the news every day. Scan the pages of your local newspaper or read the entries in the news digest of your Internet service, and you will find many topics to write about. In a sin- gle issue of the *New York Times* (Thursday, November 21, 1996), for example, the following four news excerpts were found.* Each of them raises issues that might interest you. As you read the excerpts, think about aspects of the prob- lems that you might want to investigate.

In Boston, Nothing Is Something:
No Youths Slain by Guns in 16 Months; New Tactics Get Credit
by Fox Butterfield (page A8)

BOSTON, Nov. 20—At a time when experts are trying to understand why homicide rates in many cities are dropping, Boston has one of the most impressive statistics of all: not a single juvenile under 17 has been killed by gunfire since July 1995.

Given the complexity of the crime problem, no one can say definitively why so few young people have been killed here, and one or two years is too short a time to pronounce success. But the police, public officials and crim- inal justice experts point to an innovative and inexpensive set of strategies that Boston has adopted in the last few years.

First, the city gave a small number of probation officers enhanced power to make arrests by putting them in patrol cars with police officers. More recently, city officials have also intensified their focus on controlling gangs and guns after computer-aided research from Harvard found that three- quarters of juvenile killers and their victims had been involved with gangs and that firearms dealers who were illegally selling significant numbers of guns to young people could be identified.

The number of juveniles killed by firearms in Boston has never been large—the figure was 5 in 1994, and the highest number recorded in recent years was 10. But the drop to zero surprises analysts nonetheless; the only

---

juveniles killed by any means in Boston since July 1995 have been three young children beaten to death by adult relatives.

Moreover, the figures for people 24 and younger are showing the same trend: since the city put all the components of its new plan into place in May, the homicide rate for that age group has dropped 71 percent, police statistics show, to just 8 homicides, from the 28 committed in the same five-month period the previous year. For the entire year of 1995, there were 46 people age 24 and younger murdered in Boston.

Fattening of America: Less Is No More
by Donna St.George (page B1)

The next time you hear about a friend's low-fat diet, the next time you see a kitchen stocked with low-fat cookbooks and fat-free snacks, consider this: Three of the fastest growing foods in America are hamburgers, french fries, and chicken nuggets.

Several years after low-fat eating became a full-fledged national obsession, there are signs that many Americans may have had their fill of fatlessness.

For the fourth year in a row, America is not eating more better-for-you foods, even as new low-fat items show up daily on supermarket shelves, according to a survey published this week by the NPD Group in Rosemont, Ill., a marketing research company that has tracked eating habits for 16 years.

At the same time, America is big on restaurant junk food, feasting on almost eight million more orders of french fries, nearly six million more hamburgers and five million more servings of chicken nuggets in a two-week period this year than last, the survey found.

U.S. Gets "Average" Grades in Math and Science Studies
by Peter Applebome (page A1)

In the most comprehensive study of science and mathematics achievement by students around the world, students in the United States ranked slightly below average in mathematics and slightly above average in science, according to an international comparison of 41 countries released yesterday.

Singapore, South Korea, Japan, Hong Kong and the Czech Republic were among the top-ranking nations of those surveyed. Colombia and South Africa were among the lowest. The United States results did not differ significantly from some other Western nations like Canada, England and Germany.

The survey reflected neither the most extreme proclamations of persistent educational decline that have become part of the political landscape, nor the hopes of some educators that a decade of education "reform" would have produced more striking gains by students in the United States.

But the results are further proof that the United States has virtually no chance of meeting the national goal set out in 1990 to make its students first in the world in mathematics and science by the year 2000. And it reflects the degree to which any education progress in this country is being matched or exceeded by many other countries around the world.

<u>**Romania's Communist Legacy: "Abortion Culture"**</u>
<u>**by Jane Perlez (page A3)**</u>

BUCHAREST, Romania, Nov. 19—Dorina Ciuplan, a 40-year-old mother of three teen-agers, recalled with a mixture of terror and emotion the nine self-induced abortions she endured during Communist rule under Nicolae Ceausescu.

"I sometimes think I'm lucky to be alive," said Mrs. Ciuplan, her eyes watering as she described forcing miscarriages at home and then going to a hospital, where doctors and nurses tormented her with abusive words and rough treatment as they finished terminating the pregnancies rather than let her die.

For more than two decades, contraception and abortions were strictly forbidden by Mr. Ceausescu in an attempt to build his country into a colossus through population growth. His government was overthrown in 1989, and one of its legacies was orphanages filled with unwanted and neglected children.

Another legacy of those horrific years, for Romania's women, is abortion. Some 10,000 women are believed to have died from complications of illegal abortions, and many more were permanently maimed.

Abortions were legalized as soon as Mr. Ceausescu was toppled, and contraception is theoretically available through the state health system.

But overwhelmingly, Romania remains what Western doctors call an "abortion culture," with an abortion rate that remains the highest in Europe. It also has by far the highest rate of pregnancy-related mortality, the strongest indication that Romania continues to lag far behind the rest of Europe and Russia in providing reproductive health services for women.

According to the United Nations Population Fund, Romania had 3.2 abortions for every live birth in 1990. By last year, the rate was 2.2 abortions per live birth. In 1995, the equivalent rate was 2.0 in Russia, 0.67 in the Czech Republic and Hungary and 0.2 in Germany.

Narrowing the Focus for Your Social Issue Paper   With assistance from your instructor, you should be able to narrow the issue and select a specific topic that is right for you. For example, the news is filled with reports on gangs and gang behavior, which can easily translate into many meaningful topics, including the following:

- Gangs and the Family
- Gangs and Violence in New York City
- Gangs, Drugs, and Minority Self-Concept

Suppose that you select the family as the general issue area that you would like to study. You can narrow your topic by selecting a specific focus for your paper. You may want to select, for example, one of the following:

- *A Definitional Focus:* What is the traditional family and how does it differ from other forms of family organization?
- *A Geographic Focus:* What is family life like in Concord, New Hampshire? Is it different from family life in Papua, New Guinea?

- *An Historical Focus:* How has the traditional family changed over time?
- *A Systems Focus:* How does the traditional family as an American institution interact with other basic systems or institutions in society, such churches, schools, or government agencies?
- *An Interaction Focus:* What are the roles played in the family? What social, economic, political or environmental forces affect these roles?
- *A Future Focus:* What does the future hold for the family? What can be projected from what you have learned about the issue?

10.1.3 THE CONTENTS OF A SOCIAL ISSUE ANALYSIS PAPER

Your social issue analysis paper should contain the following elements. The format for each is described in Chapter 3 of this manual.

- title page
- abstract, outline, or table of contents (Ask your instructor which of these to include.)
- the body or text of the paper, which includes source citations
- references page
- appendices (where applicable)

10.2 ADVANCED SOCIAL ISSUE ANALYSIS PAPERS

10.2.1 SELECTING A THEORETICAL PERSPECTIVE

To write an issue analysis paper for upper level or graduate classes in sociology, you need to do the following:

- Follow all directions for writing an introductory social issue analysis paper, as described in the preceding sections of this chapter.
- Conduct your analysis through a sociological theoretical perspective.

What is a sociological theoretical perspective? Sociologists have long known that it is impossible to conduct social analysis without making some assumptions about what people are like and how they behave. It is also impossible to analyze social issues or conditions without a plan or approach for tackling the issues involved. As they study social phenomena, sociologists devise approaches to analysis known as theoretical perspectives. Three major sociological theoretical perspectives (functionalism, conflict theory, and symbolic interactionism) are briefly described in the introduction to this manual. If you are writing an advance issue analysis paper for an upper level sociology course, it is likely that you have already learned much about these and other theoretical perspectives. If you feel that you are not sufficiently familiar with them, ask your instructor for information before you proceed with this paper. It is not not within the scope of this manual to describe them in detail.

In your paper, you will need to select one of two general approaches:

1. Select a single theoretical perspective from which to conduct your analysis, or
2. Compare the results when you apply more than one perspective to the issue you have chosen.

To apply the theoretical perspective that you have selected to an issue, take the following steps:

- Clearly define the issue you are examining.
- Summarize the pertinent facts about the issue that you have discovered.
- Announce which theoretical perspective you will apply to your issue.
- State the major assumptions of the theoretical perspective.
- Using the theoretical perspective that you have selected as an "interpretive lens" through which you are seeing the issue, analyze the issue by defining the implications of the results of your research.

Let us look at an example of how these steps may be accomplished. Corliss Lindell's paper (on pages 185–188) analyzed marital satisfaction. She applied two theoretical perspectives—conflict theory and symbolic interactionism—to her topic. Notice how Corliss applies conflict theory and symbolic interactionism to develop more insights about marital satisfaction than she would have, had she not applied the two perspectives.

SAMPLE ISSUE ANALYSIS PAPER

Marital Satisfaction

INTRODUCTION

They spot each other from across the room. Time seems to stand still as they glide past the crowd and into each other's arms. As they look deep into each other's eyes, they profess their love without words. Shortly thereafter, they marry and live happily ever after, and this is where the fairy tale ends.

Today, over 90 percent of Americans will marry at least once in their lifetime (Glenn 1993; Turner and Helms 1994). Marriage is something that most children believe they will experience, and most look forward to the day with excitement and anticipation. Many adults profess that marriage is the main goal in their lives (Glenn 1993; Kilborne, Howell, and England 1990; Wallerstein and Blakeslee 1995). In 1989, Glenn (1993) surveyed high school seniors' values and found that 90 percent believed matrimony was the most important value to have.

Those who marry seem to gain many benefits. It has consistently been found that married couples have higher levels of life satisfaction and better physical and psychological health than those who are single, divorced, or widowed (Fowers 1991; Turner and Helms 1994). Fowers (1991) remarks that "marital satisfaction scores were also consistently correlated with life satisfaction scores for both partners."

Obviously, marital happiness is the goal for all newlyweds, but this is not always attainable. After the anticipation of the wedding day is long gone and the honeymoon vacation in the Caribbean is over, reality takes over and the trials and tribulations begin. According to Whipple and White

SAMPLE ISSUE ANALYSIS PAPER, CONT.

(1995), "matrimony has been defined as a study in frustration—an intimate relation without intimacy." Although the divorce rate has seemed to level off over the past 20 years, it continues to affect over one million Americans each year (Henslin 1990; Turner and Helms 1994).

Some people refuse to admit their marriage is less than ideal. They go on living in an unhappy marriage because they see divorce as admitting to failure (Turner and Helms 1994). Further, they may stay in the marriage because they have children, and the probability of this occurring rises with the increasing number of children (Lauer and Lauer 1986). The major factors in marital dissatisfaction include extramarital affairs, financial problems, lack of intimacy, and personality problems (Allbritton 1982; Lauer and Lauer 1986).

Lower satisfaction rates in a marriage may also be the result of inequalities between the sexes. Fowers (1991) remarks that "satisfaction scores are directly related to the degree of task sharing among both men and women. Other research has found that inequalities in couples are associated with lower satisfaction." In fact, Campbell (1989) noted that when the wife has the most power in the relationship, "both partners are less likely to report that relationship is satisfying."

Regardless, many couples report that they are happily married. Lauer and Lauer (1986) found that those with a high degree of marital satisfaction believe that the "qualities of the spouse, the 'best friend' nature of the relationship, and their commitment to the relationship are the most important factors in their marriages." In addition, it is agreed that communication, a sense of humor, intimacy, and good conflict-management skills are mandatory in a "healthy" marriage (Gordon 1993; Israeloff 1993; Rosen 1994; Satran 1995; Wallerstein and Blakeslee 1995).

THEORETICAL PERSPECTIVE

Some components of marital satisfaction and dissatisfaction seem best interpreted from a symbolic interactionism perspective, while others fall more readily into the conflict model.

Symbolic interactionists noted back in 1933 that personality was of

SAMPLE ISSUE ANALYSIS PAPER, CONT.

increasing concern in the mate-selection process in America. According to Henslin (1990), "family solidarity was increasingly coming to depend on mutual affection, sympathetic understanding, and temperamental compatibility." Thus, the institution of marriage underwent a dramatic change in the degree of intimacy and companionship expected.

Today, symbolic interactionists often depict marriage as an "overloaded institution" (Henslin 1990). Increasingly, both men and women have come to expect each other to take care of every emotional and physical need. LaPatra (1980) describes marriage in the following manner:

> The love of a husband and wife in our society is a remarkable fusion of sex, domesticity, and comradeship. It is also self-sufficient; in theory, neither partner needs emotional satisfaction outside the warm walls of the family. This is a unique and perhaps dangerous situation. No other society, as far as I know, attempts to satisfy all the emotional needs of two persons within such a restricted framework.

Although it is nonexistent in some cultures, love is the primary basis for marital happiness in American society today (Henslin 1990; Turner and Helms 1994). This can create expectations in a marriage that are often unrealistic and unattainable. Thus, when problems begin to surface, spouses tend to place blame on the other partner. Henslin (1990) notes that "their engulfment in the symbol of love blinds them to the basic unreality of their expectations."

Conflict theorists emphasize the inequalities between the genders and believe that this is the underlying reason for marital dissatisfaction. For example, men are socialized to be dominant, while women are taught the value of submission in male-female relationships. This difference, along with many others, creates a problem when each depends on the other for total emotional support. In addition, the two sexes often have different expectations in the marriage. Often, the woman marries for financial stability, while the man may marry her for her beauty, sexual relations, or childbearing abilities (Kephart and Jedlicka 1991) Because of this, women often have much more to lose in the relationship. According to Firestone (1970),

SAMPLE ISSUE ANALYSIS PAPER, CONT.

"such an unequal balance of power makes the woman invest more in the relationship and makes her more dependent on its outcome."

Conflict theorists see the increased independence of women as a major factor in the increase of marital dissatisfaction. Women are more likely to seek a divorce due to unhappiness than they once were (Henslin 1990; Kephart and Jedlicka 1991). According to Henslin (1990), "conflict theorists see divorce not as a sign that the family is being weakened, but rather, as a sign that women are finally making headway in their basic historical struggle with men."

CHAPTER 11

CASE STUDIES

He who knows only his own side of the case knows little of that.
—John Stuart Mill, 1806–1873

11.1 DEFINITION AND PURPOSE

A case study is an in-depth investigation of a social unit—such as a business, a political party, or a church—undertaken to identify the factors that influence the manner in which the unit functions.

Some examples of case studies are the following:

- an evaluation of the industrial efficiency of a Western Electric plant
- a study of ritual and magic in the culture of the Trobriand Islanders
- a study of the social service agency behavior of forest rangers

Case studies have long been used in law schools, where students learn how the law develops by reading actual court case decisions. Business schools began to develop social service and business agency case studies to help students understand actual management situations. Although courses in social organization, public administration, and social institutions adopt the case study method as a primary teaching tool less often than business or law schools, case studies have become a common feature of many courses in these areas.

Psychologists have used the case histories of mental patients for many years to support or negate a particular theory. Sociologists use the case study approach to describe and draw conclusions about a wide variety of subjects, such as labor unions, police departments, medical schools, gangs, public and private bureaucracies, religious groups, cities, and social class (Philliber et al. 1980:64). The success of this type of research depends heavily on the open-mindedness, sensitivity, insights, and integrative abilities of the investigator.

Case studies fulfill many educational objectives in the social sciences. As a student in a sociology course, you may write a case study in order to improve your ability to do the following:

- carefully and objectively analyze information
- solve problems effectively
- present your ideas in clear written form, directed to a specific audience

In addition, writing a case study allows you to discover some of the problems you will face if you become involved in an actual social situation that parallels your case study. For example, writing a case study like the one on pages 198–205, which focuses on corporate organization, can help you to understand the following:

- some of the potentials and problems of society in general
- the operation of a particular cultural, ethnic, political, economic, or religious group
- the development of a particular problem, such as crime, alcoholism, or violence within a group
- the interrelationships—within a particular setting—of people, structures, rules, politics, relationship styles, and many other factors

11.2   USING CASE STUDIES IN RESEARCH

Isaac and Michael (1981:48) suggest that case studies offer several advantages to the investigator. For one thing, they provide useful background information for researchers planning a major investigation in the social sciences. Case studies often suggest fruitful hypotheses for further study, and they provide specific examples by which to test general theories. Philliber et al. (1980:64) believe that through the intensive investigation of only one case, the researcher can gain more depth and detail than might be possible by briefly examining many cases. Also, the depth of focus in the study of a single case allows investigators to recognize certain aspects of the object being studied that would otherwise go unobserved.

For example, Becker et al. (1961) noticed that medical students tend to develop a "slang" that Becker and his associates refer to as *native language*. Only after observing the behavior of the students for several weeks were the researchers able to determine that the slang word *crocks* referred to those patients who were of no help to the students professionally because they did not have an observable disease. The medical students felt the crocks were robbing them of their important time.

Bouma and Atkinson (1995:110–114) call attention to the exploratory nature of some case studies. For example, researchers may be interested in what is happening in a juvenile detention center. Before beginning the project, they may not know enough about what they will find in order to formulate testable hypotheses. The researchers' purpose in doing a case study may be to gather as much information as possible to help in the formulation of relevant hypotheses. Or the researchers may intend simply to observe and describe all that is happening within the case being studied.

11.3 LIMITATIONS OF THE CASE STUDY METHOD

Before writing a case study, you should be aware of its limitations to avoid drawing conclusions that are not justified by the knowledge you acquire. First, case studies are relatively subjective exercises. When you write a case study, you select the facts and arrange them into patterns from which you may draw conclusions. The quality of the case study will depend largely on the quality of the facts you select and the way in which you interpret those facts.

A second potential liability is that every case study—no matter how well written—is in some sense an oversimplification of the events that are described and the environment within which those events take place. To simplify an event or series of events makes it easier to understand but at the same time distorts its effect and importance. It can always be argued that the results of any case study are peculiar to that one case and, therefore, offer little as a rationale for a general explanation or prediction (Philliber et al. 1980:65). A third caution about case studies pertains strictly to their use as a learning tool in the classroom: Remember that any interpretations you come up with for a case study in your class—no matter how astute or sincere—are essentially parts of an academic exercise and therefore may not be applicable in an actual situation.

11.4 TYPES OF CASE STUDIES WRITTEN IN SOCIOLOGY

Sociology case studies usually take one of two basic forms. The first might be called a didactic case study, because it is written for use in a classroom. It describes a situation or a problem in a certain setting but performs no analysis and draws no conclusions. Instead, a didactic case study normally lists questions for the students to consider and then answer, either individually or in class discussion. This type of case study allows the teacher to evaluate student analysis skills, and—if the case is discussed in class—to give students an opportunity to compare ideas with other students.

The second form, an analytical case study, provides not only a description but an analysis of the case as well. This is the form of case study most often assigned in a sociology class, and it is the form described in detail in this chapter.

Sociologists conduct case studies for a variety of specific purposes. An ethnographic case study, for example, is an in-depth examination of people—an organization, or a group—over time. Its main purpose is to lead the researchers to a better understanding of human behavior through observations of the interweaving of people, events, conditions, and means in natural settings or subcultures.

Ethnographic case studies examine behavior in a community or—in the case of some technologically primitive societies—an entire society. The term *ethnography* means "a portrait of a people," and the ethnographic approach was historically an anthropological tool for describing societies whose cultural evolution was very primitive when compared to the "civilized" world (Hunter and Whitten 1976:147). Anthropologists would sometimes live within the society under scrutiny for several months or even years, interviewing and observing the people being studied. The in-the-field component of ethnographies has caused them to sometimes be referred to as field studies.

11.5   HOW TO CONDUCT A SOCIAL SERVICE AGENCY CASE STUDY

Unlike an ethnographic study, which looks at a community or a society as a whole, a social service agency case study focuses on a formal organization that provides a specific service or set of services either to a section of a society or society as a whole. This type of case study usually describes and explains some aspect of a social service agency's operation; case studies do not attempt to explain everything there is to know about the organization. To conduct a social service agency case study, you undertake the following tasks:

1. Select a particular social service agency to study.
2. Formulate a general goal, for example, to better understand how the agency works.
3. Describe in general terms the agency and how it operates.
4. Describe the structure, practices, and procedures of the agency.
5. Select a specific objective—for example, to discover the responsiveness to the agency's programs of the people the agency serves.
6. Describe your methodology—that is, the procedures you will use to conduct your investigation.
7. Describe the results of your study, the observations you have made.
8. Draw conclusions about your findings.

The specific goal of your case study is to explain the effectiveness or ineffectiveness of some aspect of the agency's operation. This focused inquiry will in turn contribute to a general understanding of how the selected agency works. You may select any social service agency—such as the United Way, the Social Security Administration, the American Red Cross, or your state's Department of Human Services—as long as its personnel are directly accessible to you for interviews.

After you have chosen a social service agency to examine, you need to focus on a specific topic related to the agency—some characteristic procedure or situation—and write a description of how it has developed within the agency. For example, if your agency focus is a county health department and your topic focus is recruitment problems, you might choose to describe how the recruitment problems evolved within the overall operations of the department.

Most social service agency case studies assigned in sociology classes are not fictional. They are based on your investigation of an actual current or recent situation in a public or private agency. Keep in mind that to make the case study exercise meaningful to you, you need to choose an agency and a topic in which you have a personal interest.

11.5.1   SELECTING A TOPIC

In seeking a topic, you are looking for a situation that is likely to provide some interesting insights about how social service agencies affect people's lives. There are two ways to begin your search. The first is to contact an agency involved with a matter that interests you, and then inquire about recent events. For example, if you are interested in the welfare system, you would contact a local office of your state welfare agency or a national or local welfare agency. Explain that you are a student who wants to write a course paper about the agency and ask to talk to someone who can explain the organization's current programs. Ask for an appointment for an interview with that person. When you arrive for the interview, tell the person you are interviewing that you are interested in doing a case study on some aspect of the agency's operations and that your purpose is to better understand how government agencies operate. Then ask a series of questions aimed at helping you find a topic to pursue. These questions might include the following:

- What recent successes has your agency had?
- What is the greatest challenge facing your agency at the moment?
- What are some of the agency's goals for this year?
- What are some of the obstacles to meeting these goals?

You should follow up these questions with others until you identify a situation in the agency appropriate for your study. There will probably be many.

Consider the following examples:

- The agency faces budget cuts, and the director may have to decide among competing political pressures which services she must reduce.
- The agency faces a reorganization.
- The agency receives criticism from the people it serves.
- The agency initiates a controversial policy.

Another way to select a topic is to find an article of interest in your local newspaper. Hardly a day goes by that a suitable topic does not appear. The successes, failures, challenges, and mistakes of government and private agencies are always in the news. The benefit of finding a topic in the newspaper is that when you contact the agency involved, you will already have a subject to discuss. The disadvantage is that, on some publicized topics, agency officials may be reluctant to provide detailed information.

11.5.2   INTERVIEWS

The goal of your first interview is to obtain enough information for a series of other interviews. The answers to questions you pose in these interviews will allow you to understand the course of events and the agency interactions that have resulted in the situation you are studying. Remember that you are writing a story, but the story you are writing must be accurate and factual. Do not accept the first version of a course of events that you hear; ask several qualified people the same basic questions.

Take notes constantly. Do not use a tape recorder, because they tend to inhibit people from giving you as much information as they would without a recorder present. At every interview, ask about documents relevant to the case. These documents may include committee reports, meeting minutes, letters, or organizational rules and procedures. Sort out fact from fiction. When the facts are straight, you will be ready to organize your thoughts first into an outline, and then into the first draft of your paper.

11.5.3   ELEMENTS OF THE CASE STUDY PAPER

Overview of Contents   Your case study will consist of four basic parts:

1. title page
2. executive summary
3. text
4. references page

The title page, executive summary, and references page should all conform to the directions in the preceding chapters of this manual.

Text   The text of a social service agency case study includes the following elements:

- the facts of the case
- the environment, context, and participants of the case
- topic analysis
- conclusions

Text elements should appear more or less in this order, but to some extent elements will overlap. In general, case studies should be brief and concise. They may include information from numerous interviews and documents, but only material that is essential to understanding the case. A case study can be any length, but a paper of about fifteen pages in length, double-spaced, will be adequate to accurately describe and analyze a case situation. Ask your instructor for the assigned length of the paper.

The Facts of the Case   Write the facts of the case in narrative-story form. Accuracy is the most important quality a case study should have, but writing style will determine in large part the benefit the reader receives from reading it. Include in the facts of the case a description of the events, the major actors and their relationships with one another, and the external and internal agency environments and contexts within which the events of the situation developed.

The Environment, Context, and Participants of the Case   In your account, consider the following aspects of a situation and relate to your readers those items that are relevant to the case:

- political and economic factors of the agency's external environment: political parties, interest groups, ideologies, and economic interests
- political and economic factors of the agency's internal environment: power and influence, budget constraints, agency structure, rules, role, and mission
- elements of the agency's internal social service agency environment: social service agency style, tone, preferences, and procedures

Give your story's actors anonymity. Without altering the essential facts of the course of events, alter or delete the names of the actors and the agencies for which they work. Accuracy of facts in a case study is essential for a correct interpretation, but the identities of the individuals involved is irrelevant, and people may want their identities protected. Any change of facts for this purpose should be done in a manner that does not alter the content of the story.

A well-written social service agency case study will reveal much about how public and/or private agencies conduct business in the United States, and even more about the agency selected for study. Public and private administrators face many of the same problems: They must recruit personnel, establish goals and objectives, account for expenditures, and abide by hundreds of rules and regulations. In several important respects, however, public agencies are very different from private businesses. A public administrator will often serve several bosses (governor, legislators) and have several competing clientele (interest groups, the general public). Public officials are more susceptible than private business to changes in political administrations. They also face more legal constraints and are held accountable to higher ethical standards. In addition, public administrators are more likely to be held under the light of public surveillance; and, finally, they are held accountable to a different "bottom line."

The goal of most businesses is—first and foremost—to earn profits for their owners. The amount of these profits is normally easy to quantify. The success of public agencies, however, can be hard to measure. Criteria used to evaluate public programs—such as effectiveness and efficiency—often contradict one another. The nation's space program has accomplished some remarkable achievements, but not many people acclaim the program's economic efficiency. Some of these differences and similarities may become evident in your case study.

Topic Analysis   Your analysis should explore and explain the events in your selected situation, concentrating on the strategies and practices used by the primary actors in the social service agency. Your analysis should answer questions such as the following:

- How did the situation or problem at the heart of the case arise?
- What were the important external and internal factors that directed what transpired?
- What were the major sources of power and influence in the situation, and how were they used?
- What social service agency styles and practices were employed, and were they effective and appropriate within the situation described?
- How did relationships within the organization affect the conduct of other public or private programs?

Conclusions   To the fullest extent possible, your conclusions should use what you have learned about the nature of administrative practices to explain causes and effects, summarize events and their results, and interpret the actions of administrators. One major purpose of a social service agency case study is to gives its readers an opportunity to benefit from the successes and mistakes of others. In your conclusion, explain what you have learned from this situation, what you would imitate in your own social service agency practice, and what you would do differently if you found yourself in a similar situation.

11.6   SAMPLE CASE STUDY: "SECRETARIES IN THE CORPORATION"

In her case study of "Secretaries in the Corporation," Rosabeth Kanter (1977) examines the position of secretary in a corporation called Indsco, focusing especially on its relationship with the position of "boss." According to Kanter, "the secretary-boss relationship is the most striking instance of the retention of patrimony within the bureaucracy. Fewer bureaucratic 'safeguards' apply here than in any other part of the system." She proceeds to support this clearly stated thesis with evidence accumulated in her investigation. The result is a case study that makes an interesting point.

Kanter begins by introducing Max Weber's analysis of bureaucracy and patrimony. The secretary is an example of patrimony in modern bureaucracy, meaning that the secretary's position is more subject to the whims of the boss than are other corporate positions.

Read Kanter's analysis of structure, position, and power—"Secretaries in the Corporation"* (on pages 198–205). As you read, try to identify the aspects of the study that make it successful. If you had written it, how would you improve it?

---

*Case study on pages 198–205 is from Rosabeth Kanter, "Secretaries in the Corporation," in *Men and Women of the Corporation*, ed. Rosabeth Kanter. New York: Basic Books, 1977. Reprinted with permission.

SAMPLE CASE STUDY

Secretaries in the Corporation

by Rosabeth Kanter

PATRIMONY IN BUREAUCRACY

... Max Weber, in his classic rendering of the character of modern organizational life, considered the universalism, legalistic standards, specialization, and routinization of tasks in the bureaucracy the antithesis of traditional feudal systems ruled by patrimonial lords. As Weber saw it, bureaucracy vested authority in offices rather than in persons and rendered power impersonal, thereby undercutting personal privilege that stood in the way of efficient decisions. But despite Weber's claims, not all relationships in modern organizations have been rationalized, depersonalized, and subjected to universal standards to the same degree. The secretary-boss relationship is the most striking instance of the retention of patrimony within the bureaucracy. Fewer bureaucratic "safeguards" apply here than in any other part of the system. When bosses make demands at their own discretion and arbitrarily choose secretaries on grounds that enhance their own personal status rather than meeting organizational efficiency tests; expect personal service with limits negotiated privately; exact loyalty; and make the secretary a part of their private retinue, moving when they move—then the relationship has elements of patrimony....

[In Indsco,] secretaries were bound to bosses in ways that were largely unregulated by rules of the larger system and that made the relationship a highly personalized one.

There were three important aspects of the social organization of the relationship: status contingency (the fact that secretaries, primarily, and

SAMPLE CASE STUDY, CONT.

bosses, secondarily, derived status in relation to the other); principled arbitrariness (the absence of limits on managerial discretion); and fealty (the demands of personal loyalty, generating a nonutilitarian aura around communication and rewards).

STATUS CONTINGENCY

Reflected status was part of the primary definition of the secretarial position. Secretaries derived their formal card and level of reward not from the skills they utilized and the tasks they performed but from the formal rank of their bosses. A promotion for secretaries meant that they had acquired a higher status boss, not that their own work was more skilled or valuable. Most often, above the early grades, secretaries were not actually promoted at all on their own; they just remained with a boss who himself received a promotion. It was common practice at Indsco for secretaries to move with their bosses within the same geographic area, as though they were part of the private retinue of a patrimonial dignitary....

There were small ways in which greater responsibility revolved around secretaries in the upper grades; a few administrative duties, the fact that mistakes might have larger ramifications. But for the most part, life got easier as the bosses' status rose. Secretaries could stop worrying about improving their own skills and work on their relationship with the boss. They could orient their work life around their connection with this one person. Some executive secretaries acquired their own crops of typists to do routine work, devoting their time to the social and interpersonal aspects of their jobs. They acquired more privileges and perquisites through their bosses: freedom to come and go, to set their own hours; office status symbols such as drapes, outside offices with windows special ashtrays, and steel file trays. They got gifts that no one else did. If there was a cocktail party for people who worked on a project, for example, the top secretary was invited, not the lower level nonexempts who actually worked directly on the tasks.

Even more important was the fact that the boss's status determined the power of the secretary. Even on the lowest levels, secretaries had some influence through their bosses, mostly in terms of people: the secretaries' assessment of other people in the office or their evaluation of new candi-

SAMPLE CASE STUDY, CONT.

dates for clerical jobs. Higher up, secretaries' power derived from control of bosses' calendars. They could make it easy or difficult to see a top executive. They could affect what managers read first, setting priorities for them without their knowing it. They could help or hurt someone's career by the ease with which they allowed that person access.

If the secretary reflected the status of the boss, she also contributed in minor ways to his status.

Some people have argued that secretaries function as "status symbols" for executives, holding that the traditional secretarial role is developed and preserved because of its impact on managerial egos, not its contribution to organizational efficiency....

Derived status between secretaries and bosses spilled over in informal as well as formal ways. The parties became fused in the awareness of other organization members. Secretaries become identified with bosses in a number of personal and informal ways. Secretaries could get respect from their peers because of feelings about their bosses, but they could also be disliked and avoided if their bosses were disliked. "There are problems for secretaries if they become trapped in their manager's fights," a secretary said. "They are usually the ones who are caught, and they have few resources with which to defend themselves." There were also "shadow hierarchies" at Indsco, in which secretaries to higher level executives received deference at informal social events from the secretaries of lower level staff and [were] more likely to assume leadership of employee events. At the same time, a socially skillful secretary could help smooth over some relationships for difficult bosses.

Despite the fact that bosses could derive some informal status from characteristics of their secretaries, status contingency operated in largely nonreciprocal ways. It was the boss's formal position that gave the secretary formal rank: he, in turn, wanted to choose someone whose personal attributes made her suitable for the status he would be conferring. As in the patrimonial official's private ownership of his servants, the secretary was seen by the boss as "my girl." This attitude was made clear to a personnel administrator who was finding secretaries for two vice presidents under the new, centralized system. She located two candidates and sent them both to see both men, who called her in anger when they discovered

SAMPLE CASE STUDY, CONT.

this: "You mean the women are making the choice?" One of the executives made an offer to a candidate, only to find that she still wanted to see the other manager. He told the administrator, "If she looks at the other job, I don't want her." (The secretary made her own angry retort, and took the second job.)

The secretaries' position in the organization, then—their reward level, privileges, prospects for advancement, and even treatment by others—was contingent upon relationships to particular bosses, much more than on the formal tasks associated with the job itself.

PRINCIPLED ARBITRARINESS

The second patrimonial feature of secretarial role relations was the absence of limits on managerial discretion, except those limits dictated by custom or by abstract principles of fair treatment. Within the general constraints of Indsco tradition and the practice of other managers, bosses had enormous personal latitude around secretaries. The absence of job descriptions, before the new personnel administration began to generate them, meant that there was no way to insure some uniformity of demands across jobs with the same general outlines. There was no way for personnel staff to help match secretaries' skills to the job, or to compare positions so as to determine whether and how a secretary could be moved. Thus, it was left to bosses to determine what secretaries did, how they spent their time, and whether they were to be given opportunities for movement. There was no such thing as career reviews for secretaries, or for nonexempt personnel in general. A secretary's fortunes, especially in finding other work in the corporation, were in the hands of the boss. Bosses received notices of job openings for nonexempts in envelopes marked "private and confidential," and it was their choice whether or not to share this information with their secretaries. Only a rare and lucky secretary, like one who was finally promoted into an exempt job, had a boss who would help her find another job because he had reached his level and she would go no further if she stayed with him.

Furthermore, until the advent of the centralized nonexempt administration, bosses prepared their own salary-budgets for the nonexempts reporting to them. This made the reward system seem to secretaries even more arbitrary than it actually was, increasing their sense of dependence on the whim of the manager. Central guides were invisible, and secretaries tended to feel that their salary was based on whether or not they were liked or what department they happened to be in. There were also no written company policies around personal days and vacations days, so bosses had the power to make decisions about the category into which time off fell, being thus able to punish or reward a secretary.

Managerial discretion in job demands combined with another feature of secretarial work to contribute to the sense of personal dependence on arbitrary authority. It was a job with low routinization in terms of time planning, characterized instead by a constant flow of orders. Unlike other parts of the bureaucracy, where the direct exercise of authority and the making of demands could be minimized through understood routines and schedules of expectations, secretarial work might involve only the general skeleton of a routine, onto which was grafted a continual set of specific requests and specific instructions. The boss did not merely set things in motion; he might make demands on the half hour. Even if boss and secretary developed a set of routines that reduced the number of direct face-to-face demands (e.g., he put work to be typed in an in-box; she knew to bring coffee in at 10:15), continual demands and new orders could not be eliminated entirely. Indeed, the secretarial position was often there in the first place to provide a person capable of responding to momentary demands and immediate requests generated on the spot.

Arbitrariness was embedded in the personal services expected of secretaries. The list of items included in the secretaries' own description of their duties on the first wave of performance appraisal forms for a hundred Indsco secretaries made clear how much variation there was in a secretary's understanding of her official responsibilities from boss to boss, even in the same nominal job at the same level. Some secretaries included personal services in the core definition of their job, giving them equal importance with the communication functions (like typing and telephones) for which Indsco had hired them. One secretary included among her major responsibilities: "office household duties; watering plants, cleaning cups, sharpening pencils, straightening desks, etc." (A personnel administrator

SAMPLE CASE STUDY, CONT.

commented about such items, "Does she think that's what the company is paying her for?") And despite media publicity for the controversy over whether or not secretaries should make and serve coffee, Indsco secretaries still performed this service, especially for visitors to their bosses' offices.

Resentment over personal work was the biggest single issue raised by secretaries when Industrial Supply brought an experimental group of them together with their bosses for "expectation exchanges." The secretaries felt that the official definition of their jobs was fuzzy enough that they were concerned about refusing to do personal things for their bosses even when they would have preferred not to. Demands were limited only by customary practice, the boss's conscience, or the secretary's negotiating skills or ability to embarrass her boss enough that he would stop asking for personal favors.

The secretarial job thus rested on a personal set of procedures and understandings carved out by secretary and boss. As we have seen, the corporation provided only the merest skeleton for the relationship; its substance depended on the unique qualities and agreements of the two people involved. Unlike other bureaucratic relations which certainly included some component of special understanding generated by the unique personalities of those who interact, the secretary-boss relation was defined largely by the special relationship developed by two particular individuals. Secretaries and bosses created unique relationships that did not remain, that were not necessarily institutionalized as part of the built in structure of that secretarial job. When either of the parties left, the job reverted to its skeletal outline, again to be remade....

Another aspect of principled arbitrariness in the relationship of bosses to secretaries was the use of particularistic criteria (or evaluation). Because of the absence of job descriptions, performance standards, or rationalized mechanisms for determining rewards, bosses were relatively free to determine their own standards for judging the performance of their secretaries. The first batch of forms from the pilot project to develop performance appraisals for nonexempts indicated that managers used a variety of standards for determining a clerical subordinate's worth, and such standards often depended on the unique values and preferences of the

SAMPLE CASE STUDY, CONT.

bosses themselves. As we shall see, managers often rated secretaries in terms of the quality of their relationship rather than in terms of skills that could benefit the corporation at large....

FEALTY

Fealty became the third feature of the ideal boss-secretary relationship, from the boss's perspective, making the relation a highly personal rather than a purely instrumental one. Secretaries were rewarded for loyalty and devotion to their bosses. They were expected to value nonutilitarian, symbolic rewards—which did not include individual career advancement—and to take on the emotional tasks of the relationship. Secretaries were rewarded for their attitudes rather than for their skills, for their loyalty rather than their talent. Given the low skill required by the actual tasks they were given to do, and the replaceability of personnel with basic secretarial skills, secretaries found it to their advantage to accept fealty as their route to recognition and reward.

Expectations of loyalty were bound up with the sense on the part of bosses that they were making secretaries part of their personal estate. This was behind the outrage experienced by some executives at the thought that secretaries might shop around for a job rather than wait to be chosen by a particular manager. It was also involved in the wishful statement made by some managers to a central personnel administrator that "my secretary wouldn't want another job." (The staff official indicated that she knew that many of their secretaries were indeed actively looking for other opportunities.) Members of an Indsco task force on upward mobility for clerical workers considered a major barrier to change the fact that "some men felt the secretaries worked for them personally, not for the corporation." They found managers reluctant to suggest competent secretaries for other positions; instead, bosses wanted to claim ownership and, in turn, demand loyalty. One case was presented to a new nonexempt personnel manager in which a male boss was trying to increase a secretary's salary above the pay ceiling that had just been established for that grade, limiting the discretion of bosses to pay whatever they chose. The manager pointed out the difficulties: "He wants more for her, he wants her paid for

SAMPLE CASE STUDY, CONT.

potential—she has an M.A. But she can't get paid [more] just because one person thinks she's deserving. She has to do more or move on. But the man and the secretary say they don't want to be separated." In these instances, fealty served to create a close bond, but one that worked for bosses and secretaries in different ways, in that a "loyalty oath" to a particular boss could hold back only the secretary's career, not the boss's....

In return for the secretary's devotion and emotional support, the boss may take on the traditional patrimonial ruler's attitude of caretaking toward his underlings. An Indsco manager told a group of managers, who were discussing the position of women in the company, how his feelings of responsibility changed when he acquired a secretary of his own, after years of sharing secretarial services with other bosses: "In the old job I shared a secretary with up to six people, and I didn't feel very personally responsible. Now I have this personal feeling that I am responsible for the care and feeding of that person—my secretary—the nurturing of her emotions, giving her a shoulder to cry on. I'm the one who remembers her anniversary. I'm the one constantly checking on her sensitivities, treating her emotions, stopping to notice that, hey, she's not having a good day. I have to make sure she's feeling all right." Note the certainty of this man that what his secretary wanted existed primarily in the emotional realm.

In a relationship of fealty, then, secretaries were expected to be bound by ties of personal loyalty, to value nonutilitarian rewards, and to be available as an emotional partner. The image of what secretaries wanted—and, by extension, working women—was shaped by these expectations....

CHAPTER 12

SOCIOLOGICAL SURVEY PAPERS

12.1 SCOPE AND PURPOSE OF A SOCIOLOGICAL SURVEY PAPER

A survey is simply a device for identifying and counting events, actions, perceptions, attitudes, or beliefs. Sociological surveys are the barometers of society. They describe a society's quality of life and the characteristics of its culture. They tell us who we are. There is little doubt that the skillful use of surveys dramatically increases the accuracy of our perceptions of ourselves.

As a student of sociology, you will find that writing your own sociological survey paper will serve two purposes. First, in learning how to construct, conduct, and interpret a sociological survey, you will add to your understanding of society and of one of the most basic processes of sociological research. By writing this paper you will gain a skill—if only at the introductory level—that you may actually use in your professional life. Public and private organizations often conduct surveys on attitudes and preferences in order to make their services more effective and desirable. Second, you will learn how to evaluate critically surveys that are published in periodicals. Knowing the strengths and weaknesses of the surveying process will help you to obtain some of the fundamental knowledge necessary for you to appraise the validity of surveys you read about in journals, magazines, and newspapers.

This chapter explains how to construct and conduct a simple sociological survey and how to apply to your survey results some elementary data analysis and evaluation techniques. Your instructor may want to add supplemental tasks, such as other statistical procedures, and your class text in sociology methods will explain much more about the process of sociological research. The following set of directions, however, will provide a general framework that will help you to create and interpret a sociological survey.

12.2 STEPS FOR WRITING A SOCIOLOGICAL SURVEY PAPER

12.2.1 FOCUS ON A SPECIFIC TOPIC

The first step in writing a sociological survey paper is to select a topic that is focused on one specific issue. While nationally conducted surveys sometimes cover a broad variety of topics, confining your inquiry to one narrowly focused issue will allow you to gain an appreciation for even a single topic's complexity and for the difficulties inherent in clearly identifying opinions. Precision is vital to the success of a sociological survey.

Topics for sociological papers are nearly as numerous as the titles of articles in a daily newspaper. Sociological surveys are conducted on topics pertaining to local, state, national, or international politics. You will usually increase the interest of the audience of your paper if you select an issue that is being widely discussed in the news. Many issues of health and safety are publicized on a regular basis. General topic headings found almost daily in the news include the following:

- drugs
- crime
- education
- abortion
- family life

12.2.2 FORMULATE A RESEARCH QUESTION, A HYPOTHESIS

After you have selected a topic, your task is to determine what you would like to investigate about that topic. One student who was interested in family relationships, for example, wanted to try to identify the factors that contribute to and detract from marital satisfaction. The first thing you need to understand when conducting survey research is that you must phrase your questions carefully. If you simply ask "What do you think makes for a happy marriage?" you will probably receive obvious replies from a substantial majority of your respondents, replies that may not have much to do with actual marital satisfaction. To find out what really makes for good marriages, you will need to design more specific questions. The following sections of this chapter will help you to do this.

However, to create these specific questions, you will first need to formulate a research question and a research hypothesis. Before continuing from this point, read the section in Chapter 8 entitled "Formulating and Testing Research Hypotheses."

A research question asks exactly what the researcher wants to know. Here are some examples of research questions posed by national surveys:

- What factors contribute to family stability?
- What social conditions contribute to violence?

- What are the social issues about which Americans are most concerned?

Research questions for papers for sociology classes, however, should be more specific and confined to a narrowly defined topic. Consider the following:

- What is the relationship, if any, between ethnicity and philanthropy?
- To what extent do the people surveyed believe that their own personal actions, such as working hard toward a goal, will actually make a difference in their lives?
- What is the relationship, if any, between sexual orientation and choice of vocation?

12.2.3   SELECT YOUR SAMPLE

Researchers usually conduct sociological surveys to find out how large groups of people—such as Americans in general, African Americans, women, or welfare recipients—behave in certain situations. It is normally unnecessary and too costly to obtain data on every member of the group under consideration, so most surveys question a small but representative percentage of the total group that is being studied. The individual units studied in a sociological survey are usually called *elements*. An element might be a group—an ethnic group, a social organization, a church denomination—but it is most often an individual. The population is the total number of elements covered by the research question. If the research question is "Are left-handed fifth-grade boys more likely to identify with sports heroes than right-handed fifth-grade boys?" then the population is all fifth-grade boys in the United States. The sampling frame consists of all fifth-grade boys that attend the school in which your survey will take place. The sample is the part of the population that is selected to respond to the survey. A representative sample includes numbers of elements in the same proportions as they occur in the general population. In other words, if 81 percent of the population of fifth-grade boys in America are right-handed and 19 percent left-handed, then 81 percent of a representative sample of fifth-grade boys will also be right-handed, and 19 percent will be left-handed. Conversely, nonrepresentative samples do not include numbers of elements in the same proportions as they occur in the general population.

How large must a sample be to accurately represent the population? This question is difficult to answer, but two general principles apply. The first is that a large sample is more likely, simply by chance, to be more representative of a population than a small sample. The second is that the goal of a representative sample is to include within it representatives of all of the strata that are included in the whole population.

SAMPLE SURVEY RESEARCH DESIGN

Research Question: Are left-handed fifth-grade boys more likely to identify with sports heroes than right-handed fifth-grade boys?

Research Hypothesis: Left-handed fifth-grade boys are more likely to identify with sports heroes than right-handed fifth-grade boys.

Elements: individual fifth-grade boys

Population: American fifth-grade boys

Sampling Frame: fifth-grade boys at Hoover Elementary School

Sample: 84 students in Mr. Wimbly's and Mrs. Baker's classes, out of the total population of 420 fifth-grade boys at Hoover Elementary School

For example, suppose that you find a bolt of cloth at the store. You want to make curtains for your room, but you are unsure your roommate will like the cloth you have selected. You decide to buy a sample of the bolt to take to your roommate for approval. Not having much money to spend on the curtains, you would like to buy as small a piece of cloth as possible that will still reveal the cloth's entire pattern. In this example, all the bolts of cloth of the design you have chosen make up the population; the sampling frame is the particular bolt of cloth you have found at the store; and the sample is the piece of cloth that you cut from the bolt to take back to your roommate.

Sample B   Sample A

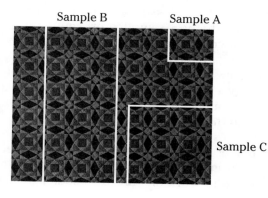

Sample C

Assume that the cloth you have selected has the pattern pictured on page 209. Notice that the diagram indicates three possible samples of the bolt of cloth. Sample A is not representative because it does not contain all of the types of objects (called *strata*) included in the pattern. Sample B is representative, but is unnecessarily large. Sample C is representative and of adequate size.

Let us consider the case of a student who has designed a research survey to determine the degree of marital satisfaction experienced by students at her college. The target population for the survey is the married students enrolled at the college. The next question becomes: How can our student researcher get a representative sample—meaning one in which the percentages of student marital satisfaction are the same as the percentages in the much larger target population? Generalizing from a sample to a population contains some error. The objective is to draw the most representative sample—one with the lowest error—from the population. A random sample has the lowest chance of error because every element in it has an equal opportunity of being selected. However, circumstances often do not allow the researcher to use this sampling technique.

Sometimes the researcher is able to control error from certain variables by stratifying the sample, or subdividing it into different layers based on prior knowledge of how these variables are distributed in the population. For example, before sampling a university population, if we know that 58 percent of the student body is female, 13 percent are minorities, the average age is 28, and 54 percent of the students attend all or part of their program at night, we can stratify the sample according to these variables before making random selections. Again, like the purely random sample, obtaining a stratified sample is very difficult—if not impossible—when the population in question is college students.

Faced with such problems, the most reasonable and economical question becomes: Can the survey be filled out in select classes that represent the student body? For example, would sampling classes that are diversified by age, sex, ethnic background, major field, and so on, lower the error enough to allow the researcher to feel comfortable generalizing to the target population as a whole? Our answer depends to some extent on the degree to which the makeup of the classes parallels the stratification of the university. While this is often the best sampling procedure available in such a complex environment as a college, the problem with the method lies in our inability to gauge the amount of error. When we read about a plus or minus 3 percent or 4 percent error in samples that have been taken for opinion polls and other scientific endeavors, it is important to understand that the researchers have applied controlled procedures to judge the error involved in generalizing to the population being sampled. So while we may have given careful thought to selecting classes that are stratified much like the student body of the university, the absence of random selection prevents us from accurately measuring the error involved in generalizing to the population.

As you begin to work on your own sociological survey, you will find it most convenient to select as your sample the class in which you are writing your paper. The disadvantage of this sample selection is that your class may not be representative of your college or university. Even if this is the case, however, using the class will enable you to learn the procedures for conducting a survey, which is the primary objective of this exercise.

Research with Human Subjects   Sociological surveys often ask people for personal information. The people whose responses are sought are then known as human subjects of the research. Most colleges and universities have policies concerning research with human subjects. Sometimes administrative offices, known as institutional review boards, are established to review proposals for research to ensure that the rights of human subjects are protected. It may be necessary for you to obtain permission from your institutional review board or college to conduct your survey. Be sure to comply with all policies of your college and university with respect to research with human subjects.

12.2.4   CONSTRUCT THE SURVEY QUESTIONNAIRE

Your research question is your primary guide for constructing survey questions. As you begin to write your questions, ask yourself what it is that you really want to know about the topic. Suppose that your research question is: "What are the views of sociology students regarding the role of the government in regulating abortions?" If you ask as one of your survey questions, "Are you for abortion?" you may get a "no" answer from 70 percent of the respondents. If you then ask, "Are you for making abortion illegal?" you may get the answer "no" from 81 percent of your respondents. These answers seem to contradict each other. By asking additional questions, you may determine that, although a majority of the respondents finds abortion is regrettable, only a minority wants to make it illegal.

But even this may not be enough information to get a clear picture of people's opinions. The portion of the population that wants to make abortion illegal may be greater or smaller according to the strength of the legal penalty to be applied for having an abortion. In addition, some of the students who want no legal penalty for having an abortion may want strict medical requirements imposed on abortion clinics, and others may not. You will need to design additional specific questions to accurately determine respondents' views on these issues.

You must consider carefully the number of questions to include in your questionnaire. The first general rule, as previously mentioned, is to ask a sufficient number of questions to find out precisely what it is you want to know. A second principle, however, conflicts with this first rule. This second principle—which may not be a problem in your sociology class—is that people generally do not like to fill out surveys. Short surveys with a small number of questions are more likely to be answered completely than long questionnaires. The questionnaire for your paper in survey research methods should normally contain between ten and twenty-five questions.

Surveys consist of two types of questions—closed and open. Closed questions restrict the response of the respondent to a specific set of answers, normally two to six. Multiple-choice examination questions are typical closed questions. Open questions do not restrict respondents to pre-selected answers, but allow them to answer in any manner they choose. Therefore, open questions call for a more active and thoughtful response than do closed questions. The increased time and effort may be a disadvantage, though, because in general the more time and effort a survey demands, the fewer responses it is likely to get. However, open questions have the advantage of providing an opportunity for unusual views to be expressed. For example, you might get the following response to the question "What should be done about gun control?"

> All firearms should be restricted to law enforcement agencies in populated areas. Special privately owned depositories should be established for hunters to be able to store rifles in hunting areas, where they can be used for target practice or outdoors during hunting season.

Open questions are preferable to closed questions when you want to expand a range of possible answers to find out how much diversity there is among opinions on an issue. For practice working with open questions, you should include at least one in your survey questionnaire.

Perhaps the greatest difficulty with open questions is quantifying the results. The researcher must examine each answer and then group responses according to their content. For example, it might be possible to differentiate responses that are clearly in favor, clearly opposed, and ambivalent to gun control. Open questions are of particular value to researchers who are doing continuing research; the responses they obtain help them to create better questions for the next survey they conduct.

In addition to the regular open and closed questions on your survey questionnaire, you will want to add what are often called *identifiers*—questions that ask for personal information about the respondents. If you ask questions about gun control, for example, you may want to know if men respond differently from women, if Caucasians respond differently from African Americans, or if young people respond differently from older people. Identifier questions concern such things as the respondent's gender, age, political party, religion, income level, or other items that may be relevant to the particular survey topic.

The student who was investigating marital satisfaction designed the questionnaire on page 213.

After you have written the survey questionnaire, you need to conduct the survey. You will need to distribute it to the class or other group of respondents. Be sure to provide on the survey form clear directions for filling it out. If the students are to fill out the survey in class, read the directions out loud to the class and ask if there are any questions before the students begin.

SAMPLE QUESTIONNAIRE

The following statements are concerned with your feelings about your marriage. Please put the number to the left of each question that indicates the degree to which your marriage possesses each of the following qualities. The number 1 represents the least degree and 5 represents the greatest degree.

Least Degree   1   2   3   4   5   Greatest Degree

___1.   Spend time doing things together.

___2.   Are very committed to each other.

___3.   Have good communication (talking, sharing feelings).

___4.   Deal with crises in a positive manner.

___5.   Express appreciation to each other.

___6.   Have a very close relationship.

___7.   Have a very happy relationship.

___8.   My spouse makes me feel good about myself.

___9.   I make my spouse feel good about himself or herself.

___10.   If I could, I would marry my current spouse again?

Please give the following information:

AGE: _____   SEX: ____male   ____female

Number of years married to current spouse? _____

Number of children? _____

Have you ever had an extramarital affair?

____yes   ____no

THANKS FOR YOUR HELP!

Source: Modified from Stinnett and DeFrain (1985)

12.2.5   TABULATE DATA

If your sample is only the size of a small sociology class, you will be able to tabulate the answers directly from the survey form. If you have a larger sample, however, you may want to use data collection forms such as those available from the Scantron Corporation. You may already be using Scantron forms when you take multiple choice tests in some of your classes now. On Scantron forms—which are separate from your survey form—respondents use a number 2 pencil to mark multiple-choice answers. The advantage of Scantron forms is that they are processed through computers that tabulate the results and sometimes provide statistical measurements. If you use Scantron sheets, you will need access to computers that process the results, and you may need someone to program the computer to provide the specific statistical measurements that you need.

12.2.6 ANALYZE DATA

After you have collected the completed survey forms, you will need to analyze the data that the forms provide. There are many statistical procedures especially designed to carry out three categories of tasks:

1. describing the data
2. comparing components of the data
3. evaluating the data

This chapter provides only a few examples of statistical methods that may be used in each category. Consult your instructor or a survey research methods textbook to learn about other types of statistical measurement tools.

12.3 Statistics

Statistics designed to describe data may be very simple or very complex. In this chapter we shall explain some simple statistical techniques. You will learn more advanced statistical techniques in your research methods or statistics classes. We will start our discussion with two examples of closed questions from the marital satisfaction survey described previously. Even though they appear in declarative form, we call the entries on a questionnaire "questions" because they require an answer.

> Question 1: Spend time doing things together.
>   Least   Less   Average   More   Greatest
> Question 6: Closeness of your relationship with your spouse.
>   Least   Less   Average   More   Greatest

Our objective in describing the data is to see how our respondent sample, as a group, answered these questions. The first step is to assign a numerical value to each answer, as follows:

Answer	Points
Least	1
Less	2
Average	3
More	4
Greatest	5

Our next step is to count our survey totals to see how many respondents marked each answer to each question. The following results are from a hypothetical sample of 42 students:

Answer	Points	Q1 Responses	Q6 Responses
Least	1	8	13
Less	2	15	10
Average	3	12	6
More	4	4	12
Greatest	5	2	1

We see in the chart, for example, that 8 people responded "Least" to question 1, and 12 people responded "More" to question 6. We may now calculate the mean (numerical average) responses by performing the following operations for each question.

1. Multiply the point value by the number of responses to determine the number of value points.
2. Add the total value points for each answer.
3. Divide the total value points by the number of respondents (42 in this case).

To see how this procedure is done, examine the table at the top of page 216. Notice the following:

- Column 1 contains the choices provided to the respondents (for Question 1).
- Column 2 contains the point value assigned to each choice.
- Column 3 contains the number of people in our sample who selected each answer.
- Column 4 contains, for each answer choice, the value points assigned, multiplied by the number of responses.

ANSWER	POINTS (VALUE ASSIGNED)	Q1 RESPONSES (FREQUENCY)	Q1 "VALUE POINTS" (Q1 VALUES X FREQUENCY)
LEAST	1	8	8
LESS	2	15	30
AVERAGE	3	12	36
MORE	4	5	20
GREATEST	5	2	10
TOTAL		42	104
MEAN			**2.48**

We can see that there are 42 total responses and 104 total value points. Dividing the number of value points (104) by the total number of responses (42), we get a mean of 2.48.

If we conduct the same operation for our hypothetical responses to Question 6 in our survey, we get the results shown in the table below.

ANSWER	POINTS (VALUE ASSIGNED)	Q6 RESPONSES (FREQUENCY)	Q6 VALUE POINTS (Q6 POINTS X FREQUENCY)
LEAST	1	13	13
LESS	2	10	20
AVERAGE	3	1	3
MORE	4	12	48
GREATEST	5	6	30
TOTAL		42	114
MEAN			**2.71**

We see from the table above that the mean of the responses for Question 6 is 2.71. Comparing the means of the two questions, we find that the mean for Question 1 (2.48) is lower than the mean for Question 6. Since the lowest value (1 point) is assigned for a response of "Least," and the highest value (5 points) is assigned for a response of "Greatest," we know that a high mean score indicates that the sample surveyed indicates that their marriages have the characteristic stated in the survey question. It is possible to conclude, therefore, that spending time doing things together is more likely to be a part of the respondents' marital experience than is closeness of the relationship with the spouse. Comparing the mean values in this fashion allows us to easily compare the results of different questions among the people surveyed.

Another frequently used statistical measure is the standard deviation, which provides a single number indicating how dispersed the responses to the question are. In other words, it indicates the extent to which the answers are grouped together in the middle ("Less," "Average," "More") or are dispersed to the extreme answers ("Least," "Greatest"). To calculate the standard deviation (S) for our example Question 1, we will follow these steps:

1. Assign a value to each response (Least = 1, Less = 2, etc.).
2. Find the mean for the question (in Question 1, the mean is 2.48).
3. Find the difference between each value and the mean.
4. Square the differences.
5. Multiply the squared differences by the frequency of each value.
6. Sum the values in step 5.
7. Divide the values in step 6 by the number of respondents.
8. Find the square root of the value in step 7.

The broadside table on page 218 shows our calculation of the standard deviation of Question 1.

The standard deviation of Question 1 is 1.26. To understand the significance of this standard deviation, we need to know that sociological samples usually correspond to what is known as a normal distribution. In a normal distribution, 68.26 percent of the responses will fall between (1) the mean minus one standard deviation (2.48 minus 1.26, or 1.22 in Question 1), and (2) the mean plus one standard deviation (2.48 plus 1.26, or 3.74 in Question 1). In other words, in a normal distribution, about two-thirds of the respondents to Question 1 will express an opinion that is between 1.22 and 3.74. Another one-third of the respondents will score less than 1.22 or more than 3.74. Remember that our assigned values for question 1 are the following:

Least	1
Less	2
Average	3
More	4
Greatest	5

For convenience, let's call the responses "Least" and "Greatest" extreme responses, and designate "Less," "Average," "and More" as moderate responses. A score of 1.22 is closest to "Less" but inclines to our first extreme, "Least." A score of 3.74 is closest to "More" but inclines to "Average." We may conclude that on the topic of Question 1 (closeness of your relationship with your spouse) that a substantial portion of the respondents (about one-third) tend to give extreme answers. We may also notice that the score 1.22, which indicates strong agreement, is closer to its absolute extreme (1.22 is only .22 away from its absolute extreme of 1.0) than is the score 3.74 (which is 1.26 points from its absolute extreme of 5). This means that the responses are

STEP 1	STEP 2	STEP 3	STEP 4	STEP 5	STEP 6	STEP 7	STEP 8
VALUE AND FREQUENCY	FIND THE MEAN	SUBTRACT THE VALUE FROM THE MEAN	SQUARE THE RESULTS OF STEP 3	RESULTS OF STEP 4 TIMES THE FREQUENCY	SUM OF VALUES OF STEP 5	STEP 6 DIVIDED BY THE NUMBER OF RESPONDENTS (42)	SQUARE ROOT OF STEP 7
LEAST VALUE = 1 FREQUENCY = 8	2.48	-1.48	2.19	17.52	17.52		
LESS VALUE = 2 FREQUENCY = 15	2.48	-.48	.23	3.45	3.45		
AVERAGE VALUE = 3 FREQUENCY = 12	2.48	.52	.27	3.24	3.24		
MORE VALUE = 4 FREQUENCY = 5	2.48	1.52	2.31	11.55	11.55		
GREATEST VALUE = 5 FREQUENCY = 2	2.48	2.52	6.35	31.75	31.75		
					67.51	1.607	1.26
THE STANDARD DEVIATION							

slightly more tightly packed towards the extreme of strong agreement. We can now see more completely the degree of extremism in the population of respondents to this question. Standard deviations become more helpful as the number of the questions in a survey increases, because they allow us to compare quickly and easily the extent of extremism in answers to different questions.

In addition to the standard deviation, there are other measures of dispersion that you will find in your statistical methods textbooks. More complex statistics will enable you to draw more conclusions from your data. Many of these statistics are easily computed with the aid of common computer programs. Ask your instructor for advice about which statistical methods to use and which statistical software package to choose. Each software package will provide its own directions for entering data and determining results.*

12.4   THE ELEMENTS OF A SOCIOLOGICAL SURVEY PAPER

A sociological survey paper is composed of five essential parts:

1. title page
2. abstract
3. text
4. references page
5. appendices

12.4.1   TITLE PAGE

The title page should follow the directions given in Chapter 3. The title of a sociological survey paper should provide the reader with two types of information: the subject matter of the survey and the population being surveyed. Examples of titles for papers based on in-class surveys are "University of South Carolina Student Opinions on Welfare Reform," or "Middlebury College Student Attitudes About Sexual Harassment," or "The 1994 Gubernatorial Election and the Student Vote."

12.4.2   ABSTRACT

Abstracts for a sociological survey paper should follow the directions given in Chapter 3. In approximately 100 words, the abstract should summarize the subject, methodology, and results of the survey. An abstract for the example used in this chapter might be like the sample abstract on page 220.

---

*Students and instructors should note that the applications of the mean and standard deviation suggested in this chapter are controversial because they are applied to ordinal data. In practice, however, such applications are common.

SAMPLE ABSTRACT

Abstract

A survey was taken at Malibu Beach College to determine the extent to which married students and their spouses spend time doing things together, experience commitment to each other, have good communication (talking, sharing feelings), deal with crises in a positive manner, express appreciation to each other, and feel closeness with each other. The results indicated that 64 percent of the respondents expressed substantial marital satisfaction, and supported a strong correlation between spending time together and feeling committed to the relationship.

12.4.3   TEXT

The text of the paper should include five sections:

1. introduction
2. literature review
3. methodology
4. results
5. discussion

Introduction   The introduction should explain the purpose of your paper, define the research question hypothesis, and describe the circumstances under which the research was undertaken. Your purpose statement will normally be a paragraph in which you explain your reasons for conducting your research. You may want to say something like the sample introduction below.

Next, the introduction should state the research question and the research hypotheses. The research question might be "Is student knowledge of federal student aid related to student attitudes about the effectiveness of the aid programs?" A hypothesis might be "Student ratings of the effectiveness of federal student aid programs is positively correlated with student knowledge of the programs."

SAMPLE INTRODUCTION

The purpose of this paper is to define Howard University student attitudes toward federal student aid programs. In particular, this study seeks to understand how students view the criteria for aid eligibility and the efficiency of application procedures. Further, the survey is expected to indicate the amount of knowledge students have about the federal student aid process. The primary reason for conducting this study is that the results will provide a basis for identifying problems in the aid application and disbursement process, and facilitate discussion among administrative officers and students about solutions to problems that are identified.

Literature Review   The purpose of a literature review is to demonstrate that the person conducting the study is familiar with the professional literature that is relevant to the survey and to summarize the content of that literature for the reader. The literature review for your sociological survey paper should address two types of information: the survey's subject matter and methodology.

For example, the subject matter of the survey may be gender discrimination in secondary education programs. In this case, the purpose of the subject matter section of your literature review would be to briefly inform your readers about (1) the history, content, and social implications of gender differences in secondary educational programs, and (2) the current status of discriminatory practices. In providing this information you will cite appropriate documents, such as previous studies on the subject.

The purpose of the methodology section of your literature review will be to cite the literature that supports the methodology of your study. If you follow the directions in this manual or your course textbook to write this paper, briefly state the procedures and statistical calculations you use in the study and the source of your information (this manual or your text) about these procedures.

Methodology   The methodology section of your paper describes how you conducted your study. It should first briefly describe the format and content of the questionnaire. How many questions were asked? What kinds of questions (open, closed, etc.) were asked, and why were these formats selected? The methodology section should also briefly address the statistical procedures used in data analysis. What statistical methods are used? Why were they selected? What information are they intended to provide?

Results   The results section of your paper should list the findings of your study. Here you report the results of your statistical calculations. You may want to construct a table that summarizes the numbers of responses to each question on the questionnaire. Next, using your statistical results, answer your research question—that is, tell your reader if your research question was answered by your results, and, if so, what the answers are.

Discussion   In your discussion section, draw out the implications of your findings. What is the meaning of the results of your study? What conclusions can you draw? What questions remain unanswered? At the end of this section, provide the reader with suggestions for further research that are derived from your research findings.

References Page   Your references page and source citations in the text should be completed according to the guidelines in Chapter 4.

Appendices   See Chapter 3 of this manual for further guidelines on including appendices at the end of your text. Appendices for a sociological survey paper should include:

- a copy of the questionnaire used in the study.
- tables of survey data not sufficiently important to be included in the text but helpful for reference.
- summaries of survey data from national surveys on the same subject, if such surveys are available and discussed in your text.

GLOSSARY

achieved status A social position within a stratification system that a person assumes voluntarily and that reflects a significant measure of personal ability and choice—for example, educational attainment.

ageism Prejudice and discrimination against the elderly.

age-sex pyramid A graphic representation of the age and sex of a population.

alienation The experience of powerlessness in social life in which the individual feels disassociated from the surrounding society.

animism The belief that natural objects—such as winds, clouds, rocks and the like—are conscious forms of life that affect humanity.

anomie A state of normlessness in which social control of individual behavior has become ineffective and society provides little moral guidance to individuals.

ascribed status A social position a person inherits at birth or assumes involuntarily later in life on the basis of characteristics over which he or she has no control.

assimilation The process by which minorities gradually take on the values of the dominant culture.

authoritarianism A political system that denies popular participation in government, or a personality syndrome that finds comfort in such structure.

authoritarian personality A personality pattern believed by social psychologists to be associated with a psychological need to be prejudiced.

authority Power people perceive to be legitimate rather than coercive.

autosystem A system or institution whose major purpose is the perpetuation of itself.

beliefs Specific statements that people hold to be true; a community held set of convictions related to a supernatural order.

blue-collar occupation Lower prestige work that involves mostly manual labor, including production, maintenance, and service workers.

bureaucracy Formal organization designed to perform tasks efficiently by explicit procedural rules.

bureaucratic inertia The tendency of bureaucratic organizations to perpetuate themselves; bureaucracies become *autosystems* that exist to maintain their existence.

bureaucratic ritualism   A preoccupation with rules and regulations to the point of obstructing organizational goals. Associated individuals are said to have "trained incapacity" or bureaucratic personality.

capitalism   An economic system in which natural resources and the means of producing goods and services are in private hands and are used to create more wealth for its owners.

capitalist   One who owns a factory or other productive enterprise and embraces the economic system of capitalism.

case studies   Observational studies of a given *social unit*, such as an individual, organization, neighborhood, community, or culture. *Ethnographic* or *field research* often describes a single unit or case.

caste system   Social stratification based on ascription.

cause and effect   A relationship between two variables in which change in one (the independent variable) causes change in another (the dependent variable).

charisma   Extraordinary personal qualities that can turn members of an audience into followers without the necessity of formal authority.

church   A formal religious organization well integrated into the larger society. A shared place of moral and ethical concerns.

cohabitation   The sharing of a household by an unmarried couple committed to a long-term relationship.

cohort   A category of people with a common characteristic, usually their age—for example, all persons born during the Great Depression (1929–1939).

colonialism   The process by which some nations enrich themselves through political and economic control of other nations.

concept   An abstract idea that represents some aspect of the world, such as descriptive properties or relations, inevitably in a somewhat simplified form.

constant   A characteristic of a sample or population that does not take on different values and is the same from one element to the next. For example, if a sample contained all males, gender would be a constant because it does not vary.

corporation   An organization with a legal existence, including rights and liabilities, apart from those of its members.

correlation   The measured strength of an association between two or more variables.

correlation coefficient   A number whose magnitude shows how strongly two or more variables are correlated, or related to one another. Values range from +1.00 to -1.00, with strength of association increasing as the value approaches either extreme.

counterculture   Cultural patterns that strongly oppose conventional culture. The individual member will usually experience alienation from the values and expectations of the dominant culture.

credentialism   Evaluating people on the basis of their credentials—especially educational degrees.

crime   The violation of a norm formally enacted into criminal law.

crimes against property (property crimes)   Crimes involving theft of property belonging to others.

crimes against the person (violent crimes)   Crimes against people that involve violence or the threat of violence.

criminal justice system   The lawful response to alleged crimes using police, courts, and state-sanctioned punishment.

criminal recidivism   A tendency by people previously convicted of crimes to commit subsequent offenses.

crude birth rate   The number of live births in a given year for every 1,000 people in a population.

crude death rate   The number of deaths in a given year for every 1,000 people in a population.

cult   A religious organization that is substantially outside the cultural traditions of a society.

cultural lag   The observation that some cultural elements (material culture/technology) change more quickly than others (values and norms), with potentially disruptive consequences.

cultural relativism   The practice of evaluating any culture by its own standards.

cultural transmission   The formal and informal learning process by which culture is passed from one generation to the next.

cultural universals   Traits found in every culture.

culture   The beliefs, values, behavior, and material objects shared by a particular people.

culture shock   The individual disorientation accompanying sudden exposure to an unfamiliar way of life.

democracy   Rule by the people.

democratic socialism   An economic and political system that combines significant government control of the economy with free elections.

demography   The scientific study of human population.

denomination   A religious group, not linked to the state, that claims doctrinal autonomy.

dependent samples   Two random samples whose elements are not mutually exclusive. An example would be when the same subjects are measured on some variable before (pre-) and after (post-) experimental manipulation; the two samples were not independently selected.

dependent variable   The variable that is being affected or influenced by another variable. In a causal analysis, the dependent variable is caused by the independent variable; it is the effect.

descent   The system by which members of a society trace kinship over generations.

descriptive statistics   Statistics (numbers) used only to describe the data—in other words, percentages, charts, graphs, and so on; no hypotheses are tested.

deterrence   The attempt to discourage criminality through fear of punishment.

deviance   The recognized violation of cultural norms.

discrimination   Treating groups of people unfavorably based on categorical, rather than individual, grounds.

distribution   A listing of all the values or outcomes for a particular variable. Often takes the form of a frequency distribution or a percentile distribution.

division of labor   Specialized economic activity separating work into distinct parts.

dramaturgical analysis   The investigation of social interaction in terms of theatrical performance.

dyad   A social group with two members involving the presentation of selves.

ecology   The study of the interaction of living organisms and their natural environment; the spatial distribution of people and activities and the resulting interdependence, as in a community.

economy   The social institution that organizes a society's production, distribution, and consumption of goods and services.

ecosystem   A physical environment composed of the interaction of all living plants and animals in it.

education   The social institution through which society provides its members with important knowledge, including facts, skills, and values.

ego   Freud's designation of a person's conscious attempts to balance the pleasure-seeking drives of the human organism and the demands of society.

element   A single member of a population.

empirical distribution   A list of the different values for a variable and the number of times each value appears in the sample. It is also referred to as a *frequency distribution*.

endogamy   Marriage between people of the same social category.

ethnocentrism   The practice of judging another culture or group by the standards of one's own culture; usually takes the position that one's own culture or group is best.

ethnomethodology   The study of the way people make sense of their everyday surroundings. Sometimes referred to as *ethnography*, it is widely utilized in *case studies*.

euthanasia (mercy killing)   Assisting in the death of a person suffering from an incurable illness.

exogamy   Marriage between people of different social categories.

experiment   A research method that investigates cause-and-effect relationships under very controlled conditions.

extended family (consanguine family)   A social unit including parents, children, and other kin.

faith   Belief anchored in conviction rather than scientific evidence.

family   A set of persons who are related to each other by blood, marriage, or adoption, and who usually live together.

feminism   A social movement that advocates social equality for men and women, in opposition to patriarchy and sexism.

feminization of poverty   The trend by which women represent an increasing proportion of the poor.

fertility   The incidence of childbearing in a society's population.

folkways   Patterns of behavior common in and typical of a group.

formal organization   A large-scale, special-purpose group that is organized to achieve specific goals.

frequency distribution   A distribution of the values of a variable and the number of times each value occurs in the data; sometimes called an *empirical distribution*.

functional illiteracy   Reading, writing, and problem-solving skills that are judged to be inadequate for everyday living.

Gemeinschaft   A type of social organization (community) in which people are bound together by kinship and tradition.

gender   The significance a society attaches to the biological categories of female and male, sometimes labeled *feminine* and *masculine*.

gender roles   Attitudes and activities that a society links to each sex; often referred to as *sex roles*.

gender stratification   The differential ranking of males and females in societies where sex determines access to scarce resources.

genocide   The systematic killing of an entire race or people.

gerontocracy   A form of social organization in which the elderly have the most wealth, power, and privileges.

gerontology   The study of aging and the elderly.

Gesellschaft A type of social organization in which relationships are contractual, impersonal, voluntary, and limited.

global economy Economic activity across national borders.

global perspective A view of the larger world and our society's place in it.

government A formal organization that directs the political life of a nation.

greenhouse effect A rise in the earth's average temperature (global warming) due to an increasing concentration of carbon dioxide in the atmosphere.

groupthink Group conformity that limits individual understanding of an issue.

hate crime A crime motivated by racial, ethical, or other bias.

hermaphrodite A human being with a combination of female and male internal and external genitalia.

high culture Cultural patterns that distinguish a society's elite.

holistic medicine An approach to health care that emphasizes prevention of illness and takes account of a person's entire physical and social environment.

homogamy Marriage between people with the same social characteristics.

horticulture The use of hand tools to raise crops.

hunting and gathering A stage of cultural evolution in which simple tools were used to hunt animals and gather vegetation.

id Freud's designation of the human being's basic drives.

ideology Cultural beliefs that justify particular social arrangements.

incest taboo A norm forbidding sexual relations or marriage between closely related family members.

income Wages or salary from work and earnings from investments.

independent variable In a causal analysis, the independent variable is the cause of the dependent variable (the effect).

industry The production of goods using sophisticated fuels and machinery.

infant mortality rate The number of children per 1,000 live births who die during their first year of life.

inferential statistics The type of statistics used to make inferences from sample data to populations through hypothesis testing. Probability is used to make a decision about the association between two or more variables; a *null hypothesis* is accepted or rejected based on the probability of an event occurring by chance.

in-group An esteemed social group commanding a member's loyalty.

institutional discrimination Discrimination against an individual or group that is supported by the values and organizations of a society.

intergenerational social mobility The social standing of children in relation to their parents.

intragenerational social mobility A change in social position occurring during a person's lifetime.

kinship A social bond, based on blood, marriage, or adoption, that joins people into families.

labeling theory The assertion that deviance and conformity result not so much from what people do as from the response of others to those actions.

language A system of symbols that allows people to communicate with one another.

latent functions The unrecognized and unintended effect of social action.

level of measurement The mathematical properties of a variable. Different levels of measurement (data) include: *nominal* (numbers are used to label mutually exclusive categories), *ordinal* (numbers are used to rank a variable on some criterion), *interval* (the distance between values is both known and constant—a unit of measurement, that allows one to add, subtract, divide, and multiply without accumulating error), and *ratio* (has all the properties of interval data, but also has a fixed meaningful zero point).

level of significance   The probability level (usually .05) used to determine the acceptance of a hypothesis or rejection of the *null hypothesis*. Sometimes referred to as *rejection level* or *alpha level.*

life expectancy   The average expectation of life at a given age, or the average number of years of life remaining for persons of a particular age.

looking-glass self   Cooley's term referring to a conception of self derived from the responses of others: We see ourselves as we think others see us.

macro-level orientation   A concern with large-scale patterns that characterize society as a whole.

manifest functions   The recognized and intended consequences of social action.

marriage   A legally sanctioned relationship, involving economic cooperation as well as normative sexual activity and childbearing, that people expect to be enduring.

mass media   Impersonal communications directed to a vast audience by means of a technological medium.

mass society   A society in which industry and bureaucracy erode traditional social ties.

master status   A social position with exceptional importance for identity, often shaping a person's entire life.

matriarchy   A form of family organization in which power and authority is vested in the hands of the females.

mean   A measure of central tendency. The mean is the arithmetic average of a group of interval level numbers (scores). Because it takes into account every score, it is affected by extremely low and extremely high scores.

mean deviation   A measure of dispersion for continuous data. In a distribution of scores, the mean deviation is the average absolute difference of each score from the mean of the scores. It measures, then, the average distance of each score from the mean. It is calculated by summing the absolute value of the difference between each score and the mean, and then dividing by the total number of scores.

measurement   The process of determining the value of a variable in a specific case.

measure of association   A statistic that indicates the strength of the relationship between two or more variables. The appropriate measure of association depends on the level of measurement of the variables involved.

measure of central tendency   Descriptive statistics that represent the most typical or representative score in a distribution of scores. The appropriate measure of central tendency depends on both the level of measurement and the dispersion of the data.

measure of dispersion   Descriptive statistics that reflect the amount of variability there is in a distribution of scores. These measures reveal how different the scores are from one another. The appropriate measure of dispersion depends on both the level of measurement and whether there are extreme scores in the data. When the magnitude of the measure of dispersion is large, it means that the scores are very different from one another and there is a substantial amount of variability in the data.

mechanical solidarity   Social bonds based on collective conformity to tradition.

median   The score that is the exact middle score in a distribution of ranked scores. It is, therefore, the score at the 50th percentile. In a rank-ordered distribution of scores, the position of the median can be found using the formula $(n + 1)/2$, where n is the number of scores.

medicalization of deviance   The transformation of moral and legal issues into medical matters.

medicine   The social institution that focuses on combating disease and improving health.

meritocracy   Social stratification based on personal merit.

micro-level orientation   A concern with small-scale patterns of social interaction in specific settings.

midpoint of a class interval   In a grouped frequency distribution, the midpoint is exactly midway between the lower and upper class limits and is determined by adding the upper and lower limits (stated or true limits) and dividing by 2. The midpoint of the class interval 100–200 would be (100 + 200)/2 = 150.

migration   The movement of people into and out of a specified territory.

military-industrial complex   A close association among the government, the military, and defense industries.

minority   A category of people, distinguished by physical or cultural traits, that is socially disadvantaged.

miscegenation   The biological process of interbreeding among racial groups.

mode   A measure of central tendency. The mode is the most frequent score in a distribution of scores or most frequently occurring interval in a grouped frequency distribution.

modernity   Social patterns linked to industrialization.

modernization   The process of social change in a society or a social institution initiated by industrialization.

modernization theory   A model of economic development that explains global inequality in terms of technological and cultural differences among societies.

monarchy   A type of political system that transfers power from generation to generation within a single family.

monogamy   Marriage involving two partners.

monopoly   Control of a market by a single producer.

mores   Norms that are widely observed and have compelling moral significance.

mortality   The incidence of death in a society's population.

multiculturalism   An educational program recognizing the cultural diversity of a population and promoting the equality of all cultural traditions.

multinational corporation   A large business that operates in many countries.

natural environment   The earth's surface and atmosphere, including various living organisms as well as the air, water, soil, and other resources necessary to sustain life.

negative correlation   A correlation or association between two variables wherein the scores co-vary in opposite directions: high scores on one variable are related to low scores on the second variable, and low scores on one variable are related to high scores on the other.

neocolonialism   The economic and/or political policies by which a nation indirectly maintains its influence over other areas.

nonverbal communication   Communication using body movements, gestures, and facial expressions rather than speech.

norms   Rules by which a society guides the behavior of its members.

nuclear family (conjugal family)   A social unit containing one, or—more commonly— two adults and any children.

null hypothesis   The hypothesis of no difference or no association that is the object of a hypothesis test. The null hypothesis is tested against the alternative or research hypothesis, and it is the one that is rejected or not rejected in favor of the alternative.

oligarchy   The rule of the many by the few.

oligopoly   Domination of a market by a few producers.

organic solidarity   Social bonds based on specialization and interdependence.

outgroup   Social group toward which one feels competition or opposition.

participant observation   A research technique in which investigators systematically observe people while joining in their routine activities.

pastoralism   The domestication of animals.

patriarchy   A form of family organization in which power and authority is vested in the hands of the males.

peer group   A group whose members have interests, social position, and age in common.

percent   A descriptive statistic obtained by dividing the frequency of a subset of events by the total number of events and dividing by 100. For example, if there are 50 property crimes out of a total of 75 crimes, the percent of property crimes is 50/75, or 66.7 percent, of the total.

personality   A individual's pattern of thoughts, motives, and self-conceptions.

personal space   The surrounding area over which a person makes a claim to privacy.

perspective   A particular theoretical model or school of thought.

pluralism   A state in which people of all races and ethnicities are distinct but have social parity.

pluralist model   An analysis of politics that views power as dispersed among many competing interest groups.

political revolution   The overthrow of one political system in order to establish another.

politics   The actual act of distributing power and making decisions.

polity   The social institution that distributes power and makes decisions.

polygamy   Plural marriage, or marriage that involves more than one spouse simultaneously.

popular culture   Cultural patterns widespread among a society's people, usually limited to the arts and entertainment.

population   The entire collection or universe of objects, events, or people that a researcher is actually interested in and from which a sample is drawn. The population is often referred to as the *universe of cases*.

positive correlation   A correlation or association between two variables wherein the attributes co-vary in the same direction. For example, as religiosity increases, faith in people increases, and vice versa.

positivism   A path to understanding based on science, not on philosophic presuppositions or metaphysics.

postindustrial economy   A productive system based on service work and high technology.

postmodernity   Social patterns typical of a postindustrial society.

power   The ability to achieve desired ends despite opposition.

power-elite model   An analysis of social life that views power as concentrated among the rich.

prejudice   A rigid and problematic generalization about a category of people.

prescribe   To set down as a rule or direction to be followed.

presentation of self   Goffman's term for the ways in which individuals, in various settings, try to create specific impressions in the minds of others.

primary group   A small social group in which relationships are close, personal, and enduring.

prioritize   The condition of ranking items in the order of their importance.

profane   That which people define as an ordinary element of everyday life.

profession   A prestigious, white-collar occupation that requires extensive formal education.

proletariat   People who sell their productive labor. Marxian term for the "masses."

public opinion   The attitudes of people throughout a society about one or more controversial issues.

puppet government   A government in one country that is under complete control of a government of another country.

qualitative variable   A variable whose values differ in quality and kind rather than quantity. With a qualitative variable you can say that one value is different from another, but numerical expressions such as "more than" or "less than" are meaningless. An example of a qualitative variable would be gender. Males are different than females, but we cannot say that males have "more gender" than females.

quantitative variable   A variable whose values differ in quantity. With a quantitative variable, you can make distinctions based on numerical properties, such as "more than" or "less than." An example of a quantitative variable would be the number of prior arrests a convicted offender has. A person with one prior arrest has fewer than a person with three prior arrests.

race   A category composed of men and women who share biologically transmitted traits that members of a society deem socially significant.

racism   The belief that one racial category is innately superior or inferior to another.

random selection   A way of ensuring that the sample selected is representative of the population from which it was drawn. In random selection, each element of the population has a known, nonzero, independent, and equal chance of being selected.

range   A measure of dispersion. With continuous data, the range is the difference between the highest score and the lowest score. With rank-ordered categorical data, the range is defined as the difference between the midpoints of the highest and lowest class intervals.

ratio-level variable   A continuous, quantitative variable in which the distance between values is both known and equal. Unlike an interval-level variable, a ratio-level variable has an absolute or true zero point, which implies the complete absence of the characteristic. An example of a ratio-level variable would be a robbery victimization rate per 100,000 for persons between the ages of 20 and 40.

rationality   Deliberate calculation of efficient means to accomplish any particular task.

rationalization   Max Weber's term for the change from tradition to rationality as the dominant mode of human thought.

recycling   Reuse of resources that we would otherwise discard as "waste."

reference group   A social group that becomes a point of reference for making evaluations and decisions.

refugees   Persons who flee their native country seeking safety from persecution.

rehabilitation   Reforming the offender to forgo further offenses.

relative deprivation   A perceived disadvantage relative to some standard of comparison.

relative poverty   The deprivation of some people in relation to others who have more.

reliability   The quality of consistency in measurement attained through repetition.

religion   A social institution involving beliefs and practices that distinguishes the sacred from the profane.

religiosity   The importance of religion in social life.

religious fundamentalism A conservative religious doctrine that opposes intellectuals and worldly accommodation in favor of restoring traditional religious systems.

replicate To reproduce, model, or simulate. In science, studies are replicated to increase or decrease confidence in their findings.

research method A strategy for systematically carrying out research. Sometimes referred to as the design of a study.

resocialization Formal or informal socialization intended to radically alter an individual's personality.

retrospective labeling The interpretation of someone's past consistent with present deviance.

robotics The field of research and development of robots.

role Normative patterns of behavior for those holding a particular status.

role conflict Incompatibility among roles corresponding to two or more statuses.

role model Someone who sets the example.

role set A number of roles attached to a single status.

role strain Incompatibility among roles corresponding to a single status.

routinization of charisma Weber's term for the development of charismatic authority into some combination of traditional and bureaucratic authority.

sacred That which people define as extraordinary, inspiring a sense of awe and reverence.

sample A subset of objects, events, or people selected from a population. A sample is selected to estimate values or characteristics (parameters) of the population or to test hypotheses about the population.

satellite country A country that is controlled by another, more powerful country.

scapegoat A person or category of people, typically with little power, whom others unfairly blame for their own troubles.

schooling Formal instruction under the direction of specially trained teachers.

science A logical system that derives knowledge from direct, systematic observation.

secondary group A large and impersonal social group based on some special interest or activity, usually of limited duration.

sect A type of religious organization that stands apart from the larger society.

secularization The historical decline in the influence of religion.

segregation The physical and social separation of categories of people.

self George Herbert Mead's term for the dimension of personality composed of an individual's self-awareness and self-image.

sex The biological distinction between females and males.

sexism The belief that one sex is innately superior to the other.

sex ratio The number of males for every hundred females in a given population.

sexual harassment Comments, gestures, or physical contact of a sexual nature that are deliberate, repeated, and unwelcome.

sexual orientation The manner in which people experience sexual arousal and achieve sexual pleasure.

sick role Patterns of behavior defined as appropriate for those who are ill.

significance level The probability of rejecting a null hypothesis when in reality it is true.

simple random sample A type of probability sample in which each element of the population has a known and equal probability of being included in the sample.

social change Any significant alteration in the structure of society.

social character Personality characteristics common to members of a society.

social-conflict paradigm   A framework for building theory based on the assumption that society is a complex system characterized by inequality and conflict that generate social change.

social construction of reality   The process by which individuals creatively build reality through social interaction.

social control   Process by which society regulates the thoughts and behaviors of individuals.

social dysfunction   The undesirable consequences of any social pattern for the operation of society.

social epidemiology   The study of how and why health and disease are distributed throughout a society's population.

social function   The consequences of any social pattern for the operation of society as a whole or in part.

social group   Two or more people who identify and interact with one another.

social institution   An organized sphere of social life such as education or the family.

social interaction   The process by which people act and react in relation to others.

socialism   An economic system in which the government owns the means of production.

socialized medicine   A medical care system in which the government owns most medical facilities and employs most physicians.

social mobility   Capability of change of position in a stratification system.

social movement   An organized effort to encourage or oppose some dimension of change.

social stratification   A system by which a society ranks categories of people in a hierarchy.

social structure   Any relatively stable pattern of social behavior.

society   A social grouping within a limited territory guided by their culture.

sociobiology   A theoretical paradigm that explains cultural patterns in terms of biological forces.

socioeconomic status (SES)   A composite social ranking based on various dimensions of inequality or inequity.

sociology   A social science concerned with the systematic study of society.

standard deviation   The square root of the variance; a commonly used measure that indicates the degree of deviation or dispersion from the mean of all the scores in the distribution. Sometimes referred to as the *standard error* of the mean.

status   A general designation of social standing as measured by income or wealth.

status consistency   The degree of consistency in a person's social standing across various dimensions of inequality.

status set   All the statuses a person holds at a particular time.

stereotype   An exaggerated belief associated with a category; a prejudiced description of a category of people.

stigma   A powerfully negative label that radically changes a person's self-concept and social identity.

structural-functional paradigm   A framework for building theory based on the assumption that society is a complex system whose parts work together to promote stability.

structural social mobility   Capability of shift in the social position of large numbers of people due less to individual efforts than to changes in society itself.

subculture   Cultural patterns that distinguish some group of a society's population.

suburbs   Urban areas beyond the political boundaries of a city but usually containing more than half the population of such areas.

superego   Freud's designation of the presence of culture within the individual in the form of internalized values and norms.

survey   A research method in which subjects selected (sampled) from a larger population respond to a series of statements or questions in a questionnaire or interview.

sustainable ecosystem   The human use of the natural environment to meet the needs of the present generation without threatening the prospects of future generations.

symbol   Anything that stands for or represents something else—for example, symbolic words, phrases, and images associated with a social movement.

symbolic-interaction perspective   A framework for building theory based on the view that society is the product of the everyday interactions of individuals and how they define the situations they are in.

technology   The body of knowledge applied to the practical tasks of living.

terrorism   Violence or the threat of violence by an individual or a group as a political strategy.

tertiary sector   The part of the economy involving services rather than goods.

theoretical paradigm   A set of fundamental assumptions that guides thinking and research; a perspective from which reality is defined.

total institution   A setting in which individuals are isolated from the rest of society and manipulated by an administrative staff.

totalitarianism   A highly centralized political system that extensively regulates people's lives.

totem   An object collectively defined as sacred or as an emblem of a clan.

tracking   The division of a school's students into different educational programs based on their achievement level.

tradition-directedness   Rigid conformity to time-honored ways of living.

tradition sentiments   Beliefs about the world that are passed from generation to generation.

transsexual   A person who feels he or she is one sex though biologically he or she is the other.

triad   A social group with three members.

urban ecology   Study of the link between the physical and social dimensions of cities.

urbanization   The concentration of humanity into cities.

validity   The quality of measurement gained by measuring exactly what one intends to measure; pertains to the accuracy of the measurement instrument.

values   Culturally defined standards of desirability, goodness, and beauty that serve as broad guidelines for social life.

variable   A concept whose value changes from case to case.

variance   A way of measuring the deviation of the scores from the mean; the amount of error involved in using the mean to represent all other scores in the distribution.

victimless crime   Violation of law in which there is assumed to be no readily apparent victim—for example, prostitution or gambling.

war   Armed conflict among people of various countries, directed by their governments.

wealth   An individual's or family's total financial assets.

white-collar crime   Crimes committed by people of high social position in the course of their occupations.

white-collar occupation   Higher prestige work that involves mostly mental activity.

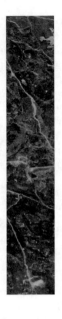

REFERENCES

Abel, E. L. 1984. *A Dictionary of Drug Abuse Terms and Terminology*. Westport, CT: Greenwood.

Abstracts in Social Gerontology. 1990. Newbury Park, CA: Sage.

Aby, S. H. 1987. *Sociology: A Guide to Reference and Information Sources*. Littleton, CO: Libraries Unlimited.

Adams, Daniel D., Thomas C. Johnson and Steven P. Cole. 1989. "Physical Fitness, Body Image, and Locus of Control in College Freshman Men and Women." *Perceptual and Motor Skills* 68:400–402.

Aday, R. H. 1988. *Crime and the Elderly: An Annotated Bibliography*. New York: Greenwood.

Adler, Patricia and Peter Adler. 1989. "Socialization and the 'Gloried Self'." *Social Psychology Quarterly* 52:299–310.

Alder, L. L., ed. 1993. *International Handbook on Gender Roles*. Westport, CT: Greenwood.

Allbritton, Cliff. 1982. *How to Get Married ... And Stay That Way*. Nashville, TN: Broadman Press.

American Journal of Sociology. 1895. Chicago, IL: University of Chicago Press.

American Sociological Association. 1996. *American Sociological Association Style Guide*. Washington, DC: American Sociological Association.

American Sociological Review. 1936. Washington, DC: American Sociological Association.

American Statistics Index. 1973. Washington, DC: Congressional Information Service.

Annual Review of Sociology. Palo Alto, CA: Annual Reviews.

Bart, P. and L. Frankel. 1986. *The Student Sociologist's Handbook*. 4th ed. New York: Random House.

Becker, Howard S., Blanche Geer, Everett C. Hughes and Anselm L. Strauss. 1961. *Boys in White: Student Culture in Medical School*. Chicago, IL: University of Chicago Press.

Berndt, J. 1986. *Rural Sociology: A Bibliography of Bibliographies*. Metuchen, NJ: Scarecrow.

Bibliographic Index. 1937. New York: H. W. Wilson.

Binstock, R. H. and L. K. George, eds. 1990. *Handbook of Aging and the Social Sciences.* San Diego, CA: Academic Press.

Blaylock, Heather S. 1996. *The Body Electric.* Cleveland, OH: Fowler.

Borgatta, E. F. and M. L. Borgatta, eds. 1992. *Encyclopedia of Sociology.* New York: Macmillan.

Boudon, R. and F. Bourricaud. 1989. *A Critical Dictionary of Sociology.* Chicago, IL: University of Chicago Press.

Bouma, Gary D. and G. B. J. Atkinson. 1995. *A Handbook of Social Science Research: A Comprehensive and Practical Guide for Students.* 2d ed. New York: Oxford University Press.

Bray, R., ed. 1996. *Guide to Reference Books.* Chicago, IL: American Library Association.

Bruhn, J. G., B. U. Philips and P. L. Levine. 1985. *Medical Sociology: An Annotated Bibliography.* New York: Garland.

Campbell, Anne. 1989. *The Opposite Sex.* Topsfield, NC: Salem House.

Charon, Joel M. 1996. *The Meaning of Sociology.* 5th ed. Upper Saddle River, NJ: Prentice Hall.

Chicago Manual of Style, 14th ed. 1993. Chicago, IL: University of Chicago Press.

Child Development Abstracts and Bibliography. 1928. Chicago, IL: University of Chicago Press.

Clark, R. E. and J. F. Clark, eds. 1989. *The Encyclopedia of Child Abuse.* New York: Facts on File.

Commager, Henry S., ed. 1963. *Documents of American History.* 7th ed. New York: Appleton-Century-Crofts.

Contemporary Sociology: A Journal of Reviews. 1971. Washington, DC: American Sociological Association.

Cooley, Charles H. [1902] 1964. *Human Nature and the Social Order.* New York: Schocken Books.

Criminal Justice Abstracts. 1968. Hackensack, NJ: National Council on Crime and Delinquency.

Cumulative Subject Index to the Monthly Catalog of United States Government Publications, 1900–1971. 1973. Washington, DC: Carrollton Press.

Darnay, A. J., ed. 1994. *Statistical Record of Older Americans.* Detroit, MI: Gale.

Demographic Yearbook. New York: United Nations/Statistical Office.

De Young, Mary. 1985. *Incest: An Annotated Bibliography.* Jefferson, NC: McFarland.

———. 1987. *Child Molestation: An Annotated Bibliography.* Jefferson, NC: McFarland.

DiCanio, M. 1993. *The Encyclopedia of Violence: Origins, Attitudes, Consequences.* New York: Facts on File.

Durkhiem, Emile. [1897] 1951. *Suicide.* Translated by J. A. Spaulding and G. Simpson. New York: The Free Press.

Engeldinger, E. A. 1986. *Spouse Abuse: An Annotated Bibliography of Violence between Mates.* Metuchen, NJ: Scarecrow.

Evans, G., R. O'Brien and S. Cohen, eds. 1991. *The Encyclopedia of Drug Abuse.* New York: Facts on File.

Fallon, April E. 1985. "Sex Differences in Perceptions of Desirable Body Shape." *Journal of Abnormal Psychology* 94:102–105.

Fallon, April E. and Paul Rozin. 1987. "Personal References: A Sexual Perspective." *Journal of Applied Psychology* 49(2):11–21.

Farley, John E. 1995. *Majority-Minority Relations*. Englewood Cliffs, NJ: Prentice Hall.

Ficke, R. C. 1992. *Digest of Data on Persons with Disabilities*. Washington, DC: National Institute on Disability and Rehabilitation Research.

Firestone, Shulamith. 1970. *The Dialectic of Sex: The Case for Feminist Revolution*. New York: Morrow.

Fowers, Blaine J. 1991. "His and Her Marriage: A Multivariate Study of Gender and Marital Satisfaction." *Sex Roles* 24(3):209–221.

Freedman, Rita J. 1984. "Reflections on Beauty as It Relates to Health in Adolescent Females." *Women and Health* 9(2):29–45.

Freud, Sigmund. 1930. *Civilization and Its Discontents*. New York: Cape and Smith.

_____. [1913] 1952. *Totem and Taboo*. Translated by James Strachey. New York: W. W. Norton.

Gall, S. B. and T. L. Gall, eds. 1993. *Statistical Record of Asian Americans*. Detroit, MI: Gale.

Ghorayshi, P. 1990. *The Sociology of Work: A Critical Annotated Bibliography*. New York: Garland.

Glamour. 1984. "Feeling Fat in a Thin Society." February, pp. 198–252.

Glenn, Norval D. 1993. "What's Happening to American Marriage?" *USA Today*, May, pp. 24–26.

Gordon, Lori H. 1993. "Intimacy: The Art of Working Out Your Relationships." *Psychology Today*, September, pp. 40–42.

Gould, J. and W. L. Kolb. 1964. *A Dictionary of the Social Sciences*. New York: Free Press.

Government Finance Statistics Yearbook. Washington, DC: International Monetary Fund.

Graves, Elliot. 1997. "Lineaments of Gratified Desire: Body English in the 1980s." Pp. 124–145 in *The Physics of Physicality*, edited by Lilly Deaver. Boston, MA: Hurstwood.

Hare, A. Paul, Edgar F. Borgatta and Robert F. Bales, eds. 1966. *Small Groups: Studies in Social Interaction*, Rev. ed. New York: Knopf.

Harris, D. K. 1988. *Dictionary of Gerontology*. New York: Greenwood.

Hartwell, Patrick. 1985. "Grammar, Grammars, and the Teaching of Grammar." *College English* 47:111.

Hawes, J. M. and E. I. Nybakken, eds. 1991. *American Families: A Research Guide and Historical Handbook*. New York: Greenwood.

Henslin, James M. 1990. "The Changing Family." Pp. 409–447 in *Social Problems*, edited by James M. Henslin. Englewood Cliffs, NJ: Prentice Hall.

Hess, Beth B., Elizabeth W. Markson and Peter J. Stein. 1988. *Sociology*. 3d ed. New York: Macmillan.

Historical Statistics of the United States: Colonial Times to 1970. Washington, DC: Government Printing Office.

Hoover, Kenneth and Todd Donovan. 1995. *The Elements of Social Science Thinking*. 6th ed. New York: St. Martin's Press.

Horton, C. P. and J. C. Smith, eds. 1990. *Statistical Record of Black America*. Detroit, MI: Gale.

Hunter, David E. and Phillip Whitten, eds. 1976. *Encyclopedia of Anthropology*. New York: Harper & Row.

Hurrelmann, K., ed. 1994. *International Handbook of Adolescence*. Westport, CT: Greenwood.

International Bibliography of Research in Marriage and the Family. St. Paul, MN: Family Social Science, University of Minnesota.

International Bibliography of Sociology. 1955. London: Tavistock.

International Encyclopedia of the Social Sciences. 1968. New York: Macmillan.

Inventory of Marriage and Family Literature. 1973. St. Paul, MN: National Council on Family Relations.

Isaac, Stephen and William B. Michael. 1981. *Handbook in Research and Evaluation.* 2d ed. San Diego, CA: EdITS Publishers.

Israeloff, Roberta. 1993. "Happy Families Are Not All Alike." *Parents,* March, pp. 129–136.

Jary, D. and J. Jary. 1991. *HarperCollins Dictionary of Sociology.* New York: HarperPerennial.

Kaiser Index to Black Resources: 1948–1986. 1992. Brooklyn, NY: Carlson.

Kanter, Rosabeth. 1977. "Secretaries in the Corporation." In *Men and Women of the Corporation,* edited by Rosabeth Kanter. New York: Basic Books.

Katz, W. 1978. *Magazines for Libraries.* 3d ed. New York: Bowker.

Kephart, William M. and Davor Jedlicka. 1991. "Marital Interaction and the Family Life Course." Pp. 239–318 in *The Family, Society, and the Individual.* New York: HarperCollins.

Kilbourne, Barbara Stanek, Frank Howell and Paula England. 1990. "A Measurement Model for Subjective Marital Solidarity: Invariance across Time, Gender, and Life Cycle Stage." *Social Science Research* 19(1):62–81.

Kinl, G. C. 1987. *Social Stratification: An Annotated Bibliography.* New York: Garland.

Kuhn, Thomas. 1970. *The Structure of Scientific Revolutions.* 2d ed. Chicago, IL: University of Chicago Press.

LaPatra, Jack. 1980. *The Age Factor.* New York: M. Evans and Company.

Lauer, Robert H. and Jeanette C. Lauer. 1986. "Factors in Long-Term Marriages." *Journal of Family Issues* 7(4):382–390.

Lerner, R., A. C. Petersen and J. Brooks-Gunn, eds. 1991. *Encyclopedia of Adolescence.* 2 vols. New York: Garland.

Levin, Jack and James Alan Fox. 1997. *Elementary Statistics in Social Research.* 7th ed. New York: Addison Wesley Longman.

Levin, Jack, Arnold Arluke and Amita Mody-Desbareau. 1986. "The Gossip Tabloid as an Agent of Social Control." Presented at the annual meeting of the American Sociological Association.

Lindsey, M. P. 1989. *Dictionary of Mental Handicap.* New York: Routledge.

Luckinbill, Gladys. [1965] 1985. *Advertising to Win: A Manual.* New York: Dalliance.

Lu, J. K. *U.S. Government Publications Relating to the Social Sciences.* Beverly Hills, CA: Sage Publications.

Maddox, G. L., ed. 1987. *The Encyclopedia of Aging.* New York: Springer.

Malinowski, B. 1948. *Magic, Science, and Religion.* Glencoe, IL: Free Press.

Mead, George H. [1934] 1962. *Mind, Self and Society.* Edited by C. W. Morris. Chicago, IL: University of Chicago Press.

Mills, C. Wright. 1956. *The Power Elite.* New York: Oxford University Press.

———. 1959. *The Sociological Imagination.* New York: Oxford University Press.

Mills, J. 1992. *Womanwords: A Dictionary of Words about Women.* New York: Free Press.

Miner, Horace. 1956. "Body Ritual Among the Nacirema." *American Anthropologist* 58(June):503–507.

Morgan, Gordon D. 1981. *Introductory Sociology: Lectures, Readings and Exercises.* Saratoga, CA: Century Twenty-One Publishing, pp. 5–6.

Murguia, Edward. 1995. [review of Isabel Valle's *Fields of Toil: A Migrant Family's Journey*]. *Rural Sociology* 60:168–169.

Nestman's Encyclopedia of Advertising Agencies: 1967. 1966. New York: Holyrod.

Newman, R. 1981. *Black Index: Afro-Americana in Selected Periodicals, 1907–1949.* New York: Garland.

NewsBank. 1975. Greenwich, CT: Urban Affairs Library.

Nordquest, J. 1988. *The Homeless in America: A Bibliography.* Santa Cruz, CA: Reference and Research Services.

———. 1991. *The Elderly in America: A Bibliography.* Santa Cruz, CA: Reference and Research Services.

O'Brien, R. and M. Chafetz, eds. 1991. *The Encyclopedia of Alcoholism.* New York: Facts on File.

Oklahoma Department of Commerce. 1991. *1989 Demographic State of the State.* Oklahoma City, OK: Publications Clearinghouse of the Oklahoma Department of Libraries.

O'Leary, Kathleen, ed. 1995. *State Rankings: A Statistical View of the 50 United States.* 6th ed. Lawrence, KS: MQ.

Philliber, Susan G., Mary R. Schwab and G. Sam Sloss. 1980. *Social Research.* Itasca, IL: F. E. Peacock.

Piaget, Jean. [1932] 1948. *The Moral Judgment of the Child.* New York: Free Press.

Popper, Karl. 1959. *The Logic of Scientific Discovery.* New York: Basic Books.

Population Index. 1935. Princeton, NJ: Office of Population Research, Princeton University and Population Association of America.

Rebach, H. M. and J. G. Bruhn, eds. 1991. *Handbook of Clinical Sociology.* New York: Plenum Press.

Reddy, M. A., ed. 1993. *Statistical Record of Hispanic Americans.* Detroit, MI: Gale Research.

———. 1993. *Statistical Record of Native North Americans.* Detroit, MI: Gale Research.

Richter, A. 1993. *Dictionary of Sexual Slang.* New York: Wiley.

Riemer, Brenda A. 1996. [review of Judith Lorber's *Paradoxes of Gender]* *Sociology of Sport Journal* 13.

Rockett, Geraldine and Kay McMinn. 1990. "You Can Never Be Too Rich or Too Thin: How Advertising Influences Body Image." *Journal of College Student Development* 31:278.

Rosen, Margery. 1994. "25 Ways to Strengthen Your Marriage." *Ladies Home Journal,* November, pp. 166–169.

Roy, F. H. and C. Russell, eds. 1992. *The Encyclopedia of Aging and the Elderly.* New York: Facts on File.

Sage Family Studies Abstracts. 1979. Beverly Hills, CA: Sage.

Sage Race Relations Abstracts. 1975. Beverly Hills, CA: Sage.

Satran, Pamela Redmond. 1995. "The 4-Minute Miracle." *Good Housekeeping,* August, pp. 88–92.

Schick, F. L. and R. Schick, eds. 1994. *Statistical Handbook on Aging Americans.* Phoenix, AZ: Oryx.

Selth, J. P. 1985. *Alternative Lifestyles: A Guide to Research Collections on Intentional Communities, Nudism, and Sexual Freedom.* Westport, CT: Greenwood.

Sheehy, E. P., ed. 1986. *Guide to Reference Books.* 10th ed. Chicago, IL: American Library Association.

Smelser, N. J., ed. 1988. *Handbook of Sociology.* Newbury Park, CA: Sage.

Social Forces. 1922. Chapel Hill, NC: University of North Carolina Press.

Social Sciences Citation Index. 1972. Philadelphia, PA: Institute for Scientific Information.

Social Sciences Index. 1974–75. New York: H. W. Wilson.

Society. 1967. New Brunswick, NJ: Rutgers University Press.

Sociological Abstracts. 1952. New York: Sociological Abstracts.

Soliday, G. L., ed. 1980. *History of the Family and Kinship: A Select International Bibliography.* Millwood, NY: Kraus International Publications.

Stanley, H. W. and R. G. Niemi, eds. 1993. *Vital Statistics on American Politics.* 5th ed. Washington, DC: Congressional Quarterly.

Statistical Reference Index Annual Abstracts. Bethesda, MD: Congressional Information Service.

Statistical Yearbook. New York: United Nations/Statistical Office.

Statistical Yearbook. Paris: UNESCO.

Stinnett, Nick and John DeFrain. 1985. *Secrets of Strong Families.* Boston, MA: Little, Brown and Company.

Substance Abuse I: Drug Abuse: A Bibliography. Santa Cruz, CA: Reference and Research Services.

Substance Abuse II: Alcohol Abuse: A Bibliography. Santa Cruz, CA: Reference and Research Services.

Sussman, M. B. and S. K. Steinmetz, eds. 1987. *Handbook of Marriage and the Family.* New York: Plenum Press.

The New York Public Library Desk Reference. 1993. New York: Stonesong Press.

The New York Times Index. 1913. New York: The New York Times.

Theodorson, G. A. and A. G. Theodorson. 1969. *A Modern Dictionary of Sociology.* New York: Barnes & Noble.

Tierney, H., ed. 1989–91. *Women's Studies Encyclopedia: Views from the Inside.* New York: Greenwood.

Turner, Jeffery S. and Donald B. Helms. 1994. *Contemporary Adulthood.* Orlando, FL: Harcourt Brace.

U.S. Bureau of the Census. 1790. *Bureau of the Census Catalog.* Washington, DC: Government Printing Office.

U.S. Bureau of the Census. 1949. *County and City Data Book.* Washington, DC: Government Printing Office.

U.S. Bureau of the Census. 1988. *County and City Data Book.* Washington, DC: Government Printing Office.

U.S. Federal Bureau of Investigation. *Uniform Crime Reports for the United States.* Washington, DC: Government Printing Office.

U.S. Library of Congress. 1950. *Subject Catalog: A Cumulative List of Works Represented by Library of Congress Printed Cards.* Washington, DC: Library of Congress.

U.S. Superintendent of Documents. 1885. *Monthly Catalog of United States Government Publications.* Washington, DC: Government Printing Office.

Vital Statistics of the United States. 2 vols. Hyattville, MD: U.S. Department of Health and Human Services.

Wallerstein, Judith S. and Sandra Blakeslee. 1995. *The Good Marriage: How and Why Love Lasts.* Boston, MA: Houghton Mifflin.

Weber, Max. 1930. *The Protestant Ethic and the Spirit of Capitalism.* London: Unwin University Books.

———. 1969. "Some Consequences of Bureaucratization." Pp. 454–455 in *Sociological Theory*, edited by L. A. Coser and B. Rosenberg. London, England: Macmillan.

Whipple, Charles M. and Edward A. White 1995. *The Ultimate Way to Match People with People*. Orlando, FL: Harcourt Brace.

White, C. 1973. *Sources of Information in the Social Sciences*. 2d ed. Chicago, IL: American Library Association.

Women's Studies Abstracts. 1972. New York: Rush.

Women's Studies Index. 1991. Boston, MA: G. K. Hall Citation Indexes.

Woods, G. 1993. *Drug Abuse in Society: A Reference Handbook*. Santa Barbara, CA: ABC-Clio.

Wortmann, Joseph. "Social Protocols, Grades 9–12." September 1996. <ftp://ftp.elp.texu/soc/libart.cite> (April 12, 1997).

Yates, John D. 1996. "The American Dream of the Self." Presented at the annual meeting of the Conference on Sociology and the Media, November 10, Austin, TX.

Yearbook of Labour Statistics. Geneva: International Labour Office.

Zophy, A. H. and F. M. Karenik, eds. 1990. *Handbook of American Women's History*. New York: Garland.

INDEX

Survey questionnaire, constructing, 211–13
Surveys, 108. *See also* Sociological survey
  papers
Sussman, M. B., 118
Symbolic interactionism, 7
Symbols, role of, 9–10, 11

Tables, 67–68, 69
Tabulating data, 213–14
Technology, as product of science, 155
Television, interview on, 87
Tertiary headings, 67
Test-retest method, 162
Text
  format for, 66
  of social service agency case study, 195–96
  of sociological survey paper, 221–23
Text citations, ASA format, 73–80
Theodorson, A. G. and G. A., 121
Theoretical perspective, selecting, 183–84
Thesis sentence, 21, 29
Thesis/theses
  citing and referencing, 88, 98
  developing, 21–22
  finding, 20–21
  working, 105
Thomas, W. I., 11
Tierney, H., 122
Time, colon used in, 44
Title
  of illustration, 68
  of table, 67
Title page
  format for, 63, 64
  for social service agency case study, 194
  of sociological survey paper, 219
Toennies, Ferdinand, 8
Tone of writing, 31
Topic
  establishing, 101
  narrowing your, 19–20, 21
  selecting, 19, 193–94, 207
  social issue analysis paper, 179–82
  social service agency case study, 193–94,
    196
  sociological survey paper, 207
Topical indexes, 124–25
Transitional elements, 34
Translator, citing and referencing, 75, 81–82,
  95
Turner, Jeffery S., 185, 186, 187

U.S. Census Bureau publications, 144–45
Unity, checking for, 34
Unpublished materials, citing and referenc-
  ing, 75, 87, 88, 98
Untranslated book, referencing, 81–82
URL (Universal Resource Locator), 151

Vague pronoun reference, 51–52
Valid measurements, 159
Valle, Isabel, 168, 171–73, 175
Variables, 158–59, 160
Verbs
  passive voice, 48–49
  sentence fragments lacking, 56

Wallerstein, Judith S., 185, 186
Weber, Max, 7–8, 197, 198
Whipple Charles M., 185–86
White, Edward A., 185–86
Whitten, Phillip, 192
Woods, G., 118
Wording, repetition of, 34–35
Word-processor "spell check" feature, 57
Working bibliography, 105–8
Working papers, 88
Working thesis, 105
World Wide Web, 146–54
  bibliographical reference for site on, 89
  how to access, 147–49
Writing process, 18–37
  drafts, 30–33, 35
  editing, 35–36
  invention strategies, 25–28
  outlining, 28–30
  planning, 19–25, 28
  proofreading, 37
  revising, 33–35
Writing to learn, 13–18

Yahoo sociology link page, 149–50
Yahoo sociology search page, 150–51
Yearbooks, 118–20
Yurasits, Andrea, 117

Znaniecki, Florian, 11
Zophy, A. H., 118